RATIONAL ECONOMIC MAN

RATIONAL ECONOMIC MAN

A PHILOSOPHICAL CRITIQUE OF NEO-CLASSICAL ECONOMICS

MARTIN HOLLIS

Senior Lecturer in Philosophy, University of East Anglia

EDWARD J. NELL

Professor of Economics, The Graduate Faculty of
the New School for Social Research, New York

CAMBRIDGE UNIVERSITY PRESS

Published by the Syndics of the Cambridge University Press
Bentley House, 200 Euston Road, London NW1 2DB
American Branch: 32 East 57th Street, New York, N.Y. 10022

Library of Congress Catalogue Card Number: 73-90649

ISBN: 0 521 20408 9

First published 1975
Reprinted 1976

Composed in Malta by
St Paul's Press Ltd
and printed in the U.S.A.

CONTENTS

PREFACE

Philosophers and economists rarely find much common ground, and we gave the seminar, which fathered this book, with more curiosity than confidence. The results were a welcome surprise, and subsequent discussions with colleagues have helped to trace further philosophical threads in the web of orthodox economic theory. In a sense the book is a tribute to the hopes of the Oxford P.P.E. school, through which we have both passed. Admittedly Hollis has only hazy recollections of genial hours with his economics tutors, but Nell is the author of several philosophical papers and has contributed much more than the economics here, for which he takes sole praise or blame. Hollis is responsible for the main philosophical argument (and also for the prose in which most of the final draft has been couched). Nevertheless, at least on the philosophical side, we regard the text as a genuinely cooperative effort.

Our thanks are due to many colleagues for their invaluable criticisms of earlier drafts. In particular, we would like to mention Dr Onora Nell of Barnard College, Professors Adolph Lowe and Robert Heilbroner of the New School, New York; Robert Sutcliffe of Oxford University and David Bailey, Bryan Heading, Peter Townroe and Professor Harold Lydall of the University of East Anglia; and the nameless readers of the Cambridge University Press. We gratefully acknowledge, also, the grant which we received from the American Philosophical Society towards the preparation of the book. Finally, our thanks go to Margaret Dunbar for preparing the diagrams and to Martha Stires for assistance in preparing the index.

M.H.
E.J.N.

INTRODUCTION

Recruits to the army of orthodox Western economic science accept a twin allegiance. They swear a general empiricism in the pursuit of knowledge and, even if they would not always admit to it, a methodological individualism in the attempt to explain human behaviour. As empiricists, they are to reject the rationalist quest for necessity among truths and inevitability among events. As individualists, they are to reject the social definition of man given by medievalists and mercantilists and refurbished by Marx. In economics, the vanguard of advance, they are to work with a notion of abstract individuals, who choose among abstractly described alternatives. In epistemology they are to insist that theories are justified only by their predictive success. Neither allegiance seems to us wise. We shall argue that neo-Classical theories of economics are unsound and that they rely for defence on a Positivist theory of knowledge which is also unsound. Having sought vainly for a trustier branch of empiricism, we shall finally argue the merits of a Rationalist philosophy and a Classical or Marxian Economics.

Our ambitions and apologies

So bold a thesis needs a scholarly defence in several volumes. Each ingredient has a complex history of subtle argument and each has been studied by authorities whom we cannot hope to rival. But, if debate had to wait for a synoptic papal bull, it would never start. Besides, general judgments formed by default can be as influential as those reached by debate and the influence of empiricism, allied in economics with neo-Classical thinking, is beyond doubt. This is not to deny that empiricists and neo-Classicists have their reasons nor that general argument occurs. But we believe that methodology is usually discussed within assumptions which need to be questioned and, indeed, rejected. Lest our point be missed, we have written something of a polemic. While regretting the cost in subtlety and scholarship, we hope for enough gain in clarity to start a fight.

We are also wary of the electrified wire dividing some academic disciplines. Fortunately it is deadliest at the lateral boundaries along the frontier with ignorance. Further back, where students are taught to intermediate level, there is more interdisciplinary harmony, since standard methods of enquiry and the corpus of existing knowledge yield a united front. The doubts, modifications and limitations peculiar to each discipline are not for beginners. However diffracted the light of truth passing through the prism of the graduate student's thesis, it shines bright and steady from the textbook. It is here that economics and philosophy have joined forces. In economics a few great textbooks have ruled the classroom and tormented every generation of students since the war. These books almost all start with a section on methodology, propounding a Positivist philosophy of science. This is the influential alliance, which we propose to attack.

The crucial issues for an economic theory often arise among the most complex of its implications. Nevertheless we must beg leave to ignore, for instance, the mathematical intricacies of modern neo-Classical theory. We shall not consider the existence or the stability of general equilibrium. Nor shall we worry about its Pareto optimality.[1] We shall not try to unravel the third volume of *Das Kapital* with matrix algebra nor to pin down the Ricardian invariant measure of value nor to expound the mysteries of 'reswitching' and 'capital reversing' in modern Marxian-type models.[2] Instead we shall be concerned with simpler matters. When dealing with neo-Classicism, we shall confine ourselves to consumer behaviour (presented in indifference curves and in simple versions of revealed preference theory) and marginalist producer behaviour in both product and factor markets. Perfect markets will not be the only ones considered, since neo-Classical thinking embraces many varieties and defines a whole system of classification for them. But although our economic questions will thus arise from the textbooks, we believe their implications to be extensive, since we hope to show that death at the roots kills the fruit on the branches.

We cannot so easily, however, base our case for Classical-Marxian thought on textbooks, since relatively few exist and those, for instance in

---

[1] Those who wish can consult Gerard Debreu, *Theory of Value* (Yale University Press, 1972); J. von Neumann, A model of general economic equilibrium, *Review of Economic Studies*, vol. 13, no. 33 (1945); and T. C. Koopmans, *Three Essays on the State of Economic Science: 1st Essay* (McGraw-Hill, 1957).

[2] Cf. F. Seton, The 'transformation problem', *Review of Economic Studies*, vol. 24, no. 65 (June 1957); F. Seton and M. Morishima, Aggregation in Leontief matrices and the labour theory of value, *Econometrica*, vol. 29, no. 2 (April 1961); P. Sraffa, *Production of Commodities by Means of Commodities* (Cambridge University Press, 1960); L. Pasinetti, A mathematical formulation of the Ricardian system, *Review of Economic Studies*, vol. 27(2), no. 73 (February 1960); P. A. Samuelson, Understanding the Marxian notion of exploitation, *Journal of Economic Literature*, vol. 9, no. 2 (June 1971).

Socialist countries, are often primarily concerned with other questions.[3] Instead, we shall rely on the classic writings of Ricardo and Marx and on the modern work of Piero Sraffa and Joan Robinson. Our economic analysis will be confined to the simplest and most general propositions.

Our economic quarrel with neo-Classicism is, firstly, that it concentrates on *market* interdependence, neglecting the deeper technological interdependence, which turns out to limit the possibilities of substitution compatible with the assumed 'givens'; secondly, that it ignores institutional and especially class relationships, so misrepresenting the nature of payments to 'factors' and neglecting the economic significance of power and conflict in societies. Neither complaint is new. Hobson made the first, Marx the second and many others have added elaborations. By contrast, the Classical-Marxian view bases itself on technological interdependence between industries and class relationships between families or persons. But this economic quarrel will not occupy the centre of the book and the first bone we wish to pick on our own account is philosophical. We dispute not only the Positivist doctrines behind orthodox methodology but also empiricism in general. Yet we do not follow those recent philosophers who therefore reject all traditional epistemology. Instead, we shall uphold a theory of knowledge assigning a crucial role to *a priori* knowledge, which we take to belong to the Rationalist tradition. It seems to us as true as ever that a scientific method must reflect a philosophy of science, which must reflect a theory of knowledge.

Crucial tenets of Empiricism

We begin by tracing the alliance between Positivism and Positive economics. This means addressing philosophical remarks to economists and economic remarks to philosophers. If we seem naive to those already familiar with the subtleties on both sides, we crave indulgence and, if our remarks are disconcertingly antiphonal, we urge patience. We should also confess at once that some philosophical issues we raise throughout the book no longer seem crucial to most Anglo-Saxon philosophers, at any rate in the form we give them. This is because Positivism and indeed all traditional epistemology are in eclipse at present. Our apologia is partly that the traditional philosophic problems still beset the philosophy of social science, which remains broadly empiricist, and partly that we ourselves simply do not agree that

---

[3] Two recent books deserving special mention, however, are R. M. Goodwin, *Elementary Economics from the Higher Standpoint* (Cambridge University Press, 1970) and Andras Brody, *Proportions, Prices and Planning* (North-Holland, 1970).

the eclipse is merited. So let us begin with a sketch of Empiricism, of which Positivism is the best-worked-out variant, and a promise to our economic readers to show it as an indispensable background to standard introductory chapters on methodology.

Empiricism, is, negatively, the denial that anything can be known about the world *a priori* or without benefit of experience. The history of the world, as an empiricist sees it, is the story of a series of states in which there happen to be patterns. Nothing *must* be as it is, no event *must* have any particular cause, no state *must* be followed by any one other state. Consequently we can never know *a priori* what will happen next and science has to progress by generalising from experience. Logic or reasoning alone cannot tell us which of infinitely many possible worlds we live in, nor which of infinitely many possible continuations from the present state will, in fact, occur. Scientific laws and explanations could be discovered *a priori*, only if ours were the only possible world. Besides, all our knowledge of the world rests in the end on observation and we observe only that something is so or (if we may ignore the traditional philosophical problems about the past) was so or has always been so. We can never observe that anything *must* be as it is. There is, therefore, no room for the idea that causal laws are in any sense necessities in nature. We can thus pick out two crucial tenets of Empiricism:

(i) claims to knowledge of the world can be justified only by experience;
(ii) whatever is known by experience could have been otherwise.

It is tempting to add a third, that no statement about the objective world depends for its truth on whether it is believed. This certainly accords with most versions of Empiricism (and of Rationalism for that matter) and embodies the common view that human beings cannot make an empirical statement true by *fiat*. But it is rejected by Pragmatism, which we shall later present as the newest champion of Empiricism. So, although the usual distinction between belief and knowledge is part of the philosophical orthodoxy taught to apprentices, we cannot list it as definitive of Empiricism.

Empiricist philosphy of science cannot allow that there is any necessity about causal connections. Malthus' laws of population, for instance, even if genuine, cannot be treated as *iron* laws in the sense that they reveal what is bound to happen or that statements of them cannot be denied without contradiction. We have to be able to observe instances of causal connections. Accordingly, the notion of Cause is analysed (usually) in a way derived from Hume. At its simplest, to say that *A* causes *B* is to say that *A* is always followed by *B* in given conditions. This takes us a step beyond mere observation but an inductive licence to generalise from observed correlations to universal ones does not offend the empiricist's insistence on the primacy of observation. Generalisations can be tested by observing whether suitable instances actually occur. There can be no basic difference in kind between causal laws and confirmed empirical generalisations, even if the title of 'law' is reserved for generalisations especially broad, useful, elegant or suggestive. This may prompt the objection that the citing of causal laws is supposed to *explain*, whereas generalisations merely describe. The empiricist replies that there is no ultimate basis for such a distinction. To explain an event, it is enough to cite confirmed generalisations from which the occurrence of the event could have been predicted. Prediction is our only weapon but it suffices and to predict is to explain in advance. Induction is the only coin which buys knowledge of what lies beyond direct observation. Since it is the only coin, prediction and explanation have to be two sides of it. To predict is to deduce an instance from a generalisation; to explain is to cover an instance with a generalisation.

The analytic–synthetic distinction and Positivist method

The last paragraph can serve as a rough account of the core of nineteenth-century Positivism. The idea still retains all its importance but has become embedded in a more forceful and elegant Logical Positivism, best introduced as a theory about the meaning and truth of statements.[4] All claims to knowledge can be treated as claims to know that a statement is true. The advance of science now becomes the progressive determination of the truth or falsity of statements. This may seem an artificial way of putting it but it clears the deck for the introduction of that great engine of Logical Positivist epistemology, the analytic-synthetic distinction.

A logical positivist holds that all cognitively meaningful statements are of just two exclusive kinds, analytic or synthetic. Very roughly, the former are statements of language, the latter statements of fact. More formally, a true statement is *analytic*, if it cannot be denied without contradiction or if its truth arises from the meanings of its terms; it is *synthetic*, if there are possible circumstances in which it would be (or would have been) false. For example, the statement that 'if the elasticity of demand is greater than unity, then a reduction in the price of a good will lead to an increase in total expenditure on the good' is analytic. For, were the total expenditure to fall, then it would follow logically not that the statement was false but that

---

[4] The clearest basic exposition is still A. J. Ayer's in *Language, Truth and Logic* (Dover Publications, 1936), and, despite the many later subtleties and developments in Logical Positivist philosophy of science and language, we regard Ayer's account of the epistemology of the position as still canonical. Other and later works will be found in the bibliography.

the elasticity of demand was not greater than unity. This is a mere consequence of our defining terms like 'elasticity of demand' as we do and does not reveal some grand causal law about the working of the economy. On the other hand, the statement that 'if investment is increased, there will be a rise in employment' is (in the absence of any theoretical proof of it) synthetic. It is no less a universal statement but whether it is true depends on observation and induction and there is no logical contradiction in denying it. It states a relation which holds (if it does) as a matter of fact and so does claim to express a causal law.

This analytic-synthetic distinction guards an apparently weak flank of Empiricism. For it seems at first sight that logic alone can sometimes tell us which of infinitely many possible worlds we live in, in the sense that some truths are both necessarily true and informative about our world. For instance, that certain relations hold under imperfect competition appears to be a fact about a type of market for which no empirical evidence is needed, since the theorist can prove it *a priori*. If this interpretation were accepted, it would follow at once that experience is not always needed to justify claims to knowledge of the world. So an empiricist who admits that there are necessary or *a priori* truths must add that they do not state empirical facts. He does so by insisting that they are analytic and therefore not synthetic. This involves him, as we shall see later, in three further and separate claims about analytic truths — that they are linguistic, that they are man-made and that they make no empirical assertions. All three claims can be (and will be) disputed but, while they stand, they serve to protect the basic tenets of Empiricism from refutation by the existence of necessary truths.

This view of analytic truths is so crucial to logical positivism that it is worth spelling out how it arises. The root question concerns the relation of *a priori* and empirical in human knowledge or, for present purposes, the relation of pure theory to fact. Can pure theorising discover truths to which experience is bound to conform (on pain of being dismissed as misleading)? Empiricists are bound to say, No. The denial can be made by refusing to recognise a class of *a priori* truths at all, but this is not the logical positivists' way. Logical positivists have a positive use for *a priori* truths, once rendered harmless. So they contend that *a priori* truths make no empirical assertions. But this is not self-evident and reasons must be given for accepting it. So the next move is to deny that theorising is a process of discovery. Again, however, this is not self-evident — psychologically indeed it is plainly false. So, to give epistemological justification, systems of pure theory are construed by analogy with languages, the meanings of whose terms depend on the semantic rules for combining them. As typically with the theorems of logic, *a priori* truths are deemed to result from the definitions and rules of the systems in which they occur. Even so, however, more needs

6

to be said, since, were these rules immutable in any important sense, truths resulting from them would reveal at least immutable ways of conceptualising and ordering experience and even perhaps immutable features of the experience ordered. So it has to be shown both that *a priori* truths have as subject matter not things but concepts and that the rules they depend on are mutable. It has to be shown that a change in the rules can, by changing the meaning of sentences, change the truth of *a priori* propositions expressed by them but cannot change the truth of empirical propositions. To put it informally, different geometries involve different truths but there is just one set of facts to determine the truth of propositions in botany. (It is as if language were a system of prices for *a priori* truths and of values for empirical truths.) Hence Logical Positivism rests crucially on the claim that *a priori* truths result from man-made rules which we can, in principle, change.

All knowledge of the world can thus be expressed in synthetic statements, whose truth cannot be guaranteed *a priori* and must be established by observation and induction. Conversely, since any state of the world might have been different, analytic truths are not about the world. This is the point of saying that they depend on the meanings of their terms, are true by definition or, in a phrase to be discussed in Chapter 6, are 'true by convention'. A bold and complete distinction has been drawn between language and fact, between pure theories and hypotheses, between what we invent and what we must discover, between *a priori* and empirical knowledge. Analytic and synthetic truths have a different sort of subject matter and statements of causal laws belong strictly among those which are for observation and induction. Synthetic statements are refutable. We can summarise Logical Positivism by adding four further tenets to our list:

(iii) all cognitively meaningful statements are either analytic or synthetic but not both;
(iv) synthetic statements, being refutable, cannot be known true *a priori*;
(v) analytic statements have no factual content;
(vi) analytic truths are true by convention.

Positivism in its earlier days had hesitated about the place of logic and mathematics in empirical science. Logical and mathematical truths are part of our stock of knowledge but, being irrefutable in principle, cannot convincingly be seen as empirical generalisations. Logical Positivism removed the hesitation by dubbing all such truths analytic, as just described. By the same token, there should no longer be a puzzle about the role of theory in science. The term 'theory' has various uses but, with the help of the analytic-synthetic distinction, we should be able to reduce them to two. A 'theory' may be what we have just called a 'pure theory', in which case it serves to transform synthetic statements about data into synthetic predictions. (For instance, the theory of Exchange-rate Adjustment turns statements of the current balance of trade and other indicators into predictions of the results of a devaluation.) Or 'theory' may be a synonym for 'hypothesis' or the name of a set of hypotheses, in which case theoretical statements are synthetic. There is no mystery here, so long as we do not confuse the two uses, and what is called theory often includes both kinds of statement. This reflects the fact that the Positivist method of science is partly deductive, in that deduction helps to prepare hypotheses for testing and to interpret the results of the tests. We are thus led to ground which economists will find familiar, the famous hypothetico-deductive method, best illustrated with a diagram. Figure 1 is taken from R. G. Lipsey's *Introduction to Positive Economics* (3rd ed., Harper and Row, 1972), which presents a widely-held point of view with striking clarity.[5]

Figure 1 includes some pointers to the discussion in later chapters. Definitions and hypotheses are grouped together under the heading of 'assumptions'. 'Predictions' are equated with 'implications'. When the theory conflicts with the facts, there is apparently a choice of responses. A 'theory' is presumably a set of assumptions and their implications. Fitting these methodological points into the context of Positivism, we get two further tenets:

(vii) a known causal law is a well enough confirmed empirical hypothesis;
(viii) the test of a theory is the success of its predictions.

Finally there are two deliberate omissions. Value judgements are excluded and there is no mention whatever of economics in Figure 1. Value judgements are excluded in the spirit of the famous distinction between 'positive' and 'normative' statements, which is crucial to this view of science. 'Positive' statements are all those which a dispassionate observer could make while remaining ethically neutral. They can include facts about the ethical norms of the agents studied but must not add any ethical reckoning of those norms. 'Normative' statements are those explicitly or implicitly containing the word 'ought'. Admittedly this way of putting the distinction is less clear than it looks, since it lumps together the idea of moral judgement with that of evaluation of ends (as we shall see later when we discuss rationality), but for the present we are content to note its importance for Positive economics. There is no mention of economics in Figure 1 because,

---

[5] Analogous versions can be found in any number of other textbooks, e.g. A. A. Walters, *An Introduction to Econometrics* (Norton, 1970) and J. M. Henderson and R. E. Quandt, *Microeconomic Theory: A Mathematical Approach* (McGraw-Hill, 1971).

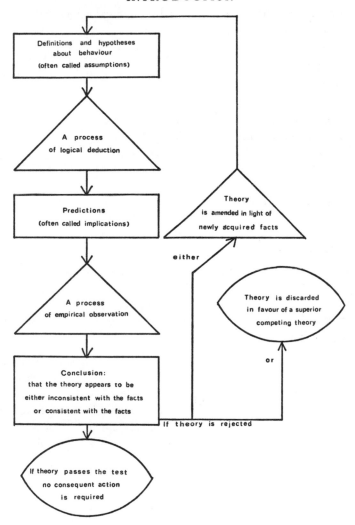

Figure 1

given the theory of knowledge already sketched, the Positivist method of science is bound to be a universal one. The difference between economics and, say, sociology or physics lies in their different subject matter and not in the method of scientific explanation which is applied. Taking these hints, we may add:

    (ix) judgements of value have no place in science;
    (x) sciences are distinguished by their subject matter and not by their methodology.

We have now staked out our main philosophical target with ten tenets, which it may be as well to repeat:

(i) claims to knowledge of the world can be justified only by experience;
(ii) whatever is known by experience could have been otherwise;
(iii) all cognitively meaningful statements are either analytic or synthetic but not both;
(iv) synthetic statements, being refutable, cannot be known true *a priori*;
(v) analytic statements have no factual content;
(vi) analytic truths are true by convention;
(vii) a known causal law is a well enough confirmed empirical hypothesis;
(viii) the test of a theory is the success of its predictions;
(ix) judgements of value have no place in science;
(x) sciences are distinguished by their subject-matter and not by their methodology.

We regard tenets (vii), (viii), (ix), (x) as defining a philosophy of science, which springs from Logical Positivism (iii), (iv), (v), (vi), which is a theory of knowledge in the empiricist tradition (i), (ii). This is our prime philosophical target (although we shall not neglect Pragmatism). To show that it is canonical, we cite Professor Samuelson:

All sciences have the common task of describing and summarizing reality. Economics is no exception. There are no separate methodological problems that face the social scientist different in kind from those that face any other scientist ... Finally it is clear that no *a priori* empirical truths can exist in any field. If a thing has *a priori* irrefutable truth, it must lack factual content. It must be regarded as a meaningless proposition in the technical sense of modern philosophy.[6]

The Inductive and Deductive problems

Before laying our economic groundwork, we shall call attention to two key epistemological problems, facing all theories of knowledge, which form the philosophical theme of the book. One concerns Induction, the other Deduction. If these problems strike our economic readers as too gruellingly philosophical to be relevant to economics, we must again urge patience. We are convinced that philosophical definitions of the role of theory partly determine the kind of theory which an economist accepts. Indeed the most hard-headed economist is secretly a philosopher too. In later chapters we

---

[6] From his *Collected Scientific Papers*, ed. J. E. Stiglitz, (M.I.T. Press, 1966), vol. II, paper no. 126, p. 1751.

shall present our own solution to the Inductive and Deductive problems as an invitation to revise the usual role assigned to theory in economics and so to adopt other criteria of theoretical success.

The Inductive problem has a general and a particular version. In general, why is a hypothesis strengthened by surviving the stages of Figure I (p. 9) and being lodged in the bottom left-hand oval? The stock answer is that what has happened in known cases will, *ceteris paribus*, happen in others. But how do we know that? It is a claim beyond the evidence of the senses alone and so is not sufficiently warranted by observation. Yet, if we claim to know it by induction, we beg the question, since previous observations count as evidence for the presence of future regularities in nature, only if we are *already* warranted in generalising from previous observations. And if we claim to know it *a priori*, then, according to positivists at least, it is true by definition and empty of all factual content. But, on the other hand, if we do not know that what holds in observed cases holds in others, then science is futile and any claim to have found a causal law falls at once. Nor can we escape by saying that science deals in probabilities rather than certainties, since there are no probabilities, unless we have inductive evidence that what holds in observed cases holds in others. We must be justified in projecting the sample into the population. If the world is about to become irregular, hypotheses are apparently not strengthened by passing the test. By Positivist canons, we cannot know *a priori* that there will not be different regularities or irregularities tomorrow. Do we know it at all? Perhaps the lack of known economic laws reflects an irregular economic world and the empirical science of economics is doomed to failure.

The particular version strikes practical men with more force. Not all generalisations inspire the same confidence. Why are we warranted in adopting some and rejecting others? For instance, we accept it as a law that when a price rises, demand tends to fall, but do not accept that the rate of profit tends to remain constant at about 12%. Yet there is much evidence for the latter hypothesis, enough to warrant a claim to have found a law in more orthodox cases. Why does successful testing confirm the hypothesis that consumption rises when income rises but, apparently, not the hypothesis that in every developed country labour receives a constant share of the national income (about 40% in the U.S. and U.K.)? Furthermore, evidence, even when accepted, always points in more than one direction, and confirms several conflicting generalisations. What warrants adoption of one over another? Again, positivists cannot know *a priori* which criteria will be best in practice. And even a general solution to the problem of Induction may not yield a particular criterion, since, even if we know that past observation is a general guide, we need not yet know how to decide what it shows. (We shall argue later that the problems are inseparable; without a particular criterion there is no general solution.)

The Deductive problem can be introduced with a dilemma about the place of pure theory in empirical science. Let us revert to Figure I (p. 9) and consider the relation between 'theory' 'logical deduction' 'definition' and 'hypothesis'. Presumably, in the spirit of Logical Positivism, definition and deduction contribute nothing on their own account to our knowledge of the world. Hypotheses, on the other hand, do contribute but only insofar as they are confirmed (and so, in general, only after the Inductive problem has been solved). The dilemma is whether a theory should be construed as a set of definitions and deductions from them or as a hypothesis (or set of related hypotheses). If a theory is a set of definitions and their consequences (such as the algorithms of maximising), then it consists of a set of analytic statements and so is, by the Positivist account, ultimately empty and optional. If it is a set of related hypotheses, economics is reduced to a wholly historical enquiry consisting of inductive generalisations, for which theorising, as the term is usually understood, provides no justification whatever, even if it helps in cutting corners.

The reader will no doubt retort that a theory is a compound of analytic and synthetic, thus apparently escaping the dilemma. Certainly neither horn by itself looks comfortable. For instance, the Identification and Specification problems at least seem to demand both that more than inductive generalisation is to be used in judging the relevance and significance of data and that econometrics consist of more than optional definitions and their consequences. But the dilemma is not escaped by choosing both horns. If induction (and historicism in general) is not sufficient to yield the criteria of economic knowledge, then the addition of optional rules for transforming statements will not be sufficient either.

The Deductive problem thus arises as soon as induction alone is found insufficient or, more subtly, as soon as deduction is given any epistemological part in solving the Inductive problem. It concerns the truths of logic, mathematics and other formal systems like kinship algebra or marginalist micro-economics and has two parts. The first is the nature of the necessity which marks such truths and how necessary truths are to be distinguished from others. The second is what, if anything, necessary truths have to do with matters of fact, how they can serve to describe a world which might have been otherwise and, if they do not have a descriptive function, what function they do have. For instance the Logical Theory of the Multiplier poses both aspects of the problem. Firstly, what sort of statements does it comprise, are they true and, if so, on what grounds? Secondly, how does the theory relate to the actual 'consequences of an expansion in the capital-goods industries, which take gradual effect, subject to time lag . . .'? These are epistemological questions but, we shall argue, crucial ones for economic theory.

Before passing on, we should perhaps indicate our own approach to the Inductive and Deductive problems. We shall argue in Chapters 6 and 7 that necessary truths are exactly what they seem, namely *a priori* truths vital to theorising, which states relations which must hold in the world market place. In other words we take the 'analytic' horn of the dilemma, arguing that theories are axiomatic systems on the geometrical model but denying that axiomatic systems are optional or empty. The axioms themselves, we then contend, are to be regarded as (putative) necessary truths and not as empirical assumptions or favoured hypotheses. Having thus claimed a truth for theoretical statements independent of the result of testing against experience and having rejected the logical positivists' account of necessary truths, we shall treat causal laws almost as if they were theorems in applied geometry. Our solution to the Inductive problem will be, in general, that without assumptions about continuity in the world scientific knowledge is impossible and, in particular, that a correlation is an instance of law only if there is a *theoretical* explanation of its significance. This approach will, we hope, lead to the rejection of some kinds of economic theory and the acceptance of others. But, since we must first overthrow some renowned theories of knowledge and then present our own, before arguing the merits of the approach, we shall withdraw into enigmatic silence for the time being.

We suggest, in short, that economic theories are to be judged partly by whether they are backed by a suitable scientific method which is itself backed by a sound theory of knowledge, which has an answer to the Inductive and Deductive problems. This is not a matter of hunting round for philosophical support for specific economic theories. It has to do with the foundations of economic theory in general. Again with apologies to scholars (this time to historians of ideas), we propose to divide economic theory into two great main streams, one flowing from the pens of Marshall and Walras, the other from Ricardo and Marx. Admittedly Marshall deemed Walras' system impractical (and so shall we) and Ricardo's politics are closer to Marshall than to Marx. Analytically, nonetheless, Marshall and Walras conceived the economy in the same way, as a set of interrelated markets, in which households and firms meet as demanders and suppliers. Their key questions concerned the interaction of demand and supply with gains and losses for households or firms in changing conditions. Ricardo and Marx, on the other hand, saw the economy as based on methods of production, controlled and operated by one class but worked by another. Their key questions concerned the division of output between the classes as conditions changed. The two visions of the economic system differ in many important ways and we do not think that they can or should be reconciled. There are grounds for choosing between them and, we shall contend, the grounds are philosophical. In our view Positivist epistemology provides crucial support for the neo-Classical picture. Indeed one version of neo-Classicism, Positive economics, stands or falls with Positivism and we shall attack this influential textbook alliance without mercy. But we shall not thereby undo the whole of neo-Classicism and so shall then have to develop our own theory of knowledge, a version of Rationalism, in order to find conceptual failings in neo-Classicism. Then, in seeking an economic theory free of such failings, we shall find ourselves proposing a rudimentary version of the Classical-Marxian conceptual scheme. Now, however, with this strategy in mind, we owe the reader a more precise definition of the neo-Classical and Classical-Marxian systems and an indication of the differences between them.

Neo-Classical versus Classical-Maxian economics

Empiricism, then, in its Positivist ramifications, supplies the general methodology of neo-Classicism, and we shall next explain what we understand by 'neo-Classicism'. (If our economic readers find what follows somewhat simple-minded, we remind them that philosophical readers probably will not and that we have therefore been content with a textbook account.) Figure 2, adapted from Samuelson and echoed in all major textbooks, shows what might be called a same-level division of society. Business and the public (producers and consumers), confront each other more or less as equals in the markets for both products and factors. (The equality is an overall one; there are some large or allied firms, some collective consumers.) Households demand final goods and services and supply the services of productive factors, in both cases in accord with what economists rather pompously call 'their given relative preference schedules', meaning what they like best. Businesses supply final goods and services according to their cost schedules in relation to the prices which consumers are prepared to pay, and demand the services of productive factors, according to their technical opportunites and needs in relation to consumer demand for products.

So goods and services flow counter-clockwise, while money flows clockwise. In each set of markets, *equivalents are traded for equivalents*, the value of goods and services flowing in one direction being just matched by the stream of revenue in the other. No exploitation is possible in competitive equilibrium. The value of household factor supplies just matches aggregate household demand and the output of goods and services by business just matches the value of productive services which business demands. This

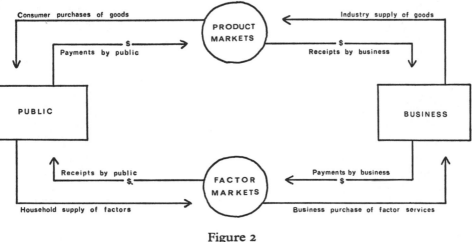

Consumer purchases of goods

PRODUCT MARKETS

Industry supply of goods

— $ —
Payments by public

— $ —
Receipts by business

PUBLIC

BUSINESS

Receipts by public
— $ —

FACTOR MARKETS

Payments by business
— $ —

Household supply of factors

Business purchase of factor services

Figure 2

may seem to ignore the fact that households save and businesses invest, meaning that some final demand flows not from the public but from business. But that is easily allowed for. To finance this demand, business must borrow household savings, by supplying bonds which the public demands. Bonds are treated as a kind of good, flowing counter-clockwise, while loans join the stream of money flowing clockwise. These points enable the micro-flow picture to be summed up as a macro-flow picture, illustrating in the simplest way how macro rests on micro foundations. It should also be clear that the market system adjusts so as to achieve the highest satisfaction possible for consumers, subject to the constraints of the technology and 'initial holdings' (meaning property arrangements). Business would be foolish to purchase factor services which are not needed, consumers to supply services for inadequate rewards. Thus factor services are all productive, in that they contribute to the efficient supply of goods which consumers demand and are offered voluntarily in the light of the reward they bring.

Obvious objections to this economic schema can easily be raised, and the standard replies illustrate the role of Positivism as defender of the economic faith. For instance, not all 'households' are on a par, since some *own* all the firms between them, while the rest merely *work for* the firms. Also the distribution of profit and similar income is not an exchange, since the only 'service' which the owner of a business, in his capacity as owner, need supply in return for its profits is that of permitting it to be owned by him. (He does bear risks, of course, but so do the employees who will be out of their jobs in the event of failure.) Other objections were mentioned earlier; for example, that orthodox neo-Classicism ignores technological

15

interdependences and institutional relationships, as the circular flow picture makes evident. Nowhere in it can one find social classes or any specific information about patterns of technical interdependence.

All these objections look at first like strong empirical problems which neo-Classicists should meet head on. In fact, however, the customary ortho-dox defence is oblique and philosophical. To the charge that their model rests on unrealistic assumptions, they reply that the *only* test of a model is the success of its predictions. So there is no *a priori* error in making un-realistic assumptions. Moreover, 'simplifying assumptions' and 'theoretical constructs' are bound to be, in some sense, 'unrealistic' and there is no predicting without them. Unrealistic assumptions may therefore be war-ranted and the warrant is philosophical, Positivism itself.

These defences will occupy us in the next few chapters. But now consider a quite different picture of capitalist society. Figure 3 epitomises the new approach, which, if the old is 'neo-Classical', could be dubbed 'Classical-Marxian'. It cannot be claimed that this is the only, or necessarily the best, distillation of an alternative picture from that tradition, but it will certainly serve to illustrate the contrasts.[7]

To keep the diagram comparable, we retain the circle for the final goods market and the box standing for industry, although we shall interpret both quite differently. 'Households' and the 'factor market' disappear altogether. Instead we have a pyramid, representing the social hierarchy, divided into two parts: a small upper class of owners and a large lower class of workers. Owners own industry and receive profits; workers work for industry and receive wages. Workers consume, but do not (in the simplified model) save; owners both consume and (save in order to) invest.

Now consider the flows of goods and services and money payments. Labour is the only 'factor input'; other inputs are produced by industry itself, which is assumed to have access to land, mines, etc. (We are lump-ing landlords and capitalists together.) Hence we might expect to be able to value the total product in terms of labour, and although the mathematics is complicated, this can indeed be done, although not in all cases. The arrows running back and forth between factories represent inter-industry transactions, the exchanges between industries necessary to replace used-up means of production. The net social product is sold for total receipts, and consists of all goods over and above those needed for replacement. These can be divided (for convenience) into necessities, luxuries and new capital goods. Necessities go for worker consumption, luxuries for capitalist

---

[7] Relatively few textbooks exist which embody this view. An old one, more Marxian than Classical, is Paul Sweezy, *Theory of Capitalist Development*, Monthly Review Press, 1942. A recent, but extremely difficult work is Goodwin, *Elementary Economics From the Higher Standpoint*.

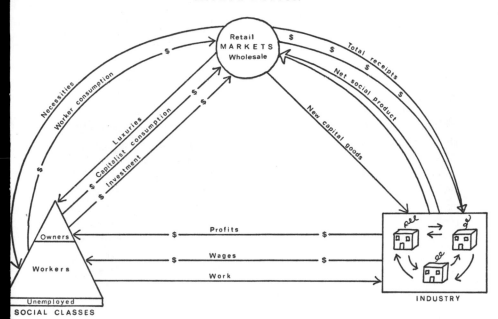

Figure 3

consumption, and new capital goods are installed in the factories in return for investment payments. Hence, the national accounts work out:

Total receipts
= net social product = wages + profits
= wage consumption + capitalist consumption + investment demand
= necessities + luxuries + new capital goods.

There are striking differences between this and the neo-Classical diagram (Figure 2). The basic constituents of the neo-Classical vision are consumers and firms, whose optimising behaviour can be described with the aid of equations. The object is to predict such behaviour and its consequences, taking for granted the circumstances in which the behaviour occurs. The alternative vision, by contrast, begins by examining what neo-Classicism takes for granted. It is concerned with structure, with dependencies between institutions, with what makes for continuance or disintegration. Its basic constituents are industries, sectors, processes and activities, defined in technological terms. The constituents do not normally coincide with the neo-Classical 'decision-making' agencies.[8] Nor is the object to predict what

---

[8] Neither 'household' nor 'firm' nor any synonym appears in Sraffa's *Production of Commodities By Means of Commodities*, the canonical foundation of the alternative vision.

17

will happen. Instead the object is to arrive at a blueprint of the economic system which explains how the system responds to institutional changes. The blueprint is essentially an analysis of the nature of production and of the social relations surrounding production.

Production, to the traditional neo-Classicist, is a 'one way street', running from 'primary' factors to 'final products'. The primary factors are land, labour and, especially, capital, each receiving in competition a reward proportional to its 'contribution'. This involves a unified theory applying to all three factors, which nineteenth-century proponents of the Marginalist Revolution saw as its great achievement. The Classical-Marxian paradigm rejects the whole approach. 'Capital', for instance, is regarded as ambiguous between legal property in the means of production, which, being a homogeneous fund of value, can be embodied in different forms, and produced means of production or heterogeneous capital goods like tools, instruments, machines and plant, created and used by labour. 'Capital', as property, is relevant to the analysis of the distribution of income; 'capital', as goods, is relevant to the study of production; but there is no unitary stuff of 'capital' which helps to set the level of the rate of profit, since the amount of 'capital' as property depends on the price of 'capital' as goods, which depends in turn on an antecedent rate of profit.

Once the role and indeed the nature of profit is called into question, other differences appear. In the neo-Classical vision profit is a payment (and a fair one when profits are 'normal') and wages plus profits are an exchange for the services of the factors of production, thereby providing a theory of the distribution of income. In the Classical-Marxian vision, distribution of income and exchange of goods are wholly different. Whereas wages as a whole are paid for work, profits as a whole are paid for nothing at all. Since payment of profit is not an exchange, there can be no equilibrium, in the usual sense, and no such thing as 'normal profit'. Nor are profit-based indicators the only or necessarily the best criteria for allocating investment, especially since what maximises growth need not maximise consumption. Correspondingly, the division of income, taken by neo-Classicists as determined in the factor market by the marginal contribution of relatively scarce factors, is related in the Classical-Marxian vision to all aspects of the economy. Labour's share is given by the real wage times the amount of work and, as Keynes emphasises in his *General Theory* (Chapter 2), the real wage is the money wage divided by an index of consumer goods prices. The money wage is set in the labour market and prices in the final goods market. Labour's share thus depends on both markets and, moreover, influences consumer demand. Consequently the Classical-Marxian economist claims to see and find crucial a host of interdependencies which play no part in neo-Classical analysis.

Neo-Classical thinkers do not deny the existence of social hierarchy; they deny only that incorporating it in economics results in useful predictions. They regard J. B. Clark's strategy for collapsing the two aspects of 'capital' into a single notion as a master-stroke which simplifies a hugely complex problem and reduces the theory of capital to a special case of price theory.[9] The claim that profit is not paid in exchange for anything is, in their view, a disguised value judgement, a 'persuasive' redefinition of exchange. There is a capital market; the price of capital is a price like any other. Profit-based indicators may not be perfect but actual markets only approximate to those of pure theory. Naturally, the real wage depends upon all other prices; neo-Classicals have always insisted that all markets are interdependent. But the interdependence cannot be portrayed in a picture which ignores marginal productivity.

We mention these differences (and there are many more) not to claim advantage for either vision but to make a philosophical point about the role of categories and concepts in theorising. Neither approach counts as a 'scientific hypothesis', by the Positivist definition of the term. For instance, in order to conduct a comparative test, an umpire would have to decide whether the payment of profits (rent, interest, etc.) is an exchange and this is a conceptual rather than (in the Positivist sense) empirical question. He would have to decide whether there is a basic social division into producers and consumers or whether the key concepts are those of hierarchy and class. Observation will not settle the point. No actual societies are as simple as these models, nor are actual institutions always easy to classify. Moreover each vision can accommodate the findings of the other, by assigning them a subordinate role. Many neo-Classical models include 'structural' relationships and many Classical-Marxian models include behavioural functions. But there remains a difference in emphasis, whose correctness cannot be judged, as we shall argue in later chapters, without making assumptions about the underlying correctness of one of the rival visions.

Our point, then, is that the assumptions and categories of each theory are paradigmatic and fall outside the scope of empirical testing of rival consequences. But this takes us into water too deep for an introductory chapter and we must leave it here with a bald synopsis. Baldly, different philosophical strategies are involved. Neo-Classicists predicate behavioural functions of individual decision-makers, paying little attention to institutional detail, except where it can be expressed in behavioural functions (as in the imperfect competitor's downward-sloping demand curve or the kinked oligopoly demand curve); Classical and Marxian theorists base their

---

[9] Cf. P. A. Samuelson, Parable and realism in capital theory: the surrogate production function, *Review of Economic Studies*, vol. 29, no. 3 (June 1962).

equations on institutional structures and may use few behavioural equations. This reflects a difference in views about the nature of society and the individual. Neo-Classicists see behaviour characteristically as the outcome of maximising decisions; Classical and Marxian theorists find behaviour expressed (as with the classical savings function) in sociological data,[10] and regard maximising as an instrument for deciding the best means to an end rather than as a description of what men do. This reflects a difference in philosophies of mind and theories of action. Neo-Classicists treat sound theory as the upshot of testing predictions with success; Classical and Marxian theorists insist that specifications and identifications be determined *a priori* by reflecting on what is essential to capitalist industrial institutions. This reflects a difference in epistemology.

Summary and preview

These are the alliances between philosophy and economics which we shall find at every turn. The first four chapters of the book will be concerned with that between Positivism and neo-Classicism. In Chapter 1 we ask why the failure of many neo-Classical predictions does not count as refuting neo-Classical theories and are met with a philosophical account of the function of *ceteris paribus* clauses. In Chapter 2 we suggest that neo-Classical theories are made viciously circular by the inclusion of maximising notions and are thus led to discuss the analytic-synthetic distinction. In Chapter 3 a query about the significance of an apparently constant capital-output ratio of 3:1 starts a debate about theories, hypotheses and induction. In Chapter 4 we find that, in attaching sense to terms like 'the price of a good', we must deny that facts are independent of theories. In each of these chapters, however, we reject the Positivist account and so, we hope, leave neo-Classicists without any coherent methodology or criteria of scientific merit. Chapters 5 to 9 survey the wreckage in a search for fresh criteria. In Chapter 5 we consider revealed preference theory as a philosophical thesis about the explanation of economic behaviour and suggest an analysis of the concept of action which favours linear programming models against revealed preference models. But the use of linear programming models needs to be backed by a fresh theory of knowledge and in Chapters 6 and 7, having rejected Pragmatism, we deploy our own solution to the problem of *a priori* knowledge. This yields the way of dealing with the Inductive and Deductive problems hinted at earlier and an axiomatic approach to theorising which favours programming and production models

---

[10] Cf. N. Kaldor, Marginal productivity and the macro-economic theories of distribution, *Review of Economic Studies*, vol. 33, no. 96 (October 1966).

against predictive models. Finally, in Chapters 8 and 9 we claim philosophical merit for Classical-Marxian economics, coming as close as we dare to asserting, in the spirit of the axiomatic method, that economics is essentially about relations of production.

We must again give warning that much has been sacrificed to clarity. Philosophically, in particular, we have confined our attention to Positivism, Pragmatism and an approach to epistemology which owes most to Leibniz and Kant. We have steered clear of much recent technical work in the philosophy of science by insisting on the primacy of unresolved epistemological issues. Our chapters on *a priori* knowledge show a reluctant disregard for many important complexities of a fascinating topic. Even so, we suspect that we have made life quite hard enough for the non-philosopher, just as non-economists may meet trouble with many passages which economists find irritatingly simple. Nevertheless we are convinced that philosophy matters to economics. Every scientific method has its metaphysics. Logical positivists used to report the death of metaphysics, but, as Mark Twain remarked on reading his own obituary in the newspapers one morning, the reports were exaggerated. We shall find metaphysical roots sustaining Positivism and so Positive economics. That is itself no fault (although positivists would presumably think it one) and our quarrel is with the nature of the metaphysics. We deny that the problems of methodology end when a philosophy of science has been propounded. The philosophy of science needs justification in its turn from a theory of knowledge. A theory of knowledge is, in our view, a general argument for general claims about what there is. This applies to Empiricism no less than to Rationalism and such general claims satisfy the logical positivists' definition of metaphysics. But such abstract reflections carry no weight unless they emerge from the dust of intellectual conflict. Let us therefore embark on our first problem, that of Relevance and Falsification.

I

RELEVANCE AND FALSIFICATION

The winds of change have been unkind to Positivism. Few professional philosophers in Britain and fairly few in America still avow it. Instead they practise what Milton calls 'a fugitive and cloistered virtue', currently known as Linguistic or Conceptual Analysis. This style of philosophising is anti-imperialist and neither has nor will make much impact on economic theory. Over the entrance to the cloister is written '*Il faut cultiver nos jardins*'.

Positivism and current economic disputes

Positivism is neither fugitive nor cloistered. It demands a say in the councils of the world both where theorists meet and where scientists go to work. Wielding the analytic-synthetic distinction, it dismisses the wisdom of the ages as metaphysical rubbish. It makes a difference to all enquiry. For, if it is well-founded, science is to be done in one way; if ill-founded, in another. Its contempt for habitual thought is vented not only against *a priori* speculation but also against ordinary language. For, since we choose what our words are to mean, the fact that language is used in a certain way never shows that it ought to be so used. Bertrand Russell has remarked that ordinary language embodies the metaphysics of the Stone Age. A positivist is likely to agree. Such cavalier tones are not for the cloister.

To cultivate a philosophical garden for its own sake is ultimately pointless. For what grows is only what is planted and the lesson of many centuries is Export or Die. We shall here support the Positivist belief that philosophy makes a difference. But Positivism makes the wrong difference.

Positive economics, according to Milton Friedman, 'is to provide a system of generalizations that can be used to make correct predictions about the consequences of any change in circumstances ... [it] is to be judged by its predictive power for the class of phenomena which it is intended to "explain"'.[1] If so, it is hard to see why economic theory is still beset with

---

[1] The methodology of Positive economics, in his *Essays in Positive Economics* (University of Chicago Press, 1953); p. 4. in the Phoenix edition of 1966.

raging disputes and why so few general laws are widely accepted or well-confirmed. Disputes, according to Positivism, are to be resolved by testing and tests will lead to a gradual accumulation of laws. Yet almost every field of economics is a battle-field with little prospect of peace by negotiation. Growth theory has at least three factions, neo-Classical, neo-Keynesian and neo-Marxist.[2] Short-term macro-theory divides between those who assert and those who deny that underemployment equilibrium with flexible wages and prices is possible[3] (those who assert and those who deny that a perfect price system works perfectly). In micro-theory the quarrel between perfect and imperfect competition grew into a larger one between the 'full cost' doctrine and marginalism in general,[4] only to see a new generation of graduate students abandon both sides for game theory and organisation theory.[5] Nor are these conflicts confined to the West, where some might seek their origin in apologetics for the capitalist system. In the Soviet Union, too, debate rages between supporters and opponents of the theory of Optimal Planning.[6] But the thickest fighting of all is around the fountain-head of analytical economics, which is distribution theory or the determination of the relative shares of wages, profits and rents. Ricardo saw this as the central question of economic theory. The criticism of neo-Classical price theory turns on its failure to explain the rate of profit and the central issue in the Soviet debate on optional planning is how to calculate profits and prices. By now much is known, little understood and a hundred flowers bloom.

Why does testing not settle these disputes? The stock answer is that tests alone are not enough. Results need proper interpretation, if only to make sure that they have not been distorted by non-economic interferences. But the practical snags of proper interpretation can hardly be

---

[2] If we may be allowed some freedom in labelling the work of economists like Robert Solow, Nicholas Kaldor and Joan Robinson.

[3] For example, D. Patinkin, in *Money, Interest and Prices* (2nd ed., Harper and Row, 1965), and others have argued that the Pigou effect in theoretically perfect markets guarantees automatic full employment, while J. G. Gurley and E. S. Shaw in *Money in a Theory of Finance* (The Brookings Institution, 1960), have argued that the existence of financial intermediaries invalidates the Pigou effect. The Pigou effect is not taken very seriously as an empirical phenomenon and A. Leijonhufvud, *Keynesian Economics and the Economics of Keynes* (Oxford University Press, 1970), gives excellent theoretical grounds for dismissing it altogether.

[4] Cf. R. Hall and C. J. Hitch, Price theory and business behaviour, in *Oxford Studies in the Price Mechanism*, ed. P. Andrews and T. Wilson (Oxford University Press, 1951).

[5] Martin Shubik, A curmudgeon's guide to micro economics, *Journal of Economic Literature*, vol. VIII, no. 2 (June 1970).

[6] Michael Ellman, *Soviet Planning Today* (Cambridge University Press, 1971); Brody, *Proportions, Press and Planning*.

the only reason for so many battles and so few known laws. Indeed the list of 'laws' seems to be shrinking. The laws of increasing and diminishing returns appear to have been expunged from the statute book and the regulations governing the relations of wages- and profit-rates to capital intensity recently withdrawn.[7] Yet nothing has replaced these once widely accepted generalisations. By the usual standards of scientific advance, this is retreat.

The difficulty, we shall contend, is to be blamed less on economics than on the Positivist canon. 'Testing' we shall argue is neither so straightforward nor so decisive a process as a simple version of Positivism suggests. It will turn out to be unclear in principle what exactly is being tested and what the test shows. Even when a prediction clearly fails to fit the facts, it is unclear whether the theory is thus refuted or whether, alternatively, the facts should be reinterpreted. Even when the theory is demonstrably at fault, it is still unclear whether rejection is called for or merely modification. At this stage we shall be addressing ourselves strictly to Positivism and we shall conclude that the notions of prediction and explanation cannot be analysed and related as positivists propose. In a later chapter we shall offer pragmatism a chance to repair the shortcomings of Positivism, but at present we are content to work with the familiar tie between Positivism and neo-Classical or Positive economics.

Positivism is a fighting philosophy. It offers both the supply and the demand sides of the neo-Classical picture a defence against some inviting (and, we argue later, largely correct) criticisms. For instance, Milton Friedman's rebuttal of the charge that the assumptions of perfect competition theory are unrealistic is a Positivist one, as we shall presently see. The doctrine of Consumer Sovereignty is guarded from scrutiny by the fact/value distinction, which makes consumer preferences into value judgements whose merits cannot be scientifically disputed. The division of market forces into those which represent the decisions of supplying (or demanding) firms and those which represent the decisions of demanding (or supplying) households rests on a Positivist case for grounding the theory of knowledge on atomic units. Institutions as social wholes, like classes, are constructed from individual propensities to behave in certain ways. Neo-Classical thinking on production, which we quarrel with in a later

---

[7] See G. C. Harcourt, *Some Cambridge Controversies in the Theory of Capital* (Cambridge University Press, 1972). Cf. also E. J. Nell, A note on *Cambridge Controversies, Journal of Economic Literature*, vol. 8, no. 1 (March 1970); L. Pasinetti, Switches of technique and the rate of return in capital theory, *Economic Journal*, vol. 79, no. 315 (Sept. 1969); J. Robinson, *Economic Heresies: Some Old-Fashioned Questions in Economic Theory* (Basic Books, 1971), Ch. 4.

chapter, has leant heavily on Positivism for defence. Positivism makes a difference, and, we shall maintain, the wrong difference.

Testing: criteria of application, 'ceteris paribus' clauses and true values of variables

Let us begin with the account of testing implied in the model of our introductory chapter. All statements, we have proposed on the positivists' behalf, are either analytic and vacuous or synthetic and empirically refutable. Predictions are got by deducing them logically (with the help of mathematics) from hypotheses. There is therefore no point in testing a 'prediction', unless whatever it was deduced from is synthetic. Indeed it would be impossible to do so, since a statement, to be empirically testable, must be synthetic and analytic statements imply only other analytic statements. Hypotheses are therefore synthetic and are to be tested by testing their implications. The implications (or predictions) are synthetic and so suitable for testing the hypotheses. Or so positivists would have us believe.

But how is the testing of an economist's predictions to be done? The history of the world is the history of contingently connected states, almost none of which is purely economic. Presumably the economist is interested not so much in economic events as in economic aspects of events which also have other aspects of interest to all sorts of other enquirers. And, whether he deals with events or aspects of events, it is surely false that economic effects have only economic causes. Changes in the level of output, for instance, may occur when not predicted by economists or not occur when predicted by economists for countless non-economic reasons. So the economist needs to stake out his ground, in order to specify what is to count as a decisive test of an economic theory. In other words, recalling that 'sciences are distinguished by their subject matter and not by their methodology' (tenet (x) of our introductory account of Positive science), he must distinguish economics and specify conditions in which the success or failure of prediction is decisive. This involves three related steps; firstly to give criteria of application for his theoretical terms, secondly to specify *ceteris paribus* clauses excluding external interference, thirdly to give rules for adjusting the observed values of his variables so as to remove distortion. Each step raises tricky methodological issues.

First then, theoretical terms need criteria of application, if they are to function as *economic* terms at all. The point is best made with an example, all too familiar to economists, however arcane it may seem to philosophers. Consider a small maximising problem, starting with the function

$$u = n(q_1, q_2, \ldots, q_n)$$

25

whose first derivatives are positive and second negative (as the qs increase, u increases, but ever more slowly), and the side condition

$$y = p_1 q_1 + \ldots + p_n q_n.$$

To maximise u subject to y we form the expression

$$v = u + \lambda(y - p_1 q_1 - \ldots - p_n q_n)$$

which we differentiate, setting the derivative equal to zero:

$$\frac{\delta v}{\delta q_1} = u_1 - \lambda p_1 = 0$$

$$\ldots \frac{\delta v}{\delta q_n} = u_n - \lambda p_n = 0$$

$$\frac{\delta v}{\delta \lambda} = y - p_1 q_1 - \ldots - p_n q_n = 0$$

where λ is a La Grangean multiplier. The solution of this set of equations will give the set of qs which will maximise u subject to y, where the p_i are given.

So far there is no breath of economics in this. It is simply a well known algorithm in the differential calculus. To infuse it with economics, we must interpret it. So let u stand for utility, q_i for the quantity of the ith commodity, p_i for its price and y for income. But this is still not economics as philosophers will readily see. It is simply an instruction to replace some symbols with others. The new symbols need interpretation in their turn, if the whole is to be a significant and true theorem about the maximising of a consumer's utility. Moreover, the whole, when interpreted, must be able to be understood as describing the behaviour of Mr Hollis, Mr Nell or some other actual economic agent. The utility is the consumer's utility, the income is his income, the quantities consumed are his quantities. The variables in the model are action-variables and represent the actions of a suitable agent. (We shall see later how problems may arise when we try to apply action-variables from the model to actual agents and shall argue that some puzzles about the role of assumptions in economic models can be solved by distinguishing a special class of assumptions which characterise economic agents.)

A term like 'utility' becomes an economic term, only if it is either directly applicable, with the help of empirical criteria, to economic behaviour or conceptually linked to other terms which are directly applicable. Criteria will therefore be needed both to identify suitable economic agents and to determine which of their actions count as exemplifying the variables in the model. To give the formal apparatus just cited an economic interpretation we must be able to identify the consumer behaviour which this formal algorithm is to represent. Otherwise terms like 'utility', 'commodity' 'price' and 'income' are merely interdefined and do not yet function as economic terms.

Insistence that theoretical terms need criteria of application is especially important to Positivists, on account of their doctrine that to know the meaning of a term is to know the conditions for the truth of statements containing it. Thus in saying 'Let u stand for utility', we give the term 'utility' only a formal meaning; whereas, in supplying the two sets of criteria just mentioned for its application, we license its use as an economic term and give it what might be called empirical sense. The criteria are likely to be complex – 'utility', for instance, is to denote something continuous and infinitely divisible, which can increase at a decreasing rate or decrease at an increasing rate – and it cannot be assumed that any actual economic phenomena satisfy them. But no model is an economic model unless it includes criteria which make it applicable in principle.

To introduce the second requirement, that *ceteris paribus* clauses are needed, let us notice that these criteria of application are, furthermore, selective and even regulative. Economic theories are not to be refuted by the intrusion of non-economic factors into economic data. No test is decisive, unless *ceteris* are *paribus*. For example, the proposition that 'less will be bought at a higher price' is not refuted by panic buying, set off by rising prices, taken to signify the imminence of invasion. Nor is it confirmed by organised consumer boycotts. *Ceteris paribus* clauses are therefore needed both to distinguish economic from non-economic influences and, within the economic realm, to distinguish relevant from irrelevant influences. Their role is in effect to state the conditions under which the test of a theory is to count as decisive. To fulfil the role, they must be finite in number and be specific and directly applicable. It must also be possible to decide independently of the theory whether they hold in a given case or not. Otherwise, and here we are giving warning of our line of attack, there will be no way of knowing whether a discrepancy between theory and facts refutes the theory or merely shows that *ceteris* were *imparibus*.

The difficulty shows the Inductive problem in action, although philosophers may find the connection more evident than economists. A *ceteris paribus* clause is used to assert that some well-defined exogenous variable remains constant and exerts no influence during the observation period. (Frictionless Motion provides a revealing case study, which we discuss in an appendix to this chapter.) Standardly, however, this is not true and so, to test a theory, we must have a way of discounting the outside influence. Since this means being able to assess the influence of the exogenous on the endogenous variables, we need in effect an interdisciplinary theory, which will be more sophisticated than the theory we are trying to test and which, moreover, will need to be already well-confirmed. In order for the interdisciplinary theory to have been already confirmed, it must already have been successfully tested. Yet, if it has any *ceteris paribus* clauses, this re-creates the same problem in more general form. If it (or any more general theory) has no *ceteris paribus* clauses, then how do we know? The only answer is that we would already have to have a solution to the Inductive problem, without which no theory can be tested at all.[8]

Thirdly, even when *ceteris* are *paribus*, a test may have a dubious result because statisticians cannot measure with sufficient nicety. Precise measurement is costly and the agencies, such as tax-collection bureaux, which collect data, are often not working primarily for economists. Yet such agencies often produce the only facts to be had. Calling this sort of partly raw data 'the observed value of economic variables', we may note that the observed values may not be wholly accurate. But that is a practical difficulty, serving mainly to introduce a point which is crucial to our argu-ment. For the observed values of variables are not the decisive test. They must be corrected for measurement error and non-economic interferences and then redefined, to yield what we shall call 'the true values of the variables'.

Let us restate the point more fully. The categories of observation are only rarely the categories of theory and hence observations must be ad-justed to yield the true variables. Observations occur in particular circum-stances subject to myriad local or temporary influences; the variables are defined for the general case and can be arrived at only after adjusting the results of observation. As Haavelmo puts it, 'The true variables are variables such that, if their behaviour should contradict a theory, the theory would be rejected as false.'[9] Despite a risk of circularity, every econometrician knows that he must distinguish true from observed values of variables and that is why criteria of application are selective and even regulative.

Two illustrative cases: racial discrimination and
estimating a demand curve

An illustration may help to drive the point home. Taking a theory about 'human capital' and the economic effects of racial discrimination,[10] sup-

---

[8] It may be objected that this argument overlooks the role of observation statements and of 'brute atomic facts' in testing. After all, *ceteris* are surely *paribus*, when an observer reports a brute fact without interpretation? Our reply, however, is that infer-ence is always involved in judging the relevance of 'brute facts' and indeed, in anticipation of our argument in Chapter 4, that theory is involved even in identifying 'brute facts'.

[9] T. Haavelmo, The inadequacy of testing dynamic theory by comparing theoretical solu-tions and observed cycles, *Econometrica*, vol. 8, no. 3 (Jan. 1940).

[10] See Jacob Mincer (ed.), *Economic Forecasts and Expectations* (National Bureau of Economic Research, 1969).

pose we derive the hypothesis that extra years of education increase earning power in all classes but increase it less among urban blacks in the same proportion as any other investment earns less for urban blacks. Income forgone during schooling is treated as the investment and extra discounted life-time earnings are treated as the return. The return will be lower for urban blacks than for urban whites, but, because of discrimination, so will the rate of return in any other line of investment open to blacks. Within the black ghetto community, competition prevails and returns at the margin will be equal. With all this in mind, let us reflect on a recent study,[11] which found the rate of return on extra education to be zero, or even negative, for ghetto blacks. The finding requires at least three hypotheses to be rejected or modified, namely that returns at the margin are not equal in the black ghetto, since there is a positive, if low, rate to be had on savings deposits; that discrimination does not affect all investment opportunities equally; that the decision to undertake education may not be adequately understood as an investment decision. That is apparently the upshot of the study referred to.

But is it? The finding is open to serious criticism.[12] Data on black earnings were not adjusted for age or changes of residence. Change in the composition by age of the earning population would have affected the pattern of earnings and the people, whose earnings were shown, were not necessarily the same people or the same kind of people who were being educated. Those successful at school, for instance, may have moved out of the ghetto. In brief, the earnings series used to test the original proposition was incorrectly defined and the observations were not strictly appropriate to the theoretical questions. These criticisms serve to illustrate our point that, even if *ceteris* are *paribus*, so that there is no interference from non-economic and other irrelevant influences, nevertheless observed values of variables may seriously mislead, until corrected to true values.

How are these corrections to be made? The case is different from that of discounting external influence. Here we are adjusting the results of observation to suit the terms of the theory. (Frictionless Motion this time provides a revealing contrast as we discuss in the appendix to the present chapter.) To make the adjustment, the econometrician must do more than simply regroup his data – otherwise the present problem would not have arisen at all. Yet, if he appeals to a further theory, that theory must be already well-confirmed, which raises the threat of a regress just discussed. So it seems that he must follow normal practice by making the ad-

[11] See Bennet W. Harrison, *Education, Training and the Urban Ghetto* (Johns Hopkins University Press, 1972).
[12] See Elizabeth Durbin, Education and earnings in the urban ghettoes: comment, *The American Economist* (Spring 1970).

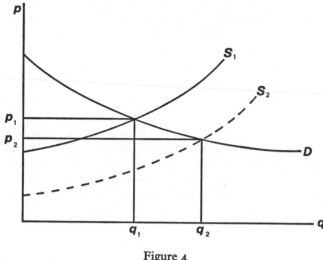

Figure 4

justments on the basis of the theory being tested itself. This is wholly illicit, however, by the Positivist canon and so those who wish to do it have a reason, and indeed a duty, to object to the canon.

To study the tactics of adjustment in a more general case, let us recall the model of consumer behaviour introduced a few pages back. From that model a demand curve can be derived by letting prices vary and the market demand curve can be got by summing over individuals. Now suppose the supply curve for the industry is given.[13] Equilibrium price and quantity will be found at the intersection of the curves. Suppose next that the supply curve shifts downward, owing to a new invention. The new equilibrium will be at a lower price and larger quantity. Just such a shift is a test of the statement that the demand curve falls from left to right (Figure 4). The questions are, firstly, what *ceteris paribus* clauses are involved in conducting the test properly and, secondly, how can we ensure that our observations are rightly presented as 'true values of variables'? Let us here concentrate on the latter issue.

The usual assumptions are needed about competition, perfect information and sufficiently rapid adjustment by consumers and producers. (Allowance must be made for the fact that these assumptions are standardly

---

[13] We are assuming, strictly for present purposes, that industries coincide with markets, or that, where they do not, suitable adjustments can be made in applying the model. (This is another example of how criteria can be selective and even regulative.) The assumption conceals a huge theoretical problem, some aspect of which will be tackled in Chapters 8 and 9 but will serve for the moment.

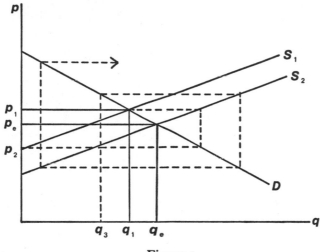

Figure 5

false!) But that is not all. Suppose, for instance, that the demand curve does slope down from left to right but the test appears to show something different. Thus suppose both curves are linear, the supply curve being slightly the flatter, and that quantity and price adjust to one another with a one-period lag. Initially price is p_1 and quantity q_1. From exogenous causes, the supply curve shifts and quantity adjusts itself but in excess of the demand at p_1. So price falls to p_2, which after one period calls forth a lesser quantity q_3. Demand now exceeds supply and price rises above p_i and a 'hog cycle' is generated (see Figure 5).

Now suppose the test were run when p_2 and q_3 were the market position. We should have to say that, when the supply curve shifts outwards and price falls, quantity also falls, which would imply that the demand curve slopes upwards from left to right more steeply than the supply curve (see Figure 6).

This case reminds us that any actual test situation is dynamic, as it must be when the test is a test of the effects of change. Hence allowance must be made for the effects of adjustment to the new equilibrium. But that lands us in a hornet's nest. To test a simple static proposition we would wish to compare static positions. Static positions occur in time and hence there must be dynamic adjustment; actual variables are dynamic and hence our observations are unsuited in themselves to test the static theory. So we must adjust our observations. But on what principles?

Economists, versed in the lore of higher theory, might suggest an appeal to the 'Correspondence Principle' (doubtless unknown to most philo-

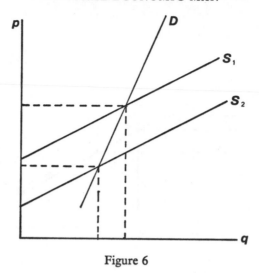

Figure 6

sophers) which states that the dynamic stability conditions of a model will determine the reaction of a static system to a displacement of one or more of its parameters. But such an appeal must be rejected by the high court of Positivism. For we can hardly assume the truth of the Correspondence Principle *a priori* and we should need to know what the comparative statics results were before we could claim to know what the dynamic stability conditions of the model were. We would have to know the equilibrium position before we could know anything about its stability. Those who are fastidious about not assuming what they are trying to prove must look elsewhere.

The traditional and sensible way to elude these difficulties is, firstly, to lay down *ceteris paribus* conditions stating that the dynamic adjustment path is not to affect the equilibrium, upon which it must converge before the other parameters of the model change (which would cause the equilibrium to shift). Secondly, to insist that the true values are those reached after the dynamic adjustment is completed. (Thus (p_1, q_1) are true values and so are (p_e, q_e); but (p_2, q_3) are not). This entails knowing how to recognise when such an adjustment is finished. These two requirements together specify the conditions under which a test will be a decisive test.

We have so far pointed out that theoretical terms need criteria of application and then removed an initial difficulty in the notion of 'testing' in two ways. One was by distinguishing between observed and true values of variables. The other was by arguing that *ceteris paribus* clauses must be included, in particular one to the effect that dynamic factors are not to be considered. In doing so, we have not strayed from the sober path of commonsense. Economists otherwise cannot conduct reliable tests. But our sobriety, far from being a testimonial for the positivism set out earlier, diverts the hornets into an attack on the positivists, which will occupy the rest of this chapter.

Falsified predictions versus unfulfilled assumptions

Tenet (viii), 'the test of a theory is the success of its predictions' originally seemed to say that a theory predicted an actual order of events and that a hypothesis was to be discarded when the predicted sequences failed to occur. But it now turns out that the theory is to predict not what will be observed to happen, but what would be observed, if the values of the variables were the true ones and if 'other things' were 'equal'. To coin a slogan, prediction is not of what will happen but of what would happen, if ... Consequently no theory can be refuted merely by showing its assumptions to be unrealistic or its predictions not to fit the facts. For predictions are standardly tested against observed values of variables in conditions where 'other things' are not 'equal'. If it further turns out that what the true values are and by how much other things are unequal depend on the theory being tested, then predictions will be standardly irrefutable. (To say that p_1, q_1, and p_e q_e are true values, whereas p_2 q_3 are not, presupposes the theory of market equilibrium; and to say that a dynamic adjustment is complete presupposes a theory of dynamic adjustment.) We contend that just this fate does befall Positivism. Statements of what will happen, we shall argue, are synthetic but statements of what would happen, if ... are analytic. The sober path of commonsense leads positivists to absurdity.

We shall state our case first simply and then more subtly. The simple version is intended to make our meaning plain and the subtle version to remove an objection. Put simply, if the test of an economic theory is that it 'make [s] correct predictions about the consequences of any change in circumstances' (Friedman, The methodology of Positive economics), then textbook Positive micro-economics is in trouble. The marginal analysis, for instance, does not predict what will happen as a result of change in demand. Instead it 'predicts' what would happen, if certain assumptions held. This is not yet objectionable, since conditional statements can be synthetic. For instance, the statement 'if Bloggs & Sons produce at $MC = MR$, they will maximise their profits' sounds synthetic. But the marginal analysis results in statements like 'if the market is perfect and cost curves are conventionally shaped and ceteris are paribus, then, if Bloggs & Sons produce at $MC = MR$, they will maximise their profits'.

33

This statement is a tautology and so, by the Positivist account of analyticity, it is devoid of all factual content, and hence cannot be tested.

Indeed the whole idea of testing the marginal analysis is absurd. For what could a test reveal? Negative results show only that the market is defective. Various interpretations can be given – observed values are not true values of variables, or there has been non-economic interference, or that cost curves, although truly recorded, are ill-behaved or that the market is imperfect in some other way. But one interpretation is not possible – that the marginal analysis has been refuted. Even if an allegedly perfect and perfectly well-behaved market were constructed, it still could not be used to test the analysis. For the test could still only reveal whether the market was as perfect as alleged. A perfect market simply is one which conforms to the model.

To generalise the point, marginalist statements to the effect that, if the assumptions of Positive micro-economics hold, then so-and-so will happen, are tautologies and their consequents are simply logical deductions from their protases. If producing at $MC = MR$ does not maximise profits, then there is not the least chance that values of variables are true and *ceteris* are *paribus*. Hence the model is untestable.

The same point arises from the suggestion made earlier that appeal to the Correspondence Principle will isolate static positions in dynamic settings. The statement of the principle is either analytic or synthetic. If it is synthetic, then our objection remains that it needs to be assumed in order to establish its truth, which is methodologically vicious. If it is analytic, then it has one effect only, namely to ensure that no test actually tests what it is supposed to. For discrepancies again reveal merely the degree of disparity between observed and true.

Our case, put simply, is thus that we cannot distinguish the failure of a model to agree with the true values of observed variables from the failure of 'other things' to be 'equal'. The former refutes the model; the latter does not. But we now need to guard against the charge that we are misconstruing the form of economic laws. In the example just discussed, we considered the equilibrium condition $MC = MR$ and earlier we compared different price-quantity situations, some of which were static equilibria and others not. It could be objected that we have created our own problems by confusing statements of equilibrium condition, like $MC = MR$, which are analytic with synthetic statements of general laws. This confusion creates the apparent puzzle that no model can be refuted by the facts; but the puzzle vanishes, when it is seen that a test never tests a whole model but, rather, only the synthetic components of a model. In reply, we agree that equilibrium conditions are to be distinguished from general empirical hypotheses (although we do not agree that statements of the former are analytic at any rate in any Positivist sense). But this does us no damage. On the contrary, drawing the distinction makes it still more difficult to say what a test is supposed to test. To show this, we shall next restate the case more subtly by considering the sorts of predictions that might be tested.

A 'general economic law' of the form beloved of positivists might be formulated:

(I) 'All business firms tend to maximise profits.'

(The phrase 'tend to' is included to allow for periods of adjustment, human error and so forth. Another formulation might be, 'In perfect markets all business firms maximise profits', even though the lurking tautology would then be more evident.)

Having been instructed that economics is a science of empirical general-isations, we set ourselves to test (I). Are we to test whether business firms do equate MC with MR? (For the long run or the short? And are claims for the 'long run' verifiable?) Or are we to test whether equating MC with MR does actually maximise profits in competitive conditions? The former test in-volves using the model to judge the firms and, regardless of whatever they say they are doing, they are not maximising profits, if they fail it. The latter test apparently involves using the firms to judge the model and, if firms in fact maximise profits without equating MC with MR, then the model presumably falls. That gives us another 'general economic law':

(II) 'Equating MC with MR maximises profits.'

Either we assume (II) in order to test (I) or we assume (I) in order to test (II). But we cannot test both. If we do assume (I) in order to test (II), we shall be treating (I) as analytic, in the sense that we refuse to count as a 'business firm' any organisation which is not a profit maximiser, except insofar as departures from the ideal are tidied away under the phrase 'tend to'. If we assume (II), then we assume it to be analytic. Whichever we assume, we use it to rule out apparent exceptions to the other. The upshot is that we cannot test either.

It might be objected at this point that, properly understood, neither (I) nor (II) represents a Positive economic law. (I), it may be said, defines the class of agents the model applies to; (II) is intended to be analytic all along, but is a truth of geometry, interpreted to fit economic phenomena, as Figure 7 shows (the shaded area is at a maximum where MC = MR). So the proper question concerns the validity of the interpretation, and turns on the behaviour of the economic variables. Here (assuming competitive demand) what counts is the Law of Increasing Marginal Costs. When prediction fails we reject not (I) or (II) but the empirical hypothesis that marginal cost rises.

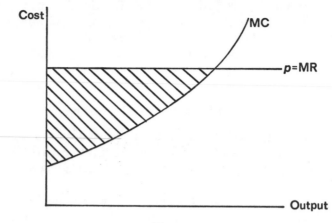

Figure 7

We are not impressed. This is not an objection but a further interpretation and it runs into the same difficulties. Why should we reject
the hypothesis of rising marginal cost rather than (I) or (II)? Marginal
costs, conceived in a *purely technological manner*, could rise (for instance,
if an assembly line were run more intensively, then breakdowns might
occur disproportionately more often), while supply price remained
constant, if (I) or (II) were false (or, if (II) is analytic, inapplicable). In
general the hypothesis that marginal costs rise yields predictions about
markets, only if the marginal cost curve, derived from technological data,
can be identified with businesses' *supply curve*, that is with their behavioural
pattern. The Law of Increasing Marginal Costs (itself no copper-bottomed
law) applies to markets only because of (I) or a suitable variant of (I). If a
test fails, we have no way of knowing which to reject. Positive economists
cannot make their escape by redefining the concept of 'law'.

Consider now a familiar problem. Suppose that businesses set their actual
prices on some form of 'full cost' or 'average cost' rule and that they estimate
their costs using some form of 'standard cost' system. To test the Law of
Increasing Marginal Costs, we must determine whether 'standard costs'
are 'true costs'. Hence we must devise a test which is independent both of
theory and of actual business behaviour, for in questioning standard costs,
we are really asking whether businesses are pursuing the most sensible
course. This is surely a good question – economists should be critical of
business practices. But they cannot be so, while claiming in the next breath
that their theories are validated by predictions of what businesses do.

Even a test which told us that standard costs were not true costs would
not be enough. We would also need to know the functional relation between
the size of deviation of observed from true values and the extent to which

the observed result deviates from true equilibrium. We would have to know, in other words, the pattern of disequilibrium behaviour; and that would mean first knowing that the model was, *ceteris paribus*, true. Since the problem is precisely how to know this, seeing that other things are standardly unequal, we are not an inch further forward.

We are left, then, with the snag that there is still no independent criterion by which to decide whether businessmen tend to maximise their profits and Positive economists can hardly use their models to judge the performance of business, while maintaining that the facts should judge the model. Nor can we distinguish between failure of 'other things' to be 'equal', failure of observed variables to take true values and failure of the hypothesis about costs.

Our claim, then, does not depend on taking any particular example or treating the concept of a 'general law' in any particular way. We rely solely on the Positivist insistence that Positive economics is a predictive science. If this is so (and it is the keystone of all versions of Positivism and perhaps of Empiricism also), then the predictions must apply to specific cases. But economic phenomena are embrangled with other social (and natural) phenomena; indeed they can better be thought of as economic aspects of behaviour which has many other significant aspects. Hence *ceteris paribus* clauses are vital, raising our earlier call for a wider, more sophisticated, interdisciplinary theory, which brings with it the threat of a regress of *ceteris paribus* clauses. To stop the regress or to prevent it from starting, we need clear cases where 'other things' are plainly seen to 'be equal'. But the data of actual observation will not do, as they have to be adjusted to yield the true values of the model's variables and, when the principles of adjustment are called for, another regress starts. Hence the economist is led, under threat of regress, to assume the correctness of some model and to base adjustments on that;[14] for instance to adjust observations of business behaviour to conform with the assumption that businessmen maximise profits. But this transforms predictive statements into covert analytic statements. A failure of prediction is a sufficient condition of values wrongly adjusted or of *ceteris paribus* conditions unsatisfied. The so called 'predictions' are no more than logical implications of assumptions predicated upon

---

[14] To complete the argument, we need to discuss whether there is a set of basic economic phenomena or 'atomic facts' which can be isolated from other influences and observed without adjustments. This will concern us in Chapter 4. For the moment we are content to ask how a positivist could arrive at any. He could not know *a priori* which they were; and if knowledge of such propositions as 'Phenomena of kind X are always free of influences Y and Z' is empirical, it will have to come from testing by showing the correlation coefficients between social and selected economic variables to be zero. Such tests will involve exclusion of outside influences and adjustments which will in turn have to be based on theory, thus reinstating the regress.

ceteris paribus clauses. Whatever fits a model, behaves as the model predicts. But that too is a tautology and, from a Positivist point of view, empty of all factual content.

If we are granted our case, we can also reduce the Positivist notion of 'explanation' to absurdity, by exploiting the philosophical thesis that prediction and explanation are two sides of the same coin. With apologies to our economic readers, let us consider a model M and a phenomenon P. By our Positivist account M can be known to explain P, only if M is known to be a good model and this can be known only after M has been successfully tested. In other words, that M is a good model is independent of the truth of the statement that M explains P. So the statement that M explains P is synthetic. But, by our Positivist account, M explains P if and only if M predicts P. It has turned out that M predicts P only if M implies P. Hence 'M implies P' is analytic and so also is 'M explains P'. So either prediction and explanation are not two sides of the same coin or there are no empirical explanations.

We have so far argued in this chapter that the difficulties of testing are not merely practical but that the whole notion of 'testing', when construed with the help of our Positivist account is incoherent. For empirical theories turn out neither testable nor explanatory. It may be well to emphasise that we are arguing strictly against Positivism. We are not contending flatly that no economic theory has any empirical value. We are saying solely that the price of insisting on the analytic-synthetic distinction is to render the prediction of what would happen, if ... vacuous. But even this bizarre conclusion will not be well received and we shall next consider possible objections.

Objections refuted

It may be objected that not all economic theories are in the same boat and that we have cheated by picking on the theory of Perfect Competition. The theory of Imperfect Competition has assumptions more realistic than those of the Perfect Competition model. An oligopolist has some control over price. Most industries have restricted entry. Information is imperfect even, or especially, in a bazaar. If all predictions were tautologous, none would be more probable than any other. Yet it is plain that the more realistic the assumptions the more probable the predictions.

In reply, we do not wish to deny the conclusion.[15] There would indeed be

---

[15] Whether neo-Classicists are wise to try to adopt it is another matter. We shall raise the question again in the Appendix to Chapter 7, where we judge that only Friedman's line is consistent with neo-Classicism, and in Chapters 8 and 9, where we try to replace the whole edifice.

little to be said for a theory which assumed that supply curves standardly sloped smoothly upwards. But we do deny that our positivists are in any position to say so. What makes one assumption more realistic than another? A possible answer is that realism is a matter of the degree of abstraction and that assumption A is more abstract than assumption B if B entails A but A does not entail B. For instance, that there is a demand for durable goods implies that there is a demand for goods but not *vice versa*. So the former is less abstract than the latter. It is then natural to say that the greater the abstraction the less the realism.[16]

Abstraction, however, whatever there may be to be said for it on other grounds, is independent of realism. All oligopolists are producers and not all producers are oligopolists but no greater realism is involved in calling a man an oligopolist than in calling him a producer. Equally all who wear socks have feet but not all who have feet wear socks. Yet, for most purposes of economic theory, there is no merit in using either the greater or the lesser abstraction.

It seems more promising, then, to hold that realism is a matter of relevance. But it is not enough to claim credit for a theory merely on grounds of relevance. The assumption that producers wear ties is (usually) irrelevant but it is at least true. The assumption that they can enter any market at any time is highly relevant and is made in the Perfect Competition model, but is undoubtedly false. So realistic assumptions are apparently those both relevant and true.

Yet what is relevance? There is no *a priori* reason why producers' neckwear should be irrelevant. Ties do not matter only because taking account of them makes no difference to economists' predictions, in that ties are not significantly correlated with profits, sales and so forth. In other words, those assumptions are to be preferred which are confirmed by testing the implications of the theory which embodies them.

This, however, puts us back where we were. Certainly a theory whose assumptions are confirmed in practice is more likely to be right than one whose assumptions are false or irrelevant. But that is analytic and so vacuous. Meanwhile nothing whatever has been said to escape our original difficulty that, within Positivism, assumptions are untestable. We are dealing with an account within which the realism of the assumptions cannot be divorced from the truth of the predictions. This is because a 'prediction' is simply an implication and because assumptions can be tested only by testing their implications. (Assumptions are general and observation is always of particulars. Besides, assumptions imply themselves.) Con-

---

[16] This yields the makings of a defence of the Perfect Competition model against the Imperfectionists, on the grounds that the greater the abstraction the greater the usefulness. See Friedman, The methodology of Positive economics, p. 4.

sequently there is no way of getting independent leverage on the notion of realism.

A more radical objection might be made to our whole line of argument. Our shift from predicting what will happen to 'predicting' what would happen, if ... was made by introducing *ceteris paribus* clauses and related assumptions. But is this necessary? The only requirement, it may be said, is an assumption that it is 'as if' *ceteris* were *paribus*. (Indeed Milton Friedman holds, in the paper cited before, that all assumptions should be interpreted to state not that something is so but that it is 'as if' it were so.)

Our reply, even if our economic readers find it hard to follow, is that the objection founders on the analytic-synthetic distinction. How are statements of the form 'X is A' related to those of the form 'It is as if X were A'? If 'X is A' entails 'It is as if X were A', then testing the latter raises the problems of testing the former. If 'It is as if X were A' entails 'X is not A', then we get the same problems again, with the odd proviso that the assumptions are to be assumed false. So the objection advances the cause, only if 'X is A' and 'It is as if X were A' are logically independent. That makes 'It is as if X were A' into a substantive assumption in its own right and we now need to know how to find out whether an assumption of this form is true. But that will again be a matter of testing the implications and again we shall want to give the same reasons for saying that the test shows the falsity of the assumption only after 'other things' are known to be 'equal'. For what would show it false that 'It is as if there were unrestricted entry to the market'? Not, apparently, that entry is in fact restricted. Nor that the market does not behave as the Perfect Competition model implies. So there has been no advance unless there is some relation (although not a logical one) between 'X is A' and 'It is as if X were A'.

But that makes the problem worse. For now we have to establish separately both whether X is A and whether it is as if X were A. Since the objection conceded that we cannot establish whether X is A, and since we find that we also cannot establish whether it is as if X were A, there is no question of relating them empirically. We suggest, therefore, that the warrant for assuming that it is as if X were A can only be either than it makes no difference whether X is A or is not A or that X is so nearly A that the adjustment is not worth making. Thus it is as if all producers wore yellow ties, in that it does not matter to economic theory what colour their ties are. It is as if there were perfect competition in some small farming communities, where oligopolies are trifling. But to assume that it is as if AC curves slope upwards, where it is significant that they do not is to court disaster (analytically so – otherwise it would not be significant). Where it is relevantly false that X is A it is also relevantly false that it is as if X were A. For both are intended as empirical statements and this is the only relation between them. The objection therefore falls.

A third objection to our claim that a shift from what will happen to what would happen, if ... renders predictions vacuous is that natural scientists can and do know what would happen, if ... A chemist does not have to drop a particular piece of sodium into water, to know what would happen, if he did. And, the objection might continue, although no one has ever seen a perfect market, any economist can tell a more perfect from a less perfect one. The theory of Perfect Competition is an extrapolation of these differences, a limiting case or ideal type. Even the theory of Imperfect Competition involves the construction of an ideal market by extrapolation from real ones. There is nothing impossible about such a scientific technique.

The objection, however, ignores the difficulty that the predictions derived from an ideal type are suspect, until shown testable. The chemist has criteria for the application of the term sodium which are non-committal about the reaction of sodium to water. The Positive economist does not have criteria for deciding what type of market he is dealing with independent of his model of how given types of market behave.

That retort is perhaps too simple and critics may reply that assumptions of a perfect market should be likened not to criteria for applying the term 'sodium' but to assumptions of frictionless motion or of a perfect vacuum. Are these not cases where an ideal type functions with success? And cannot *ceteris paribus* clauses function in the same way? To answer these questions, we note that in the cases of frictionless motion or perfect vacuum a reasonably well-defined and understood variable is held to take the value zero, in order that its influence shall be removed from the data. This is not so, however, for assumptions of economic perfection, unless there are measures of imperfection in actual markets independent of whether the theorems of marginalist analysis are true. We have already suggested that there could not possibly be but, even if there could, none has yet been produced and merely to assume that 'perfect information' can be treated like Frictionless Motion is to beg the question blatantly. There is undeniably still more to be said and we shall say it presently; but, to avoid breaking the thread of our argument, we have relegated further discussion of frictionless motion to an appendix to this chapter.

Whereas the chemist can claim to know what would happen, if..., by filling in the blank with a statement of laboratory conditions, the economist has no laboratory. He cannot be certain in the same way about what happens when a country devalues during inflation, partly because he does not know what counts as the same conditions when comparing devaluations. He predicts what would happen if the conditions of the model were satisfied, without ever having seen what happens when they are satisfied. Furthermore the chemist, when his model fails to match reality, blames the model; whereas the economist, when reality fails to match his model, has the option of blaming reality, in the sense that economic agents are not always rational. How fundamental these differences are, we do not care to say here, since the notion of 'rationality' must wait until later chapters. But there are at least *prima facie* differences. Meanwhile Adam Smith was a contemporary of Lavoisier and economics is at best *vieux jeu*; yet it has so far produced few laws and those bristling with exceptions. But we wish to contend at this stage neither that economics and chemistry do nor that they do not differ in principle, and our answer to the objection does not force us to commit ourselves on this thorny question.

Summary

Having done our best to forestall objections, we shall finish by restating the thesis of the chapter in summary form. Positive economists and positivists in general are committed to holding that the test of a scientist's model is whether its predictions fit the facts. This does not call for a simple comparison of prediction with raw fact, since that would mean wrongly discarding many sound theories. So tests of predictions are decisive only when *ceteris paribus* conditions are satisfied and only after observed variables have been adjusted to their true values. But, we have argued, the only way for a Positive economist to discover whether *ceteris* are *paribus* and to decide what adjustments to make to the observed values of variables, is to measure the degree to which the facts fail to fit the model. Tests are thus decisive only when the facts fit the model, which is like saying that verdicts are just only when they are favourable. Since irrefutable 'hypotheses' are, according to Positivism, not hypotheses at all, economic models turn out analytic and devoid of all factual content. The predictive science of Positive economics is thus reduced to absurdity.

We referred in our introductory chapter to the riddle of Induction and said that one problem facing any science was to distinguish lawlike from unlawlike statements. That problem arises only when there is a body of data amassed which show more than one possible pattern. If the argument of this chapter has been sound, Positive economics is not faced with this problem, for the embarrassing reason that there is no way of amassing such data.

The moral is not, we believe, that economists should leave philosophy to the philosophers. Nor is it that philosophers should stick to a linguistic brand of philosophy which 'leaves everything as it is'. For Positive economics is absurd without a Positivist justification for its methodology. Positivism underpins a gamut of opinions from the marginalist theory of the household and firm to the stock critique of the labour theory of value. If, as we are claiming, that justification is itself absurd, then a different philosophy is called for. The philosophy we shall advocate later is a brand of

Rationalism. But it will turn out to support not neo-Classicism but a modern approach to growth and distribution which belongs squarely to the Classical and Marxian tradition.

APPENDIX TO CHAPTER 1

FRICTIONLESS MOTION AND PERFECT COMPETITION

When critics object that key assumptions of Positive economics are unrealistic or untestable, defenders often reply by pointing to the assumption of Frictionless Motion in physics. Discussion then becomes technical and we did not try to do it justice in the preceding chapter. In this appendix, we shall give more precise reasons why appeal to Frictionless Motion does not help the Positive economist.

We have distinguished two sets of conditions which have to be met, if a test is to count as decisive. Firstly, *ceteris* must be *paribus*, in order to remove irrelevant influences; secondly, observed values of variables must be adjusted to true values. These are significantly different kinds of condition. The first picks out some reasonably well-defined and understood variables and rules that their influence shall be discounted. The second instructs the tester that the terms of the model are to be understood in a certain way and that data are to be adjusted accordingly. An example of the first kind is the assumption in partial equilibrium theory that prices and quantities of substitutes and complements remain constant. An example of the second kind is the assumption of adequate market information and mobility. In the latter case no well-defined variables are assumed to take particular values – economists have hardly begun to investigate the economics of information dispersal.[17] The point of the assumption is to ensure that 'the price of good X' shall be understood to mean the uniform price of good X, which remains uniform for all buyers and sellers during the period.[18]

With this distinction between kinds of assumption in mind, let us examine the assumption of Frictionless Motion in physics.

We shall take the simple case of a block sliding down a plane inclined at an angle θ (see Figure 8). $F = mg$ is the gravitational force acting on the body of mass m. This is resolved into two components, $mg \cos \theta$, normal

---

[17] Cf. Janos Kornai, *Anti-Equilibrium* (North Holland, 1972).
[18] Henderson and Quandt, *Microeconomic Theory*, pp. 86–7.

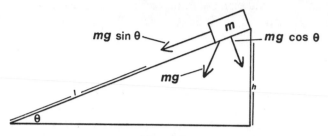

Figure 8

to the inclined plane, and $mg \sin \theta$, in the direction of the plane. From Newton's third law (Action equals reaction) the plane exerts a force equal to $mg \cos \theta$ on the block.

In the case of Frictionless Motion: the force down the plane is

$$F = mg \sin \theta = ma, \quad \text{or} \quad a = g \sin \theta.$$

The potential energy at the top equals the kinetic energy at the bottom, and since $\sin \theta = h/l$,

$$mg \sin \theta l = \tfrac{1}{2}mv^2 = mgh$$

where v is the velocity reached at the bottom. Hence,

$$v = \sqrt{(2g \sin \theta l)} = \sqrt{(2gh)}.$$

In the case of friction, however, the force down the plane is opposed by the force of friction. This depends on the force exerted by the plane on the block, $mg \cos \theta$, and upon the coefficient of friction, μ, which depends on the roughness or smoothness of the surface. The force down the plane thus is:

$$F = ma = mg \sin \theta - \mu mg \cos\theta = mg(\sin \theta - \mu \cos \theta).$$

Hence,

$$a = g \sin \theta - \mu \cos \theta.$$

The potential energy at the top equals the kinetic energy at the bottom plus the energy dissipated in overcoming friction. The energy so dissipated equals the work done by friction, wf, or the force of friction times the distance over which it acted;

$$f = \mu mg \cos \theta,$$
$$wf = l\mu mg \cos \theta = fl.$$

Hence,

$$(mg \sin \theta)l = \tfrac{1}{2}mv^2 + fl = \tfrac{1}{2}mv^2 + l\mu mg \cos \theta,$$

44

so

$$mgh = \tfrac{1}{2}mv^2 + l\mu mg \cos \theta,$$

$$2g (h - \mu \cos \theta) = v^2,$$

and

$$v = \sqrt{[2g(h - \mu a)]}.$$

It should be clear that the assumption of Frictionless Motion is an assumption of the first kind, where the value of a clearly defined variable is assumed to be zero. The variable in question is the coefficient of friction, μ. *A priori*, we know that its value range will be, $0 \leq a \leq \tan \theta$ for $u < 0$ implies that the force down the plane would be greater than $mg \sin \theta$, which is impossible, and $u > \tan \theta$ implies that the force of friction would push the block uphill, which is absurd. We know how friction is related to the other variables, for example, that it acts in opposition to the force acting down the inclined plane. We know how to measure friction, and also how to measure mass, distance, time; and assuming friction to be zero does not affect the definitions of the other terms in the analysis.

For an assumption to be of the first kind, then, it must be possible clearly to define the variable whose value is to be 0 or constant; that is, the value range of this variable must be given, which means giving both the kind of numbers (integers, rationals, or reals) and the bounds of permissible variation. To specify the kind of number the method of counting must be stated. In other words it must be shown how, in principle, the value of the variable could be found by measurement. If these rather simple conditions are not met, then no variable has been defined, and the assumption cannot be claimed to be of the first kind.

Assumptions of the first kind involve variables independent of others, in the sense that a change in their value affects neither the empirical criteria of application nor the identification of the true value of other variables. Assumptions of the second kind, in contrast, often attribute a characteristic to an economic agent in virtue of which criteria for applying a behavioural variable can be constructed. The characteristic attributed is not itself a variable, since no value range or method of counting is given for it, but is needed to explain how some variable is to be understood. Assumptions of adequate information and mobility or of uniform price function in this way.

Our objection to construing statements like 'market x is less perfect than market y' as empirical statements of what is actually the case within Positive economics, is thus that the assumptions in terms of which 'perfection' is defined are not of the first kind. That is why the model cannot be tested by comparing its success in more and in less perfect markets. Whether a market is more or less perfect depends on how well the model fits it. The objection could be met, if the assumptions could be converted to the first kind, for instance by taking the slope of the demand curve facing the firm as an indicator. But to do this, we would have to know already that the model was true *ceteris paribus*. Since the original difficulty lay precisely in how such knowledge was to be had, we are no further forward.

For these reasons, we deny that there is a helpful analogy between Frictionless Motion and Perfect Competition.

2

RATIONAL ECONOMIC MAN

The primrose path is paved with good intentions. The Positive economist intended to discover empirical economic laws by testing the implications of his theories against the facts of the world. But he found that this meant rejecting good theories for bad reasons. So he refined his methods by offering instead to test implications against the true values of variables, as measured when *ceteris* were *paribus*. Disconcertingly, this left him unable to distinguish the failure of his predictions from the failure of his *ceteris paribus* conditions or the incorrect adjustment of his observations. For, to know that failure of a prediction is to be blamed on 'other things' not being equal, he had to have an independent measure of the 'other things' based on hypotheses already confirmed. Similarly, to blame the apparent failure on incorrect adjustment, he had to know independently the relation of observed to true values. To treat such claims to knowledge as synthetic was to create a vicious regress; to treat them as analytic was to turn intendedly synthetic prediction of what will happen into analytic deduction of what would happen, if ... Theories became vacuous and laws undiscoverable.

Yet the primrose path is crowded with travellers. Able economists, both theoretical and applied, have accepted Positivism as their guide. They have been content to see it as an account of what they are doing, or trying to do and as a guide to what they ought to be doing. They have thus let Positivism cast them in an essentially passive role, ultimately as recorders and classifiers of correlations. (We shall offer them a more active role later, when we have finished with Positivism.) This chapter will begin by asking why and by showing how Positive economics has replaced an older tradition of political economy. We shall then offer and rebut some objections to the Positivist view of economics as the construction of timeless predictive models. The rebuttal will, however, involve a further shift into the subjunctive, as predictions become not of what any agent would do but of what a Rational Economic Man would do. We shall argue that assumptions of rationality are indispensable but that they also compound the confusion of the previous chapter. Finally the chapter will end with a brief and preliminary discussion of behaviourism and maximising models. Our

47

general thesis will be that rational behaviour is not 'law-like', as positivists use the term and cannot be explained by predictive models of Positive economics. In the course of this, some indication of our own view of the central role of Rationality, will, we hope, come through.

Positive economics supports an utilitarian view of the 'status quo'

The logical positivists of the thirties had the magic of success. In philosophy and much else, they carried all before them. The gloomy and decaying ramparts of absolute idealism were no match for the analytic-synthetic distinction. There were already philosophical allies in the field, encamped with the weapons of Logical Atomism under the banner of *Principia Mathematica*. Empiricism was reviving and the logical positivists were its ideal leaders. For their method was simple, clear and effective. Metaphysics must go. All genuine questions were about either language or fact. Nothing about the world could be known *a priori* and so science could dispense with philosophical assumptions. For the philosopher, it was again, as it had once been for Locke, 'ambition enough to be employed as under-labourer in clearing the ground a little, and removing some of the rubbish that lies in the way to knowledge'. The rubbish made a most satisfying bonfire and metaphysics, religion and ethics were soon consumed, along with other comforting delusions. A huge encyclopedia was begun, to record the state of human knowledge. The most general questions of method being already settled, the encyclopedia would one day without doubt need no further amendment.

The project was a deliberate echo of the Philosophes' *Encyclopédie des Sciences* written in the eighteenth century by the lamp of the Enlightenment. That lamp had burnt low in the philosophy and literature of the intervening century but it had remained the light of much social science. Comte's Positivism and English Utilitarianism, Fraser, Durkheim and Weber were all to some degree heirs of the Enlightenment. Comte, Bentham and J. S. Mill, indeed, were its silver age spokesmen (although Mill, as we shall see, also contributed to another tradition). Logical Positivism therefore drew on support outside philosophy, when it banished organic as well as moral notions from the moral sciences. Reason was again enthroned in a new return to timeless calculation and universal experiment.

In economics the triumph of Positivism was the triumph of Utility. Man, illumined by the Enlightenment and anatomised by the utilitarians, was an individual bundle of desires. He was simply a complex animal, no less part of nature than anything else and no less subject to discoverable empirical laws. His behaviour was to be explained as a series of attempts to get what he wanted. Whether his wants were metaphysical, religious, ethical or merely selfish was not to the point. For, scientifically speaking, it could simply be said that he was seeking the satisfaction of his desires. Judgements of value were irrelevant, except insofar as it could be asked scientifically whether the means chosen would secure the end, given the impact of the behaviour of each man on the aspirations of others. The rationally calculated, long-run optimum of each contributes to the long-run optimum of all. The calculation is the maximising of utility.

Utilitarians had been embarrassed by having to prove that the general optimum was a moral maximum. The pursuit of pleasure had seemed ethically suspect to religious persons in the throes of industrialisation. J. S. Mill, who embodied the conflict central to the present book, distinguished between higher and lower pleasures and argued that the 'ideal perfection of human nature' lay in achieving the former. Yet even this concession failed to persuade the Victorians that the man who succeeds in maximising his true utility is a saint. In Burke's words, the age of chivalry was gone and that of sophisters, economists and calculators had succeeded. But Logical Positivism maintains that such objections, far from being embarrassing, are instead meaningless. Normative statements not only have no place in science but also do not make sense. The proper study of mankind is human behaviour. The value-free calculus of utility becomes a natural way of applying strict scientific methods to the economic behaviour of individuals.

The triumph of utility has been at the expense of an older tradition of political economy. Admittedly that tradition made much use of the idea of Utility; but Adam Smith (and Sir William Petty before him), Malthus, Ricardo, Mill and Marx studied the interdependence between economic institutions and social classes, as defined by property rights over the means of production. How, they asked, would new knowledge, new markets, new techniques and new resources affect these interdependences. They distinguished productive from unproductive labour (and classes), divided the economy horizontally into sectors and vertically into classes and argued that the key theoretical problem of economic science was to explain the distribution of an expanding net social product among the classes.

Not only Marx but also Ricardo and Mill arrived at unpalatable conclusions. Labour worked and produced but received only a bare subsistence. Land owners were parasites, who waxed fat on rents produced during capital accumulation. Owners of capital, in addition to any fair reward for risk taking and management services, pocketed a slice of pure profit as illustrated in our second introductory diagram (Figure 3, p. 17). The rules, which gave them this simple appropriation, had no detectable justification. Meanwhile all ranks of society included many persons, like servants, lawyers, financiers, artists and marketers of luxury goods, who did nothing to increase or even to replace the basic material productive powers of society. However much they enhanced life or were respected by their fellows, such persons were to be classed as unproductive. In general, unproductive labour was a brake on the growth of society's productive powers. Since it was largely employed by owners of land and receivers of interest and profit, these classes were also a brake on social progress. Hence labour not only is exploited but also, by supporting its exploiters, assists its own exploitation.

Positive economics contains an answer to such subversive doctrines. The capitalist is shown worthy of his hire, no less than the labourer. Profit, for instance, can be construed as payment for the services of capital (making the payment flow one way and the services the other, as in Figure 2 in the introduction). It can be regarded as the due reward of saving, by postponing the pleasures of the moment and so offering the investment needed for growth. But, more basically, Positive economics contends that the analysis of society in terms of classes and institutions has to be dropped. Property rights, classes, productive and unproductive sectors are written out, first in deference to the liberal and individualist tenor of the utilitarians, later because they involve entities and values which offend the positivists' criteria of verification. Instead of classes competing for the net social product, we are shown the individual decision-maker, choosing his pattern of saving in various market conditions. Society becomes a construct out of individual behaviour and the individual is defined schematically in terms of choices made rational by presocial desires for self-evident goals. This gives the resulting theory, in its sweeping abstraction, an appearance of great generality.

Yet putting the sovereign, rational, individual economic man at the centre of the stage seems to ignore some older questions about property rights, distribution of income among social classes and the division of the labour force between productive and unproductive occupations. But Logical Positivism soon comes to the rescue of the utilitarians. Whatever exists is observable or is the short-hand name of patterns and sets of observables. Terms like 'social class', which in some of its older uses cannot be so construed, are meaningless in those uses. Terms like 'property-right' can be used descriptively but not to raise scientific questions of justice. Terms like 'productive' and 'unproductive' embody a normative distinction for which science has no place. Instead of the hierarchical triangle representing society in the Classical-Marxian diagram (Figure 3), we are offered the two boxes of rational units, namely firms and households (both constructs out of individuals) who meet, as it were, on the same level in the factor and product markets.

Positivist epistemology provides essential support for Positive economics

Models of man which depend on the rational calculation of self-interest have traditionally been harried from three quarters. Firstly, it is said, they take no account of important human ingredients like sympathy for others, moral concern, religious impulse or aesthetic endeavour. Secondly, they presuppose that means and ends are logically distinct; whereas ends are in fact determined progressively in the course of action. Thirdly, they are committed to the notion that reason is timeless and eternal, its findings universal and absolute; whereas it is a social product, limited in application and explicable by the analysis of history or the sociology of knowledge.

These charges seem to have some force. Lack of moral concern is apparently entailed by refusal to pass moral judgements. Besides the omissions are not only, so to speak, spiritual. The model also omits the intuitions, hunches and temperaments which influence economic decision-making, for profit as well as for loss. Yet a model intended to analyse rational decision-making for purposes of prediction should surely include the ingredients which do influence decisions in the best circles.[1] Moreover, means indisputably affect ends. As many studies show, large corporations rarely decide to expand, diversify or merge, in order to achieve clearly defined ends. The ends are understood and defined only afterwards and by then they have often changed. Furthermore, reason seems less eternal and timeless when it is noticed that the shift in economic pattern from small ownership to international corporations is reflected in the shift from relatively simple maximising models to more complex models, which sometimes involve finding not a maximum but a satisfactory reconciliation of conflicting objectives. Weighty opinions have it that the corporation seeks growth and security no less than profit. It cares about the community and rejoices in the soubriquet of 'soulful' – although perhaps this shows only that Burke should have mentioned 'public relations officers' along with sophisters, calculators and economists. It can, therefore, be stoutly argued that what is economically rational depends on time and place.

Positivism, however, cuts the ground from under the objectors' feet. There is only one criterion of a good model, that of whether its predictions are confirmed. Moral considerations enter only at secondhand. If the economic behaviour of consumers and producers is affected by their ideological beliefs, then this is to be dealt with by economists with *ceteris paribus* clauses and by sociologists with hypotheses about the social structure. A

---

[1] We argue in Chapters 8 and 9 that assumptions of perfect information provide no escape here.

factor belongs to the subject matter of economics, if and only if it can be specified in terms amenable to econometrics.

Socialist and Marxist critics of bourgeois economics also get short shrift. A typical complaint is that the allegedly pure and timeless analysis of the production function is cast in terms like 'capital' and 'firm'. These terms apply only in societies where the notion of private property is entrenched in the law and where returns are earned on investment. Yet there have been complex economies without firms, capital, private property or free contracts. Bourgeois models do not apply to these economies. Neo-Classical static equilibrium and steady-state growth theories in short, have little or nothing to contribute to the theory of historical development. Nor can they tell us much about equilibrium or growth in societies with different basic institutions. Or so the complaint might run. But the positivist replies that no such thesis can be proved *a priori*. The test of a model is the success of its predictions. Whether the predictions are satisfied by a given economy is always an empirical matter. They can be tested anywhere from a tribe of primitive higglers to a society where all has been nationalised. If they are falsified in a given case, then the model merely lacks generality and should be widened, rather as Einstein generalised Newton, until, ultimately, the model is so general and powerful that it applies to all men always regardless of their own self-conceptions. That the population do not themselves use the concepts of a Western economist is neither here nor there. The only conclusion from that is that the population do not understand their own economy as well as they might. There is no substitute for a successful prediction and no gainsaying its significance.

The positivist's strategy is twofold. Firstly, the merit of any coherent model is always an empirical matter. Secondly, failure of prediction can never show the concepts of economic theory to be culture-bound, since those concepts are introduced by stipulative definition or analytically derived from one another. Admittedly, conditions may not have been properly specified and significant variables may have been overlooked. But theory is a timeless analytic construct and it is an empirical question where it is most usefully applied.

Theories are composed of definitions, assumptions and hypotheses. Hypotheses assert relations between variables. We noticed in the previous chapter that behavioural economic variables need a bearer, an economic agent to whom they apply. Positive economics offers us, in the phrase of our title, 'Rational Economic Man'. Variables take their true value, when they record what a rational agent would do in the circumstances. Among the *ceteris peribus* clauses is one requiring that the agents, whose behaviour is to be predicted, be rational. This is exactly what we should expect, when we reflect that the new alternative to economic analysis by classes and institutions, was, as just mentioned, a liberal individualism.

With a strategy so neat and forceful, the attraction of Positivism is no mere historical accident. The primrose path is inviting. But, as we began to argue in the previous chapter, it leads to the everlasting bonfire. We shall continue next by contending that our positivists have, in the last few pages, covertly shifted to a still more awkward position. The previous shift was from predicting what will happen to predicting what would happen, if ... The present shift is from predicting what would happen if ... to predicting what a rational man would do, if ... We shall argue that the confusion has been compounded.

The roles of rational economic man

The original need to qualify the predictions arose because economics is only one of several social sciences, each with its proper arena. Economic hypotheses were not to be refuted by non-economic interferences. We may put this by saying that economics is the study not of man in general but of economic man. But even within the proper arena of economics, predictions may still fail for reasons which are commonly held not to refute the hypothesis from which they were generated. For instance interview and questionnaire data, confirmed by observation, indicate that businesses, both in practice and as a matter of policy, often do not go on investing until the anticipated rate of return has fallen to the current level of the rate of interest.[2] But this has been taken to show merely that not all businesses are fully rational.[3]

The predictions are, therefore, of the true values of variables, given rational behaviour and *ceteris paribus*. It is worth emphasising that the assumption of rationality is not simply another *ceteris paribus* condition. Even if all outside influences were eliminated and all observed values of variables adjusted to fit the theory, irrational behaviour, resulting for instance from an inconsistent ordering of preferences, would render prediction impossible. We may put this new qualification by saying that economics is the study of rational economic man.

Few textbooks contain a direct portrait of rational economic man. He is introduced furtively and piece by piece, which perhaps explains why the difficulties which we shall raise usually pass unnoticed. He lurks in the

---

[2] Andrews and Wilson (ed.), *Oxford Studies in the Price Mechanism*; J. R. Meyer and E. Kuh, *The Investment Decision* (Harvard, 1957).

[3] See F. Machlup's paper in *Readings in Economic Analysis*, ed. Richard V. Clemence (Addison-Wesley, 1950).

assumptions leading an enlightened existence between input and output, stimulus and response. He is neither tall nor short, fat nor thin, married nor single. There is no telling whether he loves his dog, beats his wife or prefers pushpin to poetry. We do not know what he wants. But we do know that, whatever it is, he will maximise ruthlessly to get it. We do not know what he buys, but we are sure that when prices fall he either redistributes his consumption or buys more. We cannot guess the shape of his head but we know that his indifference curves are concave to the origin. For, in lieu of his portrait, we have his Identikit picture. He is the child of the Enlightenment and so the self-seeking individualist of utility theory. He is a maximiser. As producer he maximises market-share or profit. As consumer he maximises utility by omniscient and improbable comparison of, for instance, marginal strawberries with marginal cement. (He is, to be sure, also a minimiser, but, since minimising X is maximising non-X, that need not concern us.) He is always at what he takes to be optimum, believing (however falsely) that any marginal change would be for the worse. From individual indifference to international trade, he is forever striking the best subjective balances between disincentive and reward. This is the rational *primum mobile* of neo-Classical economics.[4]

This abstract and shadowy being has two roles. First, he buckles theory to facts. His is the behaviour to be predicted; he is the bearer of the economic variables. Unlike the man in the street, he never misses an opening, ignores a price change, overrates the short-run or turns a blind eye to the unquantifiable. He therefore features, for example, in imperfect competition no less than in perfect. For an oligopolist is no less rational than the perfect competitor and the monopsonist is no less a maximiser than the mere housewife. Every model predicts the rational response. Rational economic man is both the average and the ideal, abstracted from actual marketeers with the aid of general assumptions about human desires. Yet he is not a pure fiction. Insofar as it is possible to assess the degree of irrationality in an actual situation, it is possible to predict the actual deviation from ideal behaviour. To know what rational economic man would do is to know what will actually happen 'if 'other things' are 'equal' and the degree of irrationality is given.

---

[4] 'Maximisation provides the moving force of economics. It asserts that any unit of the system will move toward an equilibrium position, as a consequence of universal efforts to maximise utility or returns. Maximisation is a general basic law that applies to the elementary units and, by the rules of composition, to larger and more complicated collections of those units' – Sherman Roy Krupp, Equilibrium theory in economics and in function analysis as types of explanation, in *Functionalism in the Social Sciences*, ed. D. Martindale (American Academy of Political and Social Science, 1965), p. 69. Quoted by R. L. Heilbroner, Is economic theory possible?, *Social Research*, vol. 33, no. 2 (Summer 1966).

Secondly he provides an escape for a theory whose predictions fail, even though 'other things' are 'equal' with respect to non-economic conditions and (rationality apart) values of variables are true. His behaviour embodies the true value of behavioural economic variables. These true values, as we have seen already, are not some sort of average of actual observed values but are those which would be exemplified by a perfectly rational agent in the conditions specified. So predictions of what is rational are not refuted even in the specified conditions, if actual economic agents fail to come up to snuff.

The rationality assumption conflicts with the prediction criterion

The difficulties raised in our last chapter now arise again. Rational economic man is not an actual man. He is, rather, any actual man who conforms to the model to be tested. So there is no question of testing an economic theory against the actual behaviour of the rational producer or consumer. Producers and consumers are rational precisely insofar as they behave as predicted and the test shows only how rational they are. There is no independent way of knowing that the guinea pigs are a suitable criterion, just as there is no independent way of knowing that 'other things' are 'equal'. Confusion is therefore compounded. Even if we could distinguish the failure of a prediction from the failure of 'other things' to be 'equal' we still could not decide whether the guinea pigs had behaved rationally. The statement of what a rational man would do, if . . . is no less vacuous than the statement of what would happen, if . . . Rational economic man's two roles as buckle and escape-hatch are incompatible.

We should perhaps emphasise once more that the last point is a limited one, addressed to the methodological framework of positivism. We are still relying on the thesis that a synthetic statement has to be refutable and that statements which are not synthetic are analytic and so empty of factual content. In later chapters we shall try to escape our own elenchus with a fresh theory of social science. But, for the present, Positivism, perhaps unwittingly, implies that whatever buckles theory to facts also closes the escape-hatch.

Philosophers will notice a further snag about the status of the statement that there are rational economic men. We confess to believing ourselves that it is a synthetic *a priori* truth; but no positivist will allow this for a moment. So is it a hypothesis, a theorem or an assumption? Construed as a hypothesis, it is untestable unless we already know that we have a correct theory and that 'other things' are 'equal'. But that is impossible, since the theory can be known to be correct, only if it is already known to predict and explain rational economic behaviour. Construed as a theorem, it is either analytic or the consequence of an assumption. If analytic, it is vacuous and tells us nothing about any real economy. If the consequence of an assumption, it can be treated as an assumption. Construed as an assumption, it is either true by definition or counts as a general hypothesis. But definitional truths are vacuous and hypotheses untestable. So in whatever way rationality is introduced, the statement of it is either vacuous or untestable. In either case, the problem of the last chapter has been made no easier.

We are in effect asking whether there are criteria of rational economic behaviour independent of the economist's model. If there are, then the model neither shows that this behaviour is rational nor provides evidence for what a rational man will do. If there are not, then the economist is reduced to saying emptily that the model predicts whatever it predicts. Neither horn of the dilemma offers any comfort, for the reason, we shall argue later, than the analytic-synthetic distinction is linked with a notion of causal explanation which forces a special sense on the term 'rational action'. But, before proposing this thesis, we must see what a positivist will do with the dilemma.

Rational agents and C.I.A. agents

The most plausible tactic is to escape between the horns by disclaiming all interest in the concept of rationality. Hempel, for instance, eliminates rationality by arguing that, granted that it is rational to do X in a given situation, we still cannot predict what George will do until we know that George is rational. In other words:

(i)   a rational agent does X in situations of type S,
(ii) the present situation is of type S;
(iii) George is a rational agent

entail that (iv) George will do X, whereas (i) and (ii) alone do not. So the prediction of what George will do requires knowing that (iii) is true. But 'rational' in the argument is doing no work. Any replacement for it throughout the argument will do. For example

(i)   a C.I.A. agent does X in situations of type S
(ii) the present situation is of type S;
(iii) George is a C.I.A. agent

is just as effective. The exact sense of 'rationality' is therefore unimportant.[5]

---

[5] C. G. Hempel, *Aspects of Scientific Explanation* (The Free Press, 1965), Section 10, esp. 10.3.1.

We are unimpressed, however. What a C.I.A. agent usually does is an empirical question. Only observation will show whether a C.I.A. agent reaches for his gun when tapped on the shoulder. If he fails to do what is usual, he does not automatically cease to be a C.I.A. agent (even if he ceases to be a live one). What a rational agent does, by contrast, is not an empirical question. The man who in textbook conditions of an everyday competitive market buys more when the price rises is simply not a rational agent. He does not satisfy the criteria of rationality supplied by the model.

To give warning of a point we shall exploit later, there is no law-like connection between being economically rational and acting as the model predicts. In the positivist scheme statements of laws are statements of regular but contingent connections. Since the connection is not contingent, it never explains economic behaviour, in the positivist sense of 'explain', to say it was rational. It never explains behaviour to say that it falls under a model, which includes criteria of rationality.[6]

Behavioural rationality and projectible generalisations

The rationality assumption thus compounds the difficulties examined earlier. Yet something must be said about rationality, if the individual choosing agent is to be the centrepiece of the analysis. So perhaps we can dispense with the strong sense of rationality, in favour of a weaker one, like 'regularity of behaviour'. Some minimal claim is needed about the habits of the agents whose behaviour is to be predicted. For unless data gathered by observation and market research are in principle an indicator for use on another occasion, predictions become fatuous. The minimal claim is that 'revealed preference' reveals not merely a previous pattern as likely to be discontinued as not but rather a disposition which will also be revealed elsewhere. Let us call consistency of preference 'behavioural rationality'.

The notion of 'behavioural rationality' we have in mind is one which will partly solve the Inductive problem of the introductory chapter by the use of maximising models. In what follows we shall restate the Inductive problem, explain the minimal sense we are giving to 'rationality', show why we use the term 'behavioural' and assess the merit of maximising models as solvents of our methodological puzzle.

Positivism recognises only one causal relation between events, that of

---

[6] Moreover, even if the connection were law-like, it could not explain why an agent acted rationally once only or for the first time. But, as we raise this point in Chapter 5, we shall not pursue it here.

correlation between earlier and later.[7] To explain an event is to cite another earlier event and an established generalisation linking the two. The link has to be a repeatedly observed empirical correlation. For all knowledge of the world rests on observation and we observe only particular events in contingent sequences. If causal relations involved any necessity, we could not know that there were any. Therefore the only generalisation we are warranted in making about two events is that they occur together in given conditions. We have not found a law unless we have found a correlation.

But finding a correlation, although necessary, is not enough. Not all correlations are law-like or, as we put it before, 'projectible'. For instance the projection of a six-month lag between rounds of the multiplier is thought warranted, while that of a 12% average rate of profit on investment is not. Predictions are warranted only if the correlation they are based on is causal and clearly identified. But not every correlation is causal and the Inductive problem is partly one of knowing which correlations to pick.

The notion of 'explanation' being tied to that of 'warranted prediction', human behaviour also is explicable only if it is warrantably predictable. Individual actions therefore need to be set within at least the agent's habits and probably the habits of a whole community, if the economist is to find generalisations to explain them by. The weakest sense of 'rational' is 'patterned'. By 'rational behaviour' in its minimal sense, we mean 'behaviour revealing a projectible pattern'. Consequently, if we knew which behaviour was rational in this sense, we would to that extent have solved the inductive problem.

There is also more to it. The demand just made that correlations be clearly identified poses the 'identification problem', since many important economic observations are generated by two or more sets of forces, those of supply and demand, and successive observations may reflect one or the other. We need a way of deciding exactly what the correlations tell us. But this problem will engage us in Chapter 3 so we shall here merely note its existence.

So our new approach, less straightforward than a strong notion of rationality but still tempting as a way of evading the difficulty that rationality assumptions make the model untestable, is to land our positivists with behaviourism. Positivism, having been coined as the philosophic currency

---

[7] This is a somewhat blunt way of putting it. J. S. Mill's *A System of Logic* (8th ed., Harper and Row, 1874), for instance, contains an elaborate variety of patterns of causal connection and any account of modern statistics seems to belie what we say. Nevertheless we unblushingly agree with Bertrand Russell, when he argues that the empiricist notion of a cause is reducible to that of a function. See B. Russell, On the notion of a cause, in *Mysticism and Logic* (Doubleday Anchor Books, 1957).

of natural science, stresses the publicly observable, and the repeatable. An agent's mental states are not publicly observable. They can apparently be changed at the agent's discretion and can apparently issue in a variety of actions, depending on the agent's free and untrammelled acts of will. The responses got by teasing an agent with stimuli are often unrepeatable. To treat an agent as a ghost in a machine is, in short, apparently to introduce an element which need not conform to any pre-ordained or discernible pattern. The agent's own reasons, which make his behaviour intellectually rational, may make nonsense of the pattern which makes his behaviour projectible.

So it is tempting to argue that human behaviour is amenable to science only insofar as it is observable. The fiercest line is to deny that there is any ghost in the machine. A man is a complex, observable servo-mechanism and has no evanid, whiffling thing within. 'Rational' is simply a predicate of certain types of behaviour. But a softer line is enough, according to which a man's thoughts, feelings and decisions are caused by external stimuli which can be correlated directly with his actions. In either case, the thesis of behavioural rationality is that the outward and visible behaviour of economic man is evidence enough for prediction. The economic behaviour of a community is rational, if it exhibits a projectible pattern; that of an individual is rational if it conforms to the pattern. This much at least must be said to justify the ordinary practice of econometrics. But why say more?

Well, again, not all patterns are projectible. They need, as it is often put, a 'rationale', a 'grounding' in 'fundamental economic behaviour' or 'central economic forces'. Otherwise there is no way of selecting from among a plethora of possible patterns those both economically relevant and economically reliable. This is one powerful reason for insisting on maximising models. The suggestion is that a generalisation is projectible only if it can be inferred from a model describing maximising behaviour.[8] The demand for money, for example, must be a consequence of choosing to hold money, rather than other assets, as a means of maximising utility or profit,[9] and not simply a mechanical consequence of the time pattern of transactions.

---

[8] For instance, 'Twenty five years after Hicks' eloquent call for a marginal revolution in monetary theory, our students still detect that their mastery of the presumed fundamental, theoretical apparatus of economics is put to very little test in their studies of monetary economics and aggregative models. As Hicks complained, anything seems to go in a subject where propositions do not have to be grounded in someone's optimising behaviour' – J. Tobin, Liquidity preference as behavior towards risk, *Review of Economic Studies*, Vol. 25, no. 67 (February 1958).

[9] Tobin, *ibid.*; J. R. Hicks, *Critical Essays in Monetary Theory* (Clarendon Press, 1967). (Notice that in the first essay Hicks appears to recant somewhat.)

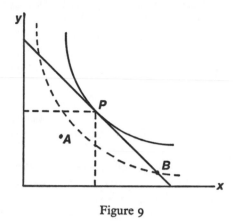

Figure 9

The division of income between consumption and saving cannot be put down to habit or custom, unless the habits or customs are shown to reflect (perhaps unconscious) economising decisions. Utility is to be maximised over a life-time and so current saving reflects a life-time's consumption plan.[10]

Why is a maximising model special? A widely-given reply would be that, without one, many basic concepts of economics do not make sense. Consider the concept of Opportunity Cost (see Figure 9). If the consumer were at B, by reducing his consumption of x and increasing that of y he would increase his utility, moving towards P along the budget line. Hence sacrificing utility by giving up x yields a net gain; measuring x and y in utility, something is got for nothing. In a world of desires for scarce resources, this does not make sense. If the consumer were at A, he could have more of both foods without any sacrifice, the opportunity cost is forgone utility being indeterminate (not zero, since trade off can be made at any ratio). Only by moving along an indifference curve do we get a true measure of the opportunity cost of y in terms of x. But only on the budget frontier is the consumer constrained so to move. Analytically he wants to be on the furthest possible indifference curve; analytically the budget line permits him to move to its perimeter. So only the maximum point gives a measure of opportunity cost in terms of forgone utility. Analogous examples could be given for concepts on the production side.

This illustrates the contention quoted above that 'maximisation provides the moving force of economics'. It does not imply that generalisations without evident roots in maximising behaviour are to be discarded forthwith.

[10] M. Friedman, *A Theory of the Consumption Function* (Princeton University Press, 1957).

But it does imply that we must find maximising roots for them. This admonition brings us to a point where the tenets of Positivism and the standard practice of most modern economists seem comfortingly to coincide.

Judging agents by models and models by agents

We began this chapter by finding a path that lead from the Philosophes by way of the utilitarians to current Positivism. To critics who urged that all concepts are culture-bound, we replied, on the positivists' behalf, that models were timeless logical structures whose applicability was always an empirical matter. The reply, however, conceded that models apply only to rational economic behaviour. The introduction of rationality compounded the confusion of the previous chapter and so we next tried to dispense with it. But some minimal claim still had to be made. We termed the minimal thesis that of 'behavioural rationality'. Models predict behaviour which can be observed to conform to a projectible pattern. That, however, leaves untouched the Inductive problem of which patterns are projectible, a problem which calls not only for a general justification of projecting patterns at all but also for a specific criterion. Can the notion of maximising provide the missing criterion for what is law-like and so leave the confusion of the previous chapter at any rate uncompounded?

The answer is surely No. Does maximising provide the 'moving force', so to speak, of the analysis or of the agent? Do we judge the agent by the model or the model by the agent? We have already argued that what might have been intended as empirical laws of rational economic behaviour turn out to be analytic statements lodged in the model. A similar dilemma rises when we ask whether maximising is built into the model or is discovered by observation of the facts. How, in other words, do we know that economic behaviour is motivated by the desire to maximise the satisfaction of one's desires? We cannot prove it *a priori*, without showing that 'satisficing' models[11] are contradictory, which there is no reason to think feasible. And, if we could, the result would be that non-maximising behaviour, like full-cost pricing or normal investment decision-making, was not the subject of economics, which would be like solving the New York slum problem by redrawing the city boundaries. Besides to prove *a priori* that maximising is the moving force of economics would be by positivist canons to render the claim vacuous, a mere matter of consequences of definitions, and so unfit it for grounding empirical explanations.

But, if the claim is synthetic, then how do we know it is both projectible

---

[11] For example, those of H. A. Simon, *Models of Man* (John Wiley and Sons 1957); or R. M. Cyert and J. G. March; *A Behavioural Theory of the Firm* (Prentice-Hall, 1963).

and true? Presumably we know, because we have enough evidence that the conditions which would refute it are not satisfied. Yet what would refute the claim that economic behaviour is motivated by the desire to maximise the satisfaction of one's desires? Translated into English, it says that men try to get as much of what they want as possible. The relevant counter-claim would be that men try to get less of what they want than they might. The relation between these hypotheses is by no means straight-forward, as our discussion of a parallel question in the previous chapter and the following paragraphs show.

Maximising behaviour

It cannot be shown that no maximising behaviour is present, without appeal to the intentions of the agent.[12] For solutions to a mathematical problem can generally be rewritten as a maximising or minimising solution. Consider, for example, the intersection of two straight lines, the solution to a pair of simultaneous linear equations (Figure 10). There is a corresponding problem of minimising the difference between the values of y corresponding to a given x or of minimising the values of x corresponding to a given y. This can be extended to any number of functions not all of them linear. Hence a mathematical algorithm, which describes an agent's behaviour, can normally be converted into an optimising (minimising or maximising) model. There is therefore a sense in which all behaviour capable of economic analysis can be regarded as maximising behaviour.

Conversely, behaviour which is apparently of a maximising kind can be regarded as non-maximising behaviour. Optimising models can usually be converted into an algorithm where maximising is not thought to be involved. For example, we can ask for the equation of the line which touches a given curve at a single point only (Figure 11). This is of course precisely the condition for an extremum,[13] which is precisely the point. No comparisons are mentioned. Optimising behaviour must involve comparison and choice. So which of the conflicting hypotheses is correct seems simply a matter of how we choose to look at it.

The consequences are disastrous. For there is now no way to decide between the hypotheses by testing and neither is refutable. Moreover any generalisation now fits a maximising model and so we have no criterion after all for distinguishing projectible from unprojectible generalisations. The suggestion that rational economic behaviour is maximising behaviour does not smooth our troubles away.

---

[12] We shall make more ambitious use of this point in Chapter 5.
[13] Neglecting points of inflexion, which can be covered by requiring that the first derivative change sign at the point.

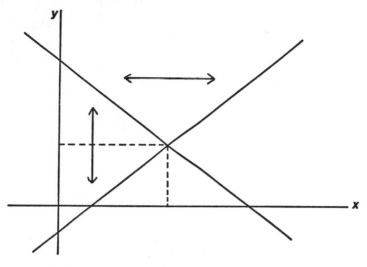

Figure 10

Once again, we do not believe that we have sunk conventional economic theory with a single broadside. Important parts of economics must involve the notions of economising, optimal achievement of goals and maximisation. Admittedly the notions need not be universally applied. The working of the material side of society, for instance, does not demand an account in terms of optimising. But the difficulty has not arisen because maximising notions need not be universal and their undoubted importance is undercut neither by this nor, when the source of the trouble is traced, by anything

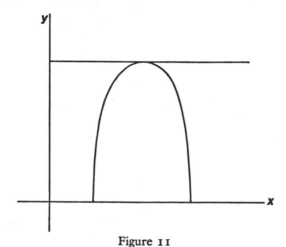

Figure 11

in this chapter. On the contrary, we believe maximising models to be one of the two major branches of economic science. (The other is the study of the material conditions for reproducing and expanding the social order.) But their use, in our view, is to judge and criticise the actions of economic agents (and only subsidiarily to predict, insofar as the agents act for the best). Consequently the agent and not the model is to blame when he does not conform and this makes it vital to establish the correctness of a useful maximising model independently of the results of applying it.

Summary

The troubles aired in this chapter have, we judge, two sources. The first is the analytic-synthetic distinction, which, we are finding, makes it impossible to apply theoretical models to economic behaviour or to give empirical criteria of application to central economic concepts. Secondly, behaviourism, into which we let Positivism beguile us, prevented our distinguishing maximising from non-maximising models. On this second score, we therefore have a debt to pay. If we can dispense with behaviourism, we can rescue much of orthodox economic theory. We shall try to pay this debt in Chapter 5, where we debate behaviourism further. Meanwhile, we believe that Positivism and behaviourism are associated probably in the logic of the Positivist position and certainly in the thinking of most Positive economists.

Confusion is therefore compounded. The prediction of what a rational man would do, if ... is no less vacuous than the prediction of what would happen, if ... Our own resolution of these difficulties must be left to later chapters, when we shall have supplied our own ground work. Meanwhile we have not finished with Positivism nor with the Positive economist's defence of neo-Classicism. Having found his account of the function of testing unacceptable and his treatment of rationality confusing, we turn now to the role of theory itself. In the next chapter we shall enquire into the nature of the support which neo-Classical theory lends to the hypotheses deduced from it.

3

THEORY AND HYPOTHESIS

The riddle of Induction is often posed by philosophers in wholly general terms. How do we know that any observed correlations will be found to hold in as yet unobserved cases? As Robbins once remarked 'however accurately [economic generalisations] describe the past, there is no presumption that they will describe the future'.[1] Such dark threats of universal scepticism rarely impress those who are not philosophers and so we also gave a more specific version of the riddle in our introduction. How are we to discriminate 'projectible' generalisations from mere correlations which just happen to have held in hitherto observed cases? Neither version arises, until we know which correlations have held in the past and, as we argued in the last chapter, a positivist cannot even assemble the candidates. Nevertheless we shall now put this awkward *nolle prosequi* on one side and turn to the problem of determining which generalisations are projectible. The question, we shall argue, is one about the relation of theory to hypothesis.

Received opinion has it that theory and hypothesis differ importantly in kind and that a hypothesis is strengthened by the endorsement of a good theory. Indeed any other view might seem a slap at the professional dignity of economists. A theory is surely a complex conceptual apparatus and so more than any mere bundle of hypotheses. If a generalisation is treated as a confirmed hypothesis, then it is projectible when endorsed by the *imprimatur* of theory. As hinted towards the end of the last chapter, the introduction of maximising models, whatever their particular merits, is surely the right sort of move to make. For such models presuppose an instinctive distinction between theory and hypothesis, in terms of which we shall be able to treat as projectible those generalisations which follow from an acceptable maximising model.

A *prima facie* case for distinguishing in kind between theory and hypothesis and then treating theoretical significance as the test of projectibility

---

[1] L. Robbins, *An Essay on the Nature and Significance of Economic Science* (Macmillan, 1932), p. 101.

65

is easily made. There are, for instance, apparently significant 'constancies' in modern industrial economies, holding for many decades and sometimes for many countries. The capital-output ratio tends to be about 3:1; the share of manual labour about $\frac{2}{5}$ of G.N.P.; the average rate of profit about 12%. Some would also claim that the velocity of circulation of money shows some constancy. Admittedly none of these highly aggregated relationships is strictly constant, but they vary oddly little compared with others. Do these constancies reflect laws? Or are they historical accidents, owing to a chance balance between opposing forces? The question is not to be answered by 'looking at the facts', since it is one about how to interpret the facts. So the answer will apparently have to depend on theory and this, in the opinion of many,[2] is the object of growth theory.

Moreover, the aggregate capital-labour ratio rises steadily over time. This and the figures just given imply a steadily rising real wage, as is in fact the case. So the measured aggregates are mutually consistent. The question now is what these highly aggregated measurements imply for the theory of growth? Do they represent trends, to be explained as consequences of the normal working of some mechanism, or might they simply be historical accidents? The question has a bite, since the neo-Classical theory of growth, at least in its most popular form, can accommodate these trends only by postulating an unexplained chance rate of technical progress, exactly offsetting the fall in the rate of profit caused by the rise in capital intensity. If there is more to these measurements than historical accident, the neo-Classical theory must be amended or rejected.

The *prima facie* case for taking these aggregate figures seriously is a strong one, simply because the record has long been consistent, while other features of the economy have been changing beyond recognition. Yet they raise a problem for neo-Classical marginal productivity theory, which is held to be highly confirmed by virtue of good performance in other areas. So, if they are not significant, it is for theoretical reasons and it is a tribute to the influence of neo-Classicism that they have been disregarded for so long. Conversely, they can be claimed to be significant after all, only insofar as there is a suitable theory to underpin them. A similar moral can be drawn from the common assertion that aggregate savings in the short run will increase with rises in the rate of interest. There is no evidence to support this, nor would it be easy to glean any, given the high proportion

[2] See, for instance, N. Kaldor, Capital accumulation and economic growth, in *The Theory of Capital*, F. Lutz and D. C. Hague (eds.) (Macmillan, 1962). L. R. Klein and R. F. Kosobud, Some econometrics of growth: Great ratios of economics, *Quarterly Journal of Economics* vol. 75, no. 2 (May 1961). R. M. Solow, *Growth Theory: An Exposition* (Oxford University Press, 1970), esp. Chapter 1.

of total savings done by business. But it follows from utility theory and so finds its way into text-books on that account.

Equally econometric methods depend much on theory. If a function is 'misspecified', a definite bias will normally be imported into the calculation, but the data do not themselves dictate how functional relationships are to be specified. A more complex problem arises in interpreting data showing changes in variables influenced by several simultaneous forces. Which forces are responsible for what? Which relationships have shifted and which are being traced out? *Prima facie* that is a matter for theory, as the received opinion suggests.

Yet Positive economists, although usually upholders of the received opinion, are in no position to support it. In this chapter we shall ask what they are to do about theory and how they are to deal with the riddle of Induction. Theory, we shall argue, must have a role in the validation of hypotheses (regardless of whether it plays a part in their discovery). For a positivist, this means that theory and hypothesis cannot differ in kind. So there is *au fond* only one epistemological task for all enquiry, that of determining which generalisations are projectible. A solution to the riddle of Induction is therefore imperative. But it is not to be found in the concept of probability nor, indeed, in any area safe for positivists. How much does this matter? Enormously, we shall contend. Not only does what economists term the 'identification' problem become insoluble but also there is no longer any need to insist that laws are confirmed empirical correlations between variables. Theories must both differ in kind from hypotheses and have a role in the validation of hypotheses. Otherwise there is no telling, for example, whether the historical constancy of the 'great ratios' just mentioned reflects underlying laws or mere historical accidents and a central issue of growth economics is rendered wholly enigmatic.

Rationalist explanation: the role of theory

That will be our theme. But, with apologies to economists, we must first examine the relation of theory to hypothesis in the empiricist tradition. We shall begin on a historical note, sketching the rationalist ancestry of the analytic-synthetic distinction and showing how empiricists accepted its methodological implications while reversing its epistemological import. The latter reversal, we shall then argue, rules out the thesis that theory can give hypotheses independent support. Once again, by 'empiricism' in this context we shall still be referring to Positivism, since, of the several rival accounts of the true method of science, none falls so sweetly on the modern ear. We shall urge that sweetness is not enough.

Francis Bacon remarks (in his *First Book of Aphorisms*, XIX):

There are and can be only two ways of searching into and discovering truth. The one flies from the senses and particulars to the most general axioms, and from these principles, the truth of which it takes for settled and immovable; proceeds to judgement and to the discovery of middle axioms. And this way is now in fashion. The other derives axioms from the senses and particulars, rising by a gradual and unbroken ascent, so that it arrives at the most general axioms last of all. This is the true way, but as yet untried.

Bacon seems to be drawing our modern distinction between analytic and synthetic or deductive and inductive. Seventeenth-century thinkers, however, saw both methods as ways of exhibiting *a priori* truths. The way of general axioms, typified by geometry was deductive and the final truth consisted in all the formal implications of an original set of true axioms. The other way was the patient discovery of rational order in particular empirical data, increase in generality and system proceeding *pari passu* with the increase in empirical data taken into account. It was widely held that both methods gave the same result, a true picture of the real order of a universe where everything happened systematically and of necessity. As Descartes remarked in his *Principles of Philosophy* (preface):

The whole philosophy is like a tree, whose roots are metaphysics, whose trunk is physics, and whose branches are all the other sciences, which can be reduced to three principal ones, namely medicine, mechanics and morals.

Most seventeenth-century rationalists preferred to work up the tree (Bacon's first way), the direction in which implications run, but working down from branches to roots would give the same result in the end, even if the scientist found it harder to see where the connections lay. The idea that deductive and inductive sciences differ in principle and perhaps apply to radically different sorts of subject matter came only later.

Crucial to this belief in the unity of all knowledge, was a theory of the nature of mathematics, which has since been rejected. Mathematical, especially geometrical, truths describe the essence of matter and so the essence of everything in the world. The great book of the universe is ever open before our eyes but it is written in mathematical symbols. Euclid's works are about space. Matter has just one essential property, Descartes held, that of occupying space. So a true account of space is a true account of what is ultimately real. This is the red-blooded version of a doctrine, since bowdlerised to read that the real properties of matter are all and only those which can be measured and quantified.

The connections in a mathematical proof are logical and so hold of necessity. Mathematical truths cannot be denied without contradiction. Therefore the ultimate order they describe is a necessary order. Causes necessitate effects and causal laws can be stated without addition or loss as mathematically necessary truths, describing what effect *must* result from what cause. No hypothesis is finally synthetic or contingent, since it is in the end either true of a necessary order or false and so contradictory. A hypothesis is, in other words, a concealed mathematical conjecture. Moreover, each state of the world must be as it is, being the necessary result of a necessary cause.[3] Not knowing whether full employment can be achieved without inflation is like not knowing whether Fermat's last theorem is true. To call a statement contingent or synthetic is not to distinguish it in kind from a necessary truth or analytic tautology. It is to say that we do not yet know enough to have a rigorous proof for it. As long as a hypothesis remains a hypothesis and has not been ennobled as a theorem, it remains imperfectly understood and we have only an inadequate idea of what it states.

Causality, then, is the expression of logical proof in the real world, and full-blooded Rationalism requires that every event has a cause. The result is liable to be, as it is in Spinoza, a world without any contingencies whatever. But room can be found for contingencies, which exist not merely because finite human minds have not yet managed to prove their necessity, but also because it is contingent which parts of mathematics apply to which subsystems of the world. For instance suppose we define a continuous function of real numbers:

$$y = y(x), \qquad y' > 0, \qquad y'' < 0.$$

This function and another, say a linear one $y = a + bx$, being given, the difference will be at a maximum when the first derivative equals the coefficient in the linear function (see Figure 12). Thus: at $\bar{x}$, $y' = b$ and $y(x) - a - bx$ is at a maximum. Given the functions, the maximum is necessarily at $\bar{x}$. If the first function represents output and the second costs, then profit will necessarily be maximised by using input $\bar{x}$. But it is contingent that $y(x)$ describes the output-input relation or $a + bx$ describes costs. Spinoza would doubtless retort that the contingency is only apparent but others are content to allow the initial description of the

---

[3] This is deliberately non-committal about the first state of the universe. Some, like Spinoza, held that everything had to be as it was. Others, like Descartes, held that God chose which initial conditions to create and could have chosen differently. All agreed however that, given the first state and the iron laws of nature, the world of our present experience is the necessary outcome of an earlier state, itself the necessary outcome of an earlier state and so on in a continuous chain, whose first link was in the hand of God.

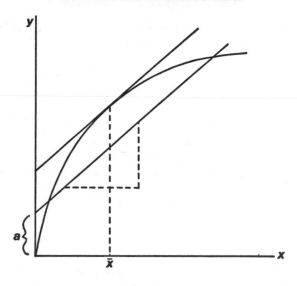

Figure 12

world to be contingent, provided that its consequences count as necessities *in rebus*. We mention this to show that rationalism can be subtle and shall return to it in later chapters.

A stock objection to rationalists' metaphysical flights is that they leave no room for scientific experiment. After all, if every statement about today's world is either necessarily true or necessarily false (even, if only hypothetically, given the initial description), what is the point of testing a hypothesis against fact? But the objection falls, as soon as it is noticed that the metaphysics of this seventeenth-century rationalism are the commonsense of the hypothetico-deductive method. For to refute a hypothesis is either to show that it was wrongly deduced or to refute whatever it was deduced from. Rationalists never supposed that the ramifications of a deductive scheme embracing the entire universe were obvious to anyone but God and rightly found scientific experiment a practical way of trying out conjectures. As with the beginners' model we presented in our introduction, refutation means that something is wrong but confirmation does not prove that everything is right. If the objection cited is thought to have greater force than this, it is because it covertly assumes that necessary truths are analytic and so void of all factual content. That would indeed render experiment fatuous but it would also beg the question. Meanwhile, experimenting in the context of our beginners' hypothetico-deductive model is very like trying out a conjectured theorem by attempting to construct a counter-case.

The Cartesian answer to the Inductive problem is now clear. It is not the only rationalist answer that can be given and we shall later distinguish another brand of rationalism, which is not committed to this sort of determinism. But the Cartesian method of science contrasts instructively with the Positivist. The Cartesian can say (however unhelpfully) that a correlation is projectible if and only if it can be formally deduced from a theorem correctly lodged further down the tree. No correlation, however frequent, not so deducible has any status, although, if the theory is incomplete, it may indicate the direction in which the theory should be developed. Any apparent correlation which conflicts with a demonstrably sound theory must result from misunderstanding or wrongly adjusted measurement. The Cartesian is exploiting the notion that genuine causal laws have the *Good-Housekeeping* Seal of necessity, whereas mere correlations do not. No such move is open to empiricists.

This grand Cartesian theory of deductive science is predicated on a necessary order of nature and few modern social scientists, working in an empirical tradition, wish to be committed to so strong a determinism. For there is a place on Descartes' tree for the moral science of economics, only if the behaviour of economic man does not depend on choice, as that word is usually understood. Moreover, the deductive method presupposes that we do not get much, or perhaps even any, genuine knowledge by observation. The senses reveal no necessities. The universe is a necessary order. So if our knowledge were confined to what we learn from sense experience, we would know nothing about the underlying universe at all and true causal laws would be in principle utterly undiscoverable. To this rationalist view, the empiricist replies that the universe is not a necessary order and that the senses reveal the world as it happens to be. And here Bacon's two ways part company and we must produce a new account of scientific investigation.

The analytic-synthetic distinction and the empiricist account of theory

So let us instead fly to the senses and argue, as we did in the last chapter, that causal laws are inductive generalisations of observed correlations. The epistemological bones of Bacon's second way have already been assembled but we have as yet no clue how to construe the idea of 'gradual and unbroken ascent' from particulars to the most general axioms. (Bacon's 'up' is Descartes' 'down', but the two metaphors are too clear to cause confusion.) In what sense is theorising ascending in the right direction?

A positivist must hold that if analytic statements ever do more than elicit implications in order to transmit the truth or probability of original premisses, then the ascent is no longer unbroken. Nor can it be resumed, since analytic statements not only differ in kind from synthetic but also are vacuous. So, insofar as 'theory' refers to logical and mathematical operations, it cannot be an explanatory notion. Definitions, rules of logic and mathematical techniques can be used to systematise statements and to elicit implications as astonishing as you please. But it is crucial that the definitions are optional, a matter of human choice and not of revealing the essence of the thing defined; that rules of logic transmit truth from true premisses to conclusions without creating or increasing it on the way; that mathematical techniques transform statements but do not show how the facts must be. The reason in brief is that logical positivists are empiricists who admit the existence of *a priori* truths. Since empiricists hold that all claims to knowledge of the world can be justified only by experience and that whatever is known by experience could have been otherwise, logical positivists are bound to add that *a priori* truths do not lay claim to knowledge of the world. To demonstrate this they must show *a priori* truths to depend only on mutable rules of language. Otherwise the admission destroys their own theory of knowledge and reinstates the search for necessary relations among matters of fact.[4] When an advocate of positive economics says he wants to know not only how but also why economic variables are related, he cannot mean that he demands a theory to unveil their real relationship. The distinction of how and why cannot be one between apparent and real. For there are no new empirical factors contained in a theory, since theory, regarded as analytic statements, has no empirical content. Truth always lies wholly in the facts.

We can perhaps best put the general point as a dilemma. Either theory and hypothesis differ in kind or they do not. If they do not, then theoretical statements are synthetic; if they do, then theoretical statements are analytic. If theoretical statements are analytic, then, by the Positivist canon, they are optional and empty and contribute nothing to the validation of hypotheses. If theoretical statements are synthetic, then they are (general or special or important or very well confirmed) hypotheses and cannot play the explanatory role assigned them by received opinion. Whichever horn the Positivist chooses, he is bound to make all his explanatory statements synthetic. He has to hold that not all the premisses, from which predictions are deduced, are analytic and that only synthetic ones can contain putative general laws. Truth about the world, however general, cannot reside in vacuous theoretical statements.

---

[4] It is vital to our case that positivism is committed to this view of definition, logic and mathematics. The matter was raised in the Introduction and will be discussed in detail in Chapters 6 and 7, where we shall argue for the contrary view that axioms and theorems can give *a priori* knowledge of the world.

Insisting that the explanatory power of an economist's handiwork must lie on the synthetic half of the analytic-synthetic divide has its merits. Suppose we meet a man who believes in fairies. 'I am well aware', he says, 'that toadstools grow in rings in certain soil conditions. What I want to know is why. My hypothesis is that fairies prefer rings, at least of that kind of toadstool in that kind of soil. You may think it unlikely, but just wait till you have heard my theory of fairies.' However systematic, elegant and comprehensive his theory of fairies, we shall still refuse to budge beyond the limits of mycology. For the theory of fairies will be no truer than its premises and, while we might feel we had settled his hash if we found contradictions in it, he has not settled ours, if it is free from contradictions. No doubt we would try to attack him by pointing out that the theory is untestable; that we do not, for instance, suffer if we fail to leave saucers of milk in the moonlight. But he can retort that 'other things' are not 'equal', that the theory tells us not what will happen but what would happen, if . . . Our reply to this awkward parry will have to be in empirical terms. Positivists cannot, in order to resolve the parallel snag we have found in Positive economics, concede that the analytic aspects of a theory have any explanatory power. For, if they do, the fairies will take up squatters' rights at the bottom of their garden too.

That does not yet account for the conceptual business of theorising. But, first, we should forestall an objection. It may be objected that the sense in which theory is explanatory is a psychological one. A statement is explanatory for anyone, whose furrowed brow it smooths. Basil Willey, for instance, is expressing a fairly common view when he writes,

To 'explain' . . . means to 'make clear', to 'render intelligible'. But wherein consists the clarity, the intelligibility? The clarity of an explanation seems to depend on the degree of satisfaction it affords. An explanation 'explains' best when it meets some need of our nature, some deep-seated demand for assurance . . . One cannot, therefore, define 'explanation' absolutely; one can say only that it is a statement which satisfies the demands of a particular place or time.[5]

Such a notion has no place in a theory of knowledge. Firstly, the merit of an explanation is made independent of its truth. If my car is out of petrol but otherwise working, then that is why it will not go, whether I believe it is out of petrol or not, whether I believe that cars need petrol or not and whether I have a need of my nature to think of cars in mechanical terms or not. Secondly, we are asking when projection of generalisations is warranted; we do not want to know merely when people are in the habit of projecting

---

[5] *The Seventeenth-Century Background* (Penguin Books, 1972), Ch. 1, p. 10f.

them. Positivism is not a psychology of belief and human need but an account of what we know and how we may warrantably claim to know it. Nor can it be transmuted into a psychology of belief without destroying its foundations. On this point we judge that Positivism is taking the right line. If theory has a role, it will be one of contributing to knowledge and not of ministering to our psychological needs. It has to help validate our advance in Bacon's 'gradual and unbroken ascent'.

Several roles, allegedly consistent with Bacon's second way, have been proposed by thinkers for economic theory. Theory, it can be said, tells the economist what to look for; it suggests the most likely or plausible relationships; it reminds him of suggestive data and rejuvenates hypotheses. Theory helps the econometrician first to specify his relationships properly and secondly to identify relationships which he could not otherwise disentangle from his data. Theory indeed (to echo a common defence of neo-Classicism against charges of ignoring or suppressing essential aspects of the economic system in framing definitions and assumptions) even plays a part in determining what are the facts to be considered. Let us next examine these proposed roles further.

Proposals turning on the suggestiveness of theory need not delay us long. No doubt theories are suggestive; but so are novels, poetry, chance conversations and pure imagination. If that is all there is to it, then the only question is which is most effective. To discover what a firm is doing it is no bad idea to ask the managing director. A good accountant has a shrewd notion of next year's prices. In fact there seem to be better sources of inspiration and information than economic theory. It will be retorted that theory codifies established and well-confirmed hypotheses, presenting them in useful form. But the retort can be met with a dilemma. Either a hypothesis is deduced from a theory or it is not. If it is not, it receives no support whatever from the theory as such. If it is, it has exactly the degree of probability which the theory has. For logical inferences only transmit truth or degrees of probability and then only if they are sound. Admittedly the results of inference can be novel and surprising and lead the enquirer into unexpected areas; but that says nothing whatever about the support which a theory lends to a hypothesis. If theory merely codifies, it lends no support, except insofar as it marshals already confirmed hypotheses. The General Theory, for instance, could have no merit or status, except perhaps as an inspired guess, in advance of empirical studies of the consumption function, the multiplier and liquidity preference. Growth theory would be vacuous without the collection and analysis of growth statistics. Yet the collection of relevant statistics and especially the estimation of parameters has been predicated on the truth of macro-theory and of growth theory. Indeed the truth of theory as we shall see presently, is a normal presupposition of specifications and identifications in econometric work.

We are in effect here distinguishing 'the logic of discovery' from 'the logic of validation'. The Inductive problem is an epistemological one and calls for a solution from the latter. A theory of knowledge need not explain how we come to hit upon causal laws but it must show how we know when we have found one. To argue that a hypothesis is rendered probable by being got from a theory of a type which has previously proved fruitful is to generate a vicious regress. For the fruitfulness of the previous theories can have lain only in their success in producing causal laws and the statement that their consequences express causal laws would have to be probable insofar as that statement has been got from a theory of a type which had previously proved fruitful. Theory, in short, does not validate merely by being suggestive and we now find ourselves saying that the hypothesis validates the theory and not the theory the hypothesis.

We do not deny that, in linking hypotheses, relationships are made more systematic and plausible. But we do insist that plausibility, being a psychological notion, is irrelevant and that probability, the epistemological notion, is a tricky one. Probability and confirmation, as we shall argue next, are derivative concepts, usable only after the riddle of Induction has been solved. As far as the concepts themselves go, hypotheses can be made more or less probable in absurd ways. To remove the absurdities, we need the missing criterion for deciding which generalisations are projectible. That, at any rate, will be the moral we shall draw from the discussion of probability which follows next.[6]

Deductions of probability from evidence are analytic

The riddle of Induction can be transformed into a problem about probability by asking how we know that statements to the effect that a given hypothesis is probable are true. At first sight, this improves matters, since it seems patent that a hypothesis is rendered more probable by an increase in the evidence for it and fairly patent what counts as evidence. On the other hand, the tenets of Positivism which imply that no hypothesis can be known true *a priori* also imply that none can be known probable *a priori*. Unless statements of probability are empirical, they do not in themselves contribute to our knowledge of the world. In terms of the analytic-synthetic distinction, probability statements had better be synthetic, but, we shall argue, are not.

A statement of probability is reached by calculation. But, as a statement of *probability*, it is more than a mere record of a calculation done. It claims

---

[6] Part of our case is beautifully put by A. J. Ayer in the two essays on probability in *The Concept of A Person* (Macmillan, 1963). See also his more recent *Probability and Evidence* (Macmillan, 1972).

not only that a figure (or degree) has been coherently derived within a calculus but also that what is predicted is in fact as likely to occur as the figure in theory indicates. These are separate claims since, for reasons given presently, statistics does not become a calculus of probabilities either merely by being mathematically sound or merely by being christened a calculus of probabilities. Unless it is in fact true that deflation during unemployment is likely to increase the unemployment, Keynesian economics are not worth the paper they are written on. Statistics is a calculus of *probabilities* only insofar as some statement that known correlations are likely to hold in unknown cases is true.

That known correlations will hold in unknown cases is a synthetic statement. That they are likely to hold, we maintain, is not. The former statement, like any universal generalisation, is shown false by an actual exception. (Admittedly there are ways of preserving an important generalisation against a single exception but that need not worry us here.) The latter is immune to empirical refutation. For, even if the sun fails to rise tomorrow, it remains true that it was likely that it would. Indeed, even if most of what we regard as laws of nature break down, it is still true now that they are likely to hold and it will still be true then that they were likely to hold. The only difference made by a general enough collapse is that it will no longer be true that the laws will probably continue to hold.

We are here following common practice in regarding probability-statements as elliptical. We take them to assign a probability to an event on the basis of evidence. Their schematic form is 'on the evidence that $n\%$ of x are y, the probability that the next x is y is $n\%$'. Statements of this form are analytic and, provided we can show that all probability statements have this form, every statement that a given hypothesis is probable will turn out analytic.

The case is clear enough where a probability is reached by pure calculation according to rules of mathematics. The probability of drawing an ace at random from a full pack of cards is $1/13$, in the sense that 4 out of 52 equiprobable outcomes are favourable. Although this need not be worded in the form 'on the evidence that $1/13$ of the cards are aces, the probability that the next card will be an ace is $1/13$', it can be so worded without damage to the calculus. Just this is intended, when the calculus is spoken of as covered by the '*A priori* theory of probability'. A pack of cards, like true dice, is constructed to make this so. A dice is biased, unless each of its six faces is equally likely to turn up; a pack is defective unless the chance of an ace is $1/13$. There is no question of testing the statements of probability got in this way against the facts, except perhaps as a test of the facts to see whether pack and dice were properly constructed.

But it may seem that the art of statistics is less abstract and that the term 'evidence' has a more empirical sense in this form of applied probability. For instance, unlike the statement of the chance of drawing an ace at random from a complete pack of properly made and so equiprobable cards, the reasoning which justifies charging extra insurance premiums to drivers of sports cars seems to apply not in all possible worlds, but only in those where sports cars happen to show significant correlation with accidents.

Here, too, however, the only processes involved in extrapolating the statistics are mathematical. The extrapolation of relative frequencies, however done, assumes and does not confirm that known correlations hold in unknown cases and, without that assumption, there are no grounds for extrapolation. The difference is only that 'probability' now enters twice into the calculation. When drawing the ace, we knew how many of all X were Y; when assessing the sports cars, we do not. So we need probability that our sample matches the whole population as well as a probability that the next sports car will have an accident. But the first probability is no less calculated than the second. The only way to find it is to extrapolate from sample to population according to the rules of statistics. It is probable that sports cars will cost the insurance company more next year precisely in the sense that they have done in the past. How probable it is is a matter for calculation, whether the upshot is stated in cardinal form or in ordinal. Calculation is therefore crucial, and it makes no difference whether or not the entire population is manufactured from a design based upon statistical requirements.

Every statement of probability involving the deduction of a probability from a statement of evidence is therefore analytic. Hence there is no statistical or mathematical reason for preferring one to another. The tautology that '70% of all sports car drivers have accidents each year so George has a 70% chance of an accident next year' is no more or less a tautology than '20% of left handed postmen have accidents each year, so George has a 20% chance of an accident next year', given that George is a left-handed postman who drives a sports car. Each indicates a different premium, each is logically impeccable and the reason for saying that the first is causal and the second is not does not belong to statistics. Statistics does not manufacture its own rules of significance, or, rather, insofar as it does, what is statistically significant is not on that account alone also empirically significant. Analytic statements, positivists assure us, are devoid of factual content.

Indeed there is no reason of any sort for preferring one tautology to another. So long as 'probability' has a purely formal sense, the logic of confirmation remains empty. Nothing about any *calculus* of probabilities makes it a calculus of *probabilities*. If we are to know that a hypothesis is confirmed by passing empirical tests, we must already know at least that hitherto observed trends tend to continue. For observed cases are supposed to be *evidence*, and, unless it is already known that trends tend to continue, the statement that a given observation was made has no general implications whatever. Indeed, we need to know more. As we said at the start, it is not enough to baffle the sceptic in general. We also need a criterion for deciding which generalisations count as trends. This is a matter of telling genuine from bogus samples and tautologies are no help.

That, we maintain, disposes of the belief that the logic of confirmation undercuts our Inductive problem. It also discharges our promise to try to show probability to be a derivative notion.

Probability statements depend upon support from established theories

We still need a solution to the Inductive problem which will explain the relation of theory to hypothesis. Granted that $n\%$ of known x are y, why is it likely that $n\%$ of all x are y?

This version of the riddle may be thought too crude and too committal. In answer to a charge of crudity, it uses the simplest wording which embodies two notions, that known cases count as evidence at all and that the evidence points in direct proportion to the distribution in known cases. These bare claims are enough to prompt our perplexity for three reasons. Firstly, not all historical economic correlations are projectible. (That inflation has run at an annual rate of 3% for the last so many months is not in itself a reason for expecting it to continue at the rate.) Secondly, it is not always clear which way the correlations point. (Verdoorn, for example, found a relation between the growth rate of output and the growth rate of productivity. Kaldor argues from this that high growth rates induce high rates of technical innovation, but others contend that high rates of technical progress induce high demand, causing growth rates to rise.[7]) Thirdly, any sample is consistent with an 'irregular' trend, for example one which alters at a later date owing to new linear programming techniques but which will, after that date and with hindsight, be seen to have been a regular trend all along.[8] There would therefore be no force in an objection that we are relying on Induction by Simple Enumeration to generate a puzzle removed by subtler brands of induction. All brands assume that known cases are evidence and that the evidence *pro tanto* points in direct proportion to the known distribution. They disagree only about how to assess the evidence.

---

[7] N. Kaldor, *Causes of the Slow Rate of Economic Growth in the U.K.* (Cambridge University Press, 1966).

[8] Cf. N. Goodman, *Fact, Fiction and Forecast* (Bobbs Merrill, 1965), esp. Ch. 3.

Our version may also be thought too committal. Instead of 'likely', we might have put 'certain' or 'reasonable to suppose'. But 'certainly' strikes us as too strong for a subject where all projections are, it seems, conditional. However mystifying the contention that the economist predicts not what will happen but what would happen, if..., we have no wish, yet at least, to drop it. On the other hand 'reasonable to suppose', strikes us as too weak. It has had a good run recently in philosophical writing on Induction, where it is often argued that a statement of the principle of Induction explicates the meaning of the term 'rational scientific procedure'. This makes it analytic that to proceed inductively is to proceed rationally. But no such dissolving of the puzzle is open to the positivist. From his standpoint analytic statements are vacuous and the meaning of their terms optional. The dirt is therefore only shifted from one corner of the carpet to another and the problem becomes why we should settle for that meaning of 'rational'. Whatever protean transformations of meaning occur, the question repeats, until it is at last answered by reference to the future course of events. At that point we may ask the original question all over again.

So, granted that $n\%$ of known x are y, why is it likely that $n\%$ of all x are y? The answer certainly ought to be that it is likely if but only if x and y are related in a well-established theory. But that answer has already been blocked by insisting on a strong analytic-synthetic distinction. So far, at least, we have found only one, tenuous, sense in which a theory strengthens a hypothesis, and that is by relating the hypothesis to a set of others. But the riddle is too general to be solved by heaping up more examples of what the riddle is about. Further correlations tell up neither why known behaviour is to be taken into account nor what conclusion we are to draw from it. And, in general, no set of analytic statements, void of factual content, can, of their positivist nature, tell us what is empirically likely to happen next.

Positivism cannot allow theories to support hypotheses

Is there any other Positivist answer? Students are often assured that there exists something called the Pragmatic Justification of Induction. Shorn of verbiage, this has it that previous success with inductive techniques is evidence of future success. As Dr Johnson might have put it, 'Sir, we know Induction works and there's an end on't.' But this is to beg the question in a way little short of blatant. For 'evidence' can only mean 'inductive evidence' and the justification reads 'past inductive success is inductive evidence of future inductive success.' No better example could be given of a statement void of all factual content.

But the tautology cannot create its own truth and to ask what guarantees it is to raise the problem afresh.[9]

Having hunted vainly for a solution, we shall now try to prove the futility of the quest within Positivism. We said (and, indeed, believe) that the answer ought to be that the sample is likely to match the population insofar as there is a sound theory linking x with y. Schematically we are saying that 'a correlation is projectible if and only if p', where p stands for any definitive account of what constitutes a sound theoretical link between x and y. Let us christen this whole propositional function S. Now, any instance of S is either analytic or synthetic. If analytic, it shows only what we mean by 'projectible', without telling us what we ought to mean or what justifies that choice of meaning. (For example, 'a correlation is projectible if and only if true counterfactuals are warrantably deducible from a statement of it'.) Moreover any further analytic gloss on S will merely transfer any difficulties in S. (For example, 'true counterfactuals are warrantably deducible from an instance of S, only if the predicates used to specify x and y make no mention of space and time'.) On the other hand, if any instance of S is synthetic, then a correlation may be projectible, when p is unsatisfied. (For example, 'a correlation is projectible if and only if it is cited in the works of Samuelson.') And even if it happened that p specified all and only the projectible correlations, we could not know this, unless we knew which they were independently of p. But that too would only shift the problem to whatever the independent criterion was. We conclude, therefore, that no solution to the riddle of Induction is possible within positivism.

Without a solution to the riddle, there is no role for theory, if theory is required to support hypotheses and winnow out the projectible generalisations. This seems to confine economics to the recording of empirical connections. Pragmatic economists will perhaps be content – if there is no systematic answer to scepticism, we must settle for what works best in practice. Why not treat theories simply as heuristic devices to be used or discarded as it suits? Why not treat 'knowledge' as tentative and particular but nevertheless handy in practice? Positivists have traditionally hoped for more but should they perhaps settle for pragmatism?

Our answer is emphatically No. To reject theory in economics is to forgo some important kinds of facts, which can be established only with the help of theory. We believe, in general, that no clear or unique line can be drawn between 'fact' and 'interpretation' and that rejection of theory leaves the

---

[9] This paragraph is intended to show only that positivists cannot find comfort in the Pragmatic Justification of Induction. The Pragmatic Justification itself merits more care, when treated in the context of Pragmatism, although we do not find it finally viable for the sorts of reason given in Chapters 6 and 7.

economist without any facts. But that will be the subject of the next chapter and we are concerned here only with a specific point about specific kinds of economic fact. We shall now take up the textbook case of supply and demand in a particular market, use it to argue the folly of being pragmatic and finish by rejecting the positivist notion of 'scientific law'.

Two econometric examples: the identification and the specification problems

Suppose we have observed the price of bread and quantity sold in a particular city for a period. These observations are the facts, although, having been adjusted to eliminate extraneous influences, they are not raw facts. The question is what to conclude from such data. A scatter diagram may suggest no particular shape (Figure 13) or it may suggest one (Figure 14). Whether it does or not, we are dealing with two categories of agents, buyers and sellers, and each price-quantity observation represents a coming together of the two under different circumstances. One question is what caused the changes in prices and quantities; another is whether the data reflect the behaviour of the buyers, the sellers or both. The questions are related. Suppose we have two observations, the difference between situations A and B being a rise in the level of employment (Figure 15). With more employed breadwinners, demand for bread rises, producing the higher price and quantity of situation B. Precisely because we know that the difference is due to the demand side, we can take the observations as reflecting the behaviour of the suppliers. As a corollary, if we did not know the causes of the difference, we would not know how to interpret the observations.

This applies, even if the observations reveal a distinct pattern. Figure 14 above may show a demand curve or may show a supply curve, where there are substantial economies of scale. Figure 15 may portray a good, demand for which increases for snobbish reasons, when its price rises.

In general, whenever an event is caused by as many behavioural forces as there are variables involved, an identification problem occurs, soluble only by finding the causes of changes in the observed variables. Scrutiny of the data alone is not enough. Other variables, causing a shift in the initial forces, must be found. A regular connection between at least one of the forces and some further variable must be established. This requires a reasonably neutral charting of the initial forces or, in short, theory. Without theory, data resulting from multiple simultaneous forces cannot even be examined for regularities or patterns.

A pragmatist might be tempted to agree, provided that all theoretical statements are treated as provisional. But this proviso would imply that confirmations or refutations were also provisional. For suppose we wished

Figure 13

Figure 14

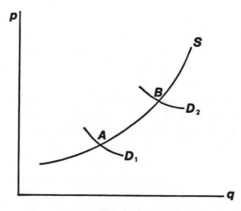

Figure 15

to test the Law of Increasing Marginal Cost (or of Rising Supply Price). Figure 14 would be an exception, only if the observations are identified as caused by shifts in demand. Similarly, Figure 15 confirms the law, only if identified as caused by shifts in demand. Identification is crucial and depends upon prior theory. So a provisional theory makes for provisional identifications and so for provisional confirmation or refutation. If everything is provisional, we shall argue, the pragmatist has no testing procedures.

Suppose next that we have good reasons for taking a group of price-quantity observations as caused by shifts in supply. In this case the observations should trace out a demand curve. It might seem natural simply to fit a line or curve to the points. But that would be a mistake. For suppose some further variable, say the price of potatoes, tends to move systematically with or against the price of bread. Now the observed change is either boosted or damped down by the other variable. Since bread and potatoes, for instance, are substitutes and both are farm products, a simple curve fitted in Figure 14 is likely to prompt an underestimate of the effect of a change in price on the demand for bread, since it latently includes the counteracting effect of the associated movement in the price of potatoes. The point can be formalised as follows, with apologies to our less mathematical readers: find the mean values of all observations and rewrite the variables as deviations from means, to eliminate constant terms.

1. Let the incorrect specification be

$$q = \overline{B}qp_1 P_1 + \overline{\epsilon} \qquad (1)$$

where q is the quantity of bread demanded, P_1 is the price of bread, Bqp_1 is the coefficient and $\overline{\epsilon}$ is a random disturbance.

2. Let the correct specification be

$$q = Bqp_1 P_1 + Bqp_2 P_2 + \epsilon \qquad (2)$$

where P_2 is the price of potatoes and Bqp_2 the coefficient showing the effect on the demand for bread of a change in the price of potatoes.

3. Multiply (1) by P_1 and sum over all observations:

$$\Sigma P_1 q = \Sigma \overline{B}qp_1 P_1^2 + \Sigma \overline{\epsilon} P_1 \qquad (3)$$

so that:

$$\overline{B}qp_1 = \frac{\Sigma P_1 q}{\Sigma P_1^2},$$

since $\Sigma \overline{\epsilon} P_1$ reduces to zero in large samples.

4. Multiply (2) by P_1 and sum over all observations:

$$\Sigma P_1 q = Bq p_1 \Sigma P_1{}^2 + Bq p_2 \Sigma P_1 P_2 + \Sigma \epsilon P_1. \qquad (4)$$

5. Divide (4) by $\Sigma P_1{}^2$ dropping $\Sigma \epsilon P_1$:

$$\frac{\Sigma P_1 q}{\Sigma P_1{}^2} = Bq p_1 + Bq p_2 \frac{\Sigma P_1 P_2}{\Sigma P_1{}^2}. \qquad (5)$$

6. The LHS is $\overline{B} q p_1$ (from (3)); and $\dfrac{\Sigma P_1 P_2}{\Sigma P_1{}^2}$ is the regression coefficient of P_2 on P_1, which we may call $B p_1 p_2$.
Hence

$$\overline{B} q p_1 = Bq p_1 + Bq p_2 \cdot B p_1 p_2 \qquad (6)$$

7. If P_1 and P_2 are uncorrelated, then $B p_1 p_2 = 0$, and (1) is adequate, even though $Bq p_2 \neq 0$. But if P_1 and P_2 are correlated, then (1) will yield false estimates of the effect of the price of bread on the demand for bread. If $B p_1 p_2 > 0$ and $Bq p_2 > 0$: the second term on the RHS will be positive, whereas both $\overline{B} q p_1$ and $Bq p_1$ are negative (a rise in price reduces demand). Hence $Bq p_1$ understates the true value.)

Here again theory must provide guidance. Before we can start to write specifications, we must know that commodities can figure as complements or substitutes in demand patterns. These are theoretical terms. If theory is merely provisional and heuristic, in other words if the whole theory of demand can be revised on less than any particular specification, then we have no way of working with data. There is no longer a way to decide whether a failure in prediction results from a wrong specification or a wholly wrong theory. The pragmatist perhaps replies that we preserve the theory because it is more deeply entrenched in our thinking. But, if entrenchment is a rational process, this presupposes that the theory has been confirmed in the past, which presupposes in turn that identifications consequent on specifications have been successfully made in the past. The pragmatist is thus begging the question in his own favour and against his own thesis that everything is always provisional.[10]

The concept of 'general law'

Positivists, failing to solve the Inductive problem, cannot therefore settle for being pragmatic. They still need a way of arriving at general laws.

---

[10] This is only a skirmish with Pragmatism, which we attack on a wider front in Chapter 6.

Problems of classification, of identification and of detecting errors in specification arise only on the assumption that there are functional relations between variables. These relations must be known to be lawlike, if they are to license what philosophers term 'counter-factual conditionals'. Unless, for instance, we may infer from a demand curve that, had the price been p, the quantity demanded would have been q, demand curves are not worth constructing. There is nothing novel about this – a projectible generalisation is one which warrants the assertion of counter-factual conditionals for cases which never actually occurred. Since the concepts of identification and specification error are applicable only with the help of theory, as we have seen, we must be able to relate laws to the workings of theory.

Let us revert for a moment to the problem mentioned at the start of this chapter. Neo-Classical theory seeks to state general laws pertaining to markets, regardless of time, place or stage of historical development. So it must be able to discount the many extraneous variables and accidents which seem to affect the phenomena it wishes to isolate. So it makes some such presumption as this:

a succession of picturesque incidents and romantic transformations, which arrest public attention ... seem to indicate a coming change of our social arrangements ... [These are] apt to be exaggerated ... many of them are little more than eddies, such as have always fluttered over the surface of progress. And though they are on a larger and more imposing scale ... than ever before; yet, now, as ever, the main body of movement depends on the deep, silent strong stream of the tendencies of normal distribution and exchange, which 'are not seen', but which control the course of those episodes which are seen.[11]

The distinction drawn here between the 'deep silent strong stream' and the fluttering eddies is crucial for theory, for the testing of theory and for policy. The claim of neo-Classical theory to embody general truths about the working of markets depends on it; so does the testing of theories which require a solution to the identification and specification problems; so does the soundness of long-term policy, designed to survive surface turbulence. The implicit recipe for making the distinction is that an apparent observed tendency is law-like or projectible, if it can be deduced from the theory of normal distribution and exchange or perhaps from an expanded version of basic theory; otherwise it is an eddy. Yet the justification for this recipe and so for the distinction itself is now crucially in doubt.

We can now take a step hinted at in Chapter 1 towards indicating the sources of this difficulty. The Positivist notion of 'general law' strikes us as

[11] Alfred Marshall, *Principles of Economics*, 9th (variorum) ed., with annotations by C. W. Guillebaud (Macmillan, 1961), vi, viii, x.

unsatisfactory, since it conflates two distinct problems. One is that of determining the form of the functional relations between variables; the other is that of deciding the scope of their application. *Prima facie*, at least, there is a distinction between the properties which a scientist finds to be interrelated and the objects or agents which bear those properties. To put it disingenuously, 'being red' and 'being round' are related properties of a cricket ball but the ball is a thing and not a property. The question is whether this distinction is genuine or relevant. The positivist holds, and must hold, that it is not. He takes all laws to assert only correlations between variables. Thus to say that cricket balls are red and round is not to predicate redness and roundness of cricket balls but to say that anything with the property of being a cricket ball has the properties of being red and being round. In general a statement of the form 'All F are G' (for instance 'All businessmen maximise profits') is equivalent to 'If anything is F, then it is also G', which is in turn equivalent to 'Everything is either not-F or G or both'.[12] The formulation conjures bearers of variables out of existence, since laws become no more than relations between variables. Positivists see virtue in this, since it accords well with the idea that causal relations are reducible to concomitant variations between atomic states of the world. We do not.

To see what is involved in formulating a law and how this differs from determining its range of application, let us consider an ideal and ideally rational consumer. He consumes according to his relative preferences, which we describe by a utility function:

$$u = u(x_1 \ldots x_n) \tag{1}$$

where $x_1 \ldots x_n$ are the n commodities available in the economy. Utility is assumed to increase with each increase in the amount consumed, hence:

$$\frac{\delta u}{\delta x_i} > 0, \qquad i = 1, \ldots, n \tag{2}$$

but at a diminishing rate; hence:

$$\frac{\delta^2 u}{\delta x_i^2} < 0, \qquad i = 1, \ldots, n. \tag{3}$$

Since utility need not be a definite amount, so long as marginal utilities can be calculated, we replace (1) by the functional $\overline{u}$ consisting of all monotonic transformations of (1):

$$\overline{u} = \overline{u}(x_1 \ldots x_n), \quad \text{where } \overline{u}'(u) > 0. \tag{4}$$

---

[12] In simple predicate logic, 'All F are G' is written as $(x)(Fx \to Gx)$, which is tautologically equivalent to $(x)(\sim Fx \vee Gx)$.

This is sometimes called the Law of Diminishing Marginal Utility. To get the consumer's equilibrium pattern, we add prices and his income y:

$$y = p_1 x_1 + p_2 x_2 + \ldots + p_n x_n. \tag{5}$$

Then we maximise the utility function, subject to the linear constraint of income. The conditions are that the marginal utilities should equal the ratio of the corresponding prices:

$$\frac{(\delta u/\delta x_1)}{p_1} = \frac{(\delta u/\delta x_2)}{p_2} = \ldots = \frac{(\delta u/\delta x_n)}{p_n} \tag{6}$$

and that marginal utility should be diminishing.[13]

Equations (1)–(6), together with the definitions of the terms, contain all that is essential to the model. From them the familiar income and substitution effects can be derived and criteria for complementary and substitutable goods formulated. Yet, strikingly, such models nowhere mention the consumer. Admittedly the utility is his, the quantities consumed are his and the model is of him. But there is no symbol for him, just as there is no symbol for gas in the gas laws. Far from quantifying over consumers, the law is formulated independently of them. They come into the picture, only when questions of application are raised.

Yet the range of application does matter to the formulation of laws. In production theory, for instance, the production function states, in effect, that *for every level of output* there is a set of input combinations which will produce it and within which a decrease in one input can be offset by a larger increase in another. This embodies the Law of Diminishing Marginal Productivity but does not mention the 'representative business firm' it is meant to characterise. The phrase 'for every level of output' is important, since 'marginal rates of substitution' are usually held to turn negative in production theory, although not in utility theory. These negative cases are excluded as economically meaningless in production theory.

Can the law of diminishing marginal utility be expressed in the positivist idiom as a general scientific law? The best we ourselves can do is:

$$(x)(y) \left[(Cx \ \& \ Gy \ \& \ Pxy) \to (\exists z)(Uzx \ \& \ Fxy) \right]$$

where Cx is 'x is a consumer', Gy is 'y is a quantity of a good', Pxy is 'x possesses y', Uzx is 'z is a degree of utility to x' and Fzy is 'z increases with y at a diminishing rate'. But, far from revealing the logical structure of the law, this compresses equations (1)–(6) into a single dyadic predicate

---

[13] Standard expositions of the theory of consumer behaviour can be found in e.g.: Henderson and Quandt, *Microeconomic Theory*, Chapter 2, or R. G. D. Allen, *Mathematical Economics*, 2nd ed. (Macmillan, 1966), Chapter 19.

F. Moreover a positivist would presumably have to accept the same logical formulation for a (presumably analytic) 'law' stating that 'if a consumer purchases a good, then there is a sum of money, which he paid and which is equal to what the good cost him'. In other words, the formulation is doing no work whatever and the burden is wholly carried by its interpretation. The logical formulation is in no sense an analysis of the statement of the law.

Positivism conflates two distinct aspects of theory, namely statements of the range of application of laws and statements of the laws themselves. Thus we found in Chapter 1 an irremediable confusion between the claim that all businessmen maximise profits and the statement that marginal costs rise as output rises. The former attempts to characterise what we shall term the proper 'bearer' of a theoretical variable ('bearers' being the agents or things forming the subject matter of a theory), the latter states a 'law' or functional relation between variables. The point of the distinction will become clear when we argue later that much of the contribution of theory consists in eliciting the sort of functional relations which must characterise the bearers of certain sorts of variables.

The moral we wish to draw is that, if laws are stated as contingent correlations between variables and if the analytic portions of theory are allowed no explanatory or validating role, then the riddle of Induction is insoluble. Without a solution, there is no way of knowing whether, for instance, the ratio of 3 : 1 between capital and output is lawlike and so reliable in explanations and predictions. The moral is thus a negative one at this stage. In later chapters we shall revive the rationalism sketched earlier and offer a theory of knowledge in which Bacon's first and second ways once again lead to the same destination. We shall also try to remove the apparent implication of rationalism, that a world can be investigated by science, only if it is wholly determined. This, coupled with a distinction between variables and their bearers, will restore us to the bosom of received opinion and theory will again have a validating role. But the economic theories suited to the task will be classical and Marxian rather than neo-Classical.

Meanwhile we can perhaps make our strategy clearer with a parable. In the next appendix, we give two ways in which chess might be made the subject of science. One is Positivist and leads to absurdity; the other points ahead to our own view. Only with the second and more Rationalist way, can the scientist know when he may project his generalisations about chess.

Finally we repeat that positivists cannot both treat theories and hypotheses as different in kind and allow theory an epistemological role in validating hypotheses. That is why Positivism cannot uphold received opinion and why it cannot solve the riddle of Induction.

A MINI-SCIENCE OF CHESS

To draw threads together and to point ahead, let us postulate a mini-science whose subject is chess, see how a positivist might set about it and ask what more promising way there might be. The argument will be rapid and without detail but it is intended only to outline points given substantial attention throughout the book.[14]

Our positivist begins, perhaps, in a behaviourist spirit, taking as his proper data all behaviour emitted by chess players and as his object the confirmation of empirical hypotheses about how players act and react in what conditions. He assembles observations of very many past games and looks for promising correlations. With the need for a typology in mind, he notes the general reciprocal binary relations between players in the pair-group conflict situation and the serial dynamic disequilibria, which progress diachronically towards a terminal state. Repeated observations begin to suggest correlations, for instance between a furrowed brow and a cramped position or between growing disparity in the opposing forces and the proximity of the terminal state. Then he moves on to more precise hypotheses about the effects of kinds of move in kinds of position.

Hypotheses generated in this manner will be shaky. But, even before we press the point, there are two objections to be deflected. The first is that interesting hypotheses are not, as a matter of fact, generated by noting correlations, since scientists are more wont to hit on ideas by guess and by God than by the sort of process just caricatured. But this objection, although true enough, need not embarrass the positivist, who replies by distinguishing the art of discovery from the logic of validation. As has been repeatedly said, Positivism is a theory of knowledge, concerned to tell us how to know when we have found a causal law and does not stand or fall by whether the hypothetico-deductive method is a fruitful heuristic device. Secondly, it may be objected that testable hypotheses cannot even be formulated, since concepts enter into the identification of data more essentially than the caricature suggests. A 'king', for instance, is not just a bit of wood of a certain shape, but an entity defined quasi-legally by reference to its role and powers and so not directly observable. Where does our positivist get his concepts from? Our positivist replies that statements of the roles and powers

[14] For a more thorough and complete version, see M. Hollis, Theory in miniature, *Mind* (1973).

of pieces are analytic (insofar as declarations of rules are statements at all) and so record only our determination to make the rules as we do. So long as the concepts involved are stipulated and mutable, their function in identifying data does not threaten the vital independence of facts. Although it will be argued in later chapters that this reply finally falls, let us take it to suffice for the moment.

Thus equipped, he applies the tenet that the test of a theory is the success of its predictions. But what exactly is to be predicted? It seems at first that he is trying to predict what particular players will do in particular positions, on the evidence of what previous players have tended to do in such positions. Prospects of success are dim, however, since players differ in skill, imagination, temperament, style, knowledge and countless other ways. Their play is affected by their respect for their opponent, fatigue, lighting, digestion, marital discord and so on. If particular actual moves are to be predicted, the mini-science would have to include all the social sciences and a working knowledge of medicine and physiology.

There must therefore be restrictions on the scope of the predictions and on the tests allowed to confirm or refute them. So our positivist introduces *ceteris paribus* clauses to remove external interference by factors belonging to other sciences. Prediction is to be not of what flatly will happen, but of what would happen, if there were no extraneous interference. Indeed he must restrict scope still further, since, within the boundary of the mini-science, some players are more rational than others and predictions will presume a given degree of rationality. Consequently they are also not to be refuted when a less rational player fails to do what he 'should'. Prediction is to be of what would happen, if there were no extraneous interference and the player were suitably rational.

This at once creates the familiar double threat of circularity. On the external front, our positivist has just issued himself a licence to preserve pet hypotheses against all failure. For, since he has no superscience, in which the boundary between chess and, say, psychology can be marked out independently of the hypotheses of each, a failure of prediction can be taken as logically sufficient to show 'other things' to be 'unequal'. The only way to prevent this disastrous consequence is to produce a criterion for deciding when failure refutes the hypothesis being tested and when it is properly blocked by the *ceteris paribus* clauses. This criterion cannot *ex hypothesei* be the success or failure of the prediction and, as a positivist, our mini-scientist cannot allow other criteria. On the internal front, the injection of rationality makes matters even worse, as there is no way of testing whether a kind of move is rational, except by comparing it to the theory being tested. Thus there is no question of testing a theory of rational play against the play of the ideally rational world champion and the actual world champion, who makes mistakes from time to time, is only as rational as the theory recognises. Just as profits cannot be maximised under perfect competition unless marginal cost equals marginal revenue, so no ideally rational player can possibly lose. So assumptions of rationality serve to add a further set of *ceteris paribus* clauses which reinforce the prior circularity and make the mini-scientist's theories simply untestable.

Our positivist will not admit to being wholly dismayed by the last paragraph, on the grounds that it shows only something he himself holds, namely that science cannot advance solely by induction. If it were solely his task to generalise from past play, then he would fail, partly because past play is a poor guide to present play in a developing game, partly because of the snag about *ceteris paribus* clauses. But, he will no doubt add, he too rejects historicism, even if many of his positivist predecessors were historicists. He himself distinguishes analysis from mere description, fruitful abstraction from mere realism, interpretation from mere history. The introduction of rationality signals the importance of model-building and theory construction, which is as much part of a sophisticated Positivism as any insistence on the facts of observation.

But he cannot escape like this. He must still hold that the test is the success of prediction, whereas he has just conceded that an analysis of rational play is theoretical. In other words, if prediction is the test, then he is lead back either to historicism or to circularity. For, if statements of his hypotheses complete with *ceteris paribus* clauses are synthetic, then his theory is an aid to inductive generalising; if they are analytic then they are untestable. So Positivism cannot produce a viable mini-science of chess, whether the aim is a summary of trends or an abstract theory.

Now let us be constructive. Two useful ideas emerge from the argument. One is that data cease to be all of equal weight when the notion of rationality is introduced. The other is that prediction is not the only criterion. Putting these ideas together, we notice that the whole enterprise has so far been conducted in a most curious way. The object of a mini-science of chess, we submit, is not to predict in principle all moves in all games but to discover how to play chess better. The question is not which moves are likely but which are rational. The answer will lie not in covering laws and statistical generalisations but in a sound maximising model, explaining how to gain comparative advantage by maximising control of, for instance, force, space and time in order to deliver checkmate.

From this perspective the data and difficulties look very different. We examine past play for sound and unsound ideas. The world champion is a source of theoretical novelties, the beginner a fund of instructive mistakes. But even the champion nods and even the beginner sometimes shines and our new problem is to tell good from bad. There is no doctrine of loser sovereignty which makes sense. Equally the problem of discerning trends in a developing game vanishes. For instance the Hypermodern System of chess, pioneered by Nimzovitch, gradually revolutionised the game. But when it first came in, it did not catch on; few knew of it and those who did were mostly contemptuous. So, had it been the job of our mini-science before Nimzovitch to predict what all players at all times tend to play, it would have been an increasingly evident failure. Were it Nimzovitch's task, as chess theorist, to predict what all players tend to play, his new theory would have been merely laughable. But Nimzovitch had the wholly different aim of reconceptualising the game for the purpose of winning. He proved his point partly by winning from positions previously regarded as inferior and partly by providing a theoretical explanation of his successes. The theoretical explanations were needed to show that the new system was genuinely better and did not merely bring good luck; in other words to distinguish significant connections from mere correlations. Yet there is still a predictive element, since Nimzovitch claimed that 'if you follow my system, you will win' but it turns not on the success of prediction but on the prediction of success.

For the mini-science of chess then, a hypothesis or general statement is projectible not if it reflects past correlations but if it can be derived from a sound theory. The sort of theory we have in mind includes:

(i) axiomatic statements introducing essential analytical concepts (e.g., the concepts of 'force', 'space' and 'time', e.g. 'A player has an advantage in time relative to a given area of the board if he can come to control it in less moves than his opponent needs to defend it');

(ii) criteria for assessing comparative advantage (e.g., 'The pieces are roughly worth pawn: 1, knight or bishop: 3, rook: 5, queen: 9 and two bishops are worth 7 on an open board');

(iii) derived principles of rational play (e.g. 'A central knight posted forward and safe from attack is well placed');

(iv) a typology of positions with advantage (e.g. 'king, bishop and pawn will usually win against king and bishop, if the bishops are on squares of the same colour and the king is ahead of and close to the pawn').

Schematically, the logical form of such a theory is (presupposing the rules of logic):

$$[(A \rightarrow T) \ \& \ (T \rightarrow (C \text{ and } ceteris \ paribus) \rightarrow (S \rightarrow R)]$$

where: A refers to axioms (including those introducing essential concepts)

T refers to theorems (including (ii), (iii), (iv) above)

C refers to a range of initial conditions $C_1, C_2 \dots C_n$
S refers to the 'best' stimulus or move $S_1, S_2 \dots S_n$
R refers to the 'best' response $R_1, R_2 \dots R_n$

and statements of analyses taking the form

$$(C_j \ \& \ cet. \ par.) \to (S_j \to R_j)$$

are themselves provable theorems of less generality than those initially derived from the axioms.

This kind of theory allows the analysis and assessment of positions. In the simplest case, it can reveal a way to checkmate an opponent by analysing all variations. The full statement of the win is an *a priori* truth, consisting of a set of conditional statements like 'if 30 ... K $-$ B$_1$ then 31. Q $-$ B$_7$ mate'. It does not predict that the better placed player will win; still less does it predict the actual sequence of moves, since that depends on the ingenuity of both parties. It asserts that 'White has a won game', which is true whether white actually finds the win or not. Yet the win is there, if the analysis is correct, and the theory explains why some moves are more rational than others. In the more usual case, there is no guarantee of checkmate and the analysis leads only to a better position. Again, however, that 'White probably has a won game' is a truth provable or partially provable upon the soundness of the theory.

So, how are we to know whether a proposed theory of chess is sound or not? Notoriously, chess has yet to be fully analysed and what is progress if not the success of prediction? At this point we need a notion of probability, to be able to say that a particular move is probably best, a particular theorem probably right or a particular concept probably basic and applicable. Two sorts of probability are involved. Firstly, success in practice in applying an incompletely proved theorem makes it more likely that the theorem will be finally provable. Here logic trumps experience, in the sense that mere observation cannot prove the theorem, whereas a final proof guarantees that observation will never contradict it. Secondly, there is always room for doubt about the range of application of even a proved theorem and experience marks out its likely limits. Here experience trumps logic in the sense that analysis is a skill, which even those with a complete grasp of theory may lack. The doubt is not whether the 'hypothesis' is indeed a theorem but whether the theorem applies. The mini-science thus advances by repelling two kinds of uncertainty with the aid of probability. On the one hand, tentative theorems are proved or discarded, on the other the art of analysis becomes systematic. A sound theory is one which can be shown to guarantee best play.

Chess in our view is an empirical maximising science in which a hypothesis is strengthened by the support of a sound theory. The final test is indeed actual success and the science is indeed predictive. But it is predictive not in the sense of projection from experience but in the sense that correct application of a sound theory is bound to succeed. The appeal to sound theory also removes threats of circularity caused by *ceteris paribus* clauses and rationality assumptions. It does so, however, only if we first reject what is done by positivists in the name of the analytic-synthetic distinction, since we are treating a sound theory as an *a priori* but by no means optional or vacuous structure which has application to the world. To make the case out we must wait until Chapters 6 and 7, where we discuss the problem of *a priori* knowledge. Meanwhile we hope that chess can serve to illustrate our doubts about Positivism and to hint at a possible alternative.

4

FACTS AND THEORIES

The Azande have a deep and systematic belief in witchcraft, oracles and magic. Witchcraft adds an uncertainty to life, which oracles dispel and magic controls. In practice, however, oracles are often inaccurate and magic often incompetent. So a decent scepticism about them might seem called for. But Zande beliefs are resilient. As Evans-Pritchard describes them in his *Witchcraft, Oracles and Magic among the Azande*:

Azande see as well as we that the failure of their oracle to prophesy truly calls for explanation, but so entangled are they in mystical notions that they must make use of them to account for the failure. The contradiction between experience and one mystical notion is explained by reference to other mystical notions.[1]

Witchcraft, oracles and magic form an intellectually coherent system. Each explains and proves the others. Death is a proof of witchcraft. It is avenged by magic. The accuracy of the poison–oracle is determined by the king's oracle, which is above suspicion.[2]

The parallel with Positive economics is too close for comfort. Failure of prediction is proof of interference. Interference is removed by *ceteris paribus* clauses and by adjusting observed variables to their true values. The scope of clauses and adjustments is determined by theory and theories are validated by checking their implications against facts. But the parallel stops, when we look for the king's oracle. A solution to the riddle of Induction would serve nicely but we have failed to find one. Without it, theories do not support hypotheses, hypotheses cannot be tested and tests show nothing. If it is a coherent world that we want, the Azande are better off than we.

We have so far argued that a Positive economist can always interpret facts in two ways, one of which does and the other of which does not refute his

---

[1] E. E. Evans-Pritchard, *Witchcraft, Oracles and Magic among the Azande* (Clarendon Press, 1937), p. 388.

[2] *Ibid.* p. 476.

hypothesis, and that he has no criterion for deciding which way is right. We have suggested also that his conception of lawlike hypotheses makes him assimilate the ascription of properties to bearers of variables to the specification of relations between variables; which presupposes implausibly that all differences between theories in the range and type of subjects they apply to can be fully expressed in the choice of variables and their range of values. In order to raise these issues, we had to credit him with knowing at least roughly what his economic facts are and which are relevant to testing which hypothesis. We are now ready to withdraw that credit and examine further the nature of individual economic facts.

In this chapter we shall discuss the relation of theoretical economic terms to the facts which are instances of them. We shall start by asking how theoretical terms get their sense and reply, at first, that they get sense by being defined. Definition, however, gives only a formal sense and criteria of application are also needed. Calling statements of such criteria 'criterial statements', we shall ask next whether criterial statements are analytic or synthetic. If they are analytic, they do not serve to anchor terms to the world; if synthetic, they do not state the sort of criteria required. We shall thus reach an impasse, which we next try to escape by defining theoretical terms first operationally and then ostensively. Neither escape will succeed; theoretical terms are explicable only in theoretical terms. What, then, becomes of the brute economic facts essential to a Positivist theory of economic knowledge? We argue that there are none. All facts are theory-laden and economic facts are 'visible' only to a man with the right economic concepts. Hence it is not surprising that the Positivist account of the testing of theories results in a confusion only compounded by treating concepts as stipulations for the use of terms. That, at any rate, will be our theme.

Theories connect terms to the world

When we explored the notion of theory before, we were looking for an epistemological role for it, to show what theory contributed to knowledge. Consequently we played down its methodological role until we proposed at the end that theory yields the interpretation of a set of observations. We shall now take the proposal further and begin here with a methodological suggestion, that theory yields the definitions of the 'true variables', whose actual values will be counted as decisive tests of hypotheses. For example, to test hypotheses about the influences of changes in the price of a good upon demand for it, we need data showing the uniform, general price (corrected for mismeasurements, particular personalities, seasonal factors and local irregularities in the prices of complements and substitutes). Similarly, to test hypotheses about the effects of change in investment spending on the level of national income, we need national income data adjusted for seasonal variation and corrected for inflation and other extraneous factors like changes in import prices and strikes. The suggestion is that we must rely on theory to arrive at uniform prices and adjusted income data. How exactly does theory help?

As a first, naive, sighting-shot, let us say that theories define variables simply and schematically in the abstract, so that we can recognise instances when we meet them in practice. They are like manuals on aircraft recognition or parables and, as with teenagers who have memorised their lectures on sex, experience becomes recognition of the schematic met in the flesh.

But how do we know an instance when we meet one? To estimate the 'price level of output', for example, do we use a retail or a wholesale index? How are we to treat variations in quality, seeing that comparative value for money depends on quality as well as on price? We need criteria for deciding these and scores of other well-known questions. The economic facts are to be described in terms which have been 'adjusted' to remove non-economic interferences and to ensure *ceteris paribus*. So we must be able to select the right facts to adjust and then to adjust them correctly. But which and how? As the example of the price level suggests, it is not straight-forward.[3] Measures of aggregate output or of growth rates of output are, despite their influence on economic policy, notoriously suspect and illustrate the same point.[4] It is the task of a sound methodology to give criteria of decision, which are clear in principle, even if sometimes tricky to apply in practice. Clear concepts, whose scope of application is precisely delimited, are essential. We need to know what is an instance of which theoretical term. There is a general philosophical problem here of the relation of meaning to reference, which we shall find neither Positivism nor Operationalism can solve.

Our naive sighting-shot relies on its being obvious what is an instance of which term. It is as if economic facts resembled pictures in economic

---

[3] 'To say that net output today is greater, but the price level lower, than ten years ago or one year ago, is a proposition of a similar character to the statement that Queen Victoria was a better queen but not a happier woman than Queen Elizabeth – a proposition not without meaning and not without interest, but unsuitable as material for the differential calculus. Our precision will be a mock precision if we try to use such partly vague and non-quantitative concepts as the basis of a quantitative analysis' – J. M. Keynes, *The General Theory of Employment, Interest and Money* (Macmillan, 1936), p. 40.

[4] T. P. Hill's preliminary studies for O.E.C.D. indicate that the normal margin of error in estimating growth rates exceeds the difference between the highest and lowest growth rates currently reported by O.E.C.D. member countries – T. P. Hill, *The Process of Economic Growth* (O.E.C.D., 1971).

models, just as aircraft resemble silhouettes in the manual. In economics, however, there are no pictures. The term 'capital', for example, does not function like a picture of say, a Boeing 707 and, besides, the same economic facts can be instances of two different terms, whereas each silhouette belongs to one aircraft only. It might seem possible to evade the difficulty by holding that official indices, like the retail price index, were to count as instances of theoretical terms, like 'the general price level'. But this would be a mistake. Even if we were satisfied that the criteria for compiling the index were criteria for applying the theoretical term, we would still want to know whether the index had been correctly compiled. Officials are fallible. Have they applied their criteria correctly? Is their index an adequate account of relative movements in retail prices? The question has merely been pushed back one stage.

The philosophical problem arises because two sorts of relation are involved in the use of a theoretical term. Firstly, the term must be related to others. To understand the concept of 'saving', for example, we need to understand others like 'consumption', 'investment', 'income' and 'price'. Secondly, if economics is to be proudly distinct from magic and demonology, we must be able to know when some empirical statements containing the term are true, which requires knowing which actual phenomena the term applies to. Thus the term 'general level of prices' can be explained partly by reference to the retail price index but the explanation is insufficient unless the term 'retail price index' can be applied to actual economic phenomena. Otherwise the explanation will be wholly formal, internal or semantic. Terms defined wholly by interrelating them cannot yet be used and criteria of application are needed for at least one of them. Theoretical terms must be attached to the world as well as to one another.

A statement interdefining theoretical terms will be analytic by the Positivist rubric; for instance 'The annual G.N.P. is the ensemble of goods and services produced by the nation during the year.' It is less clear how statements of criteria of application are to be classed. When we say for example 'A shift in the general price level is measured by comparison of relevant retail price indices', we are saying one of two things. We are saying either that to know how those retail price indices have moved is *eodem ipso* to understand some statements about the general price level or that the retail price indices just happen to be a useful guide to the general price level. The first interpretation produces an analytic statement and the second a synthetic one. There is a *prima facie* case for holding that criterial statements are analytic. The general form of such statements is that a statement containing the theoretical term is true, if another statement not containing the theoretical term is true. But not all statements of this form are criterial. For example, let us suppose, 'Baby Jane has a temperature' is true, if 'Baby Jane lets herself be put to bed without fuss' is true. This has nothing to do with the criteria of application for the term 'has a temperature', even if it is a useful guide to managing Baby Jane. The simplest way to distinguish criteria from rules of thumb is to insist that criterial statements are analytic. In other words, we would need a *theoretical* link between having a temperature and being docile.

But it now becomes hard to explain how criteria of application function. By the Positivist rubric, analytic statements have no factual content. So criterial statements, if analytic, presumably link terms with terms. Yet they were introduced because of a need to anchor terms to the world. Perhaps, therefore, the *prima facie* case is wrong. But there are also snags about taking criterial statements as synthetic. To apply a theoretical term in a synthetic statement, we must *already* know what it means. That is why 'Baby Jane has let herself be put to bed without fuss' does not explicate the meaning of 'has a temperature'. Moreover we reopen the question which a criterial statement is supposed to close, whether the criterion is a good one. If we can ask whether the retail price index is a good measure of movements in the general level of prices, we shall have to be able to test its merits. Before we could conduct the test, we should need criteria for applying both 'the general price level' and 'the retail price index'. We therefore face a dilemma. Criterial statements are either analytic or synthetic. If they are analytic, they do not connect theoretical terms to the world; if they are synthetic, they do not serve to state criteria of application.

Can we escape the dilemma by a pragmatic appeal to habits of decisions? Can we say that we simply decide upon criteria of application and that such decisions are useful or useless but not right or wrong? In itself, this suggestion is no escape, since we still have to say which decisions are useful and who is entitled to make them. If the process is a rational one and some people are better at it than others, then being useful is not an alternative to being right. If it is arbitrary, then the difficulties remain, since we have no way of knowing what we are doing. Moreover it is well to be wary when philosophers speak of what 'we' say or 'we decide' without specifying who 'we' are or how and by what right 'we' make such decisions. The first person plural and the notion of decision are too abstract, when used very generally, to have any reference and, as soon as any specification is made, the earlier questions about authority and correctness arise again. A pragmatic approach simply pushes them back a stage. But that may seem too easy an answer and we must next examine that blend of the pragmatic and positivistic, known as Operationalism. Can we advance matters by saying that theoretical terms acquire meaning by 'operational definition'?

Operational definitions

Operationalism is attractive at first sight. To know how officials compile the retail price index is now to know what that term means. Theoretical terms become constructs out of the terms used to describe measuring operations. 'True effective demand', for instance, is the name of a set of calculations with figures got by operations called 'measuring observed effective demand'. Provided we know what operations we are performing, we cannot fail to know what our theoretical terms mean and the difficulties of relating variable to instance seem to disappear.

Boldly stated, the thesis of Operationalism is that a theoretical term is fully defined by specifying operations which count as applying it. That statement, however, is too bold for four reasons. Firstly, since different operations now define different terms, it becomes forthwith impossible to test for the same property in different ways. So, for instance, we could no longer measure domestic national income (income paid out) by observing consumption, investment and government spending. Secondly, operations need to be correctly performed. But what is 'correctly' to mean here? It cannot mean that the results correctly measure the value of an operationally-defined variable, since that would presuppose our knowing what the variable is independently of the operations defining it. Nor can 'correctly' mean 'to the satisfaction of suitable officials', since officials too need justifiable rules of procedure. Besides, which officials are suitable? What happens when they disagree? Do they have to be consistent and, if so, in what sense? Are they to fulfil the Strong or the Weak Axioms of Revealed Preference? Are there no incompetent officials? We are against the deification of bureaucrats. Thirdly the distinction of 'observed' from 'true' values of a variable loses its sense, since the values are now merely different. There is no way of saying that one operation is 'truer' than another; the 'true' value of any variable is simply the result of the operations which define it. And, finally, since a new operation defines a new meaning, we can never find a new way of measuring an old variable.

Although disastrous in bold form, our Operationalist thesis cannot easily be modified. So far it has held that any variable V can be fully defined by a set of operations O, such that necessarily for every statement $V_1, \ldots V_n$ giving a value for V there is a statement $O_1, \ldots, O_n$ specifying the result of an operation. As long as this remains a thesis about the meaning of V, which is defined in terms of O, it remains impossible to doubt whether O is in general a reliable indicator of V, or whether O_j properly represents V_j. Indeed it is no longer possible even to wonder what we are testing for the presence of – 'intelligence', for instance, becomes simply a stipulated score on an 'intelligence test'. There is no room to ask whether the retail price index truly reflects the price level or the Treasury's basket of representative goods the retail price index. To modify the thesis would presumably be to make that doubt possible. But it is then no longer true that V is operationally *defined* in terms of O. Also the problem still arises of saying when O is an adequate test for V. We cannot say that O represents V when it gives a true value for V as that would be circular. To do it without circularity simply raises the original troubles again.

Even if Operationalism can steer off these reefs, it soon meets another. The whole notion of operational definition collapses without ado, unless the definiens can be stated without any of the theoretical terms in the definiendum. ('Instinct' cannot be operationally defined in terms of 'instinctual behaviour' or 'price' in terms of 'transacting behaviour'.) In other words the facts and operations specified in O must be describable without use of terms in V. We shall argue next that, insofar as this can be done at all, it leaves the positive economist without grounds for deciding which observed facts are to be adjusted or how the adjustments are to be made. We shall address the point to operationalists initially but we are also in pursuit of the deeper question, whether all facts are theory-laden.

Our case can be made with an example. Let us take the notion of 'price'. 'The price of good x' in economic theory usually means the uniform price throughout the market paid by any buyer to any seller for any item of x at any place or time in any medium of exchange in any transaction of any size, occurring as any member of any series of transactions. Admittedly the economist recognises special cases, like that of the discriminating monopolist; but even here the monopolist's price is uniform in all respects save one, relating to the buyer's ability to pay. And, even so, any buyer of given ability is charged the same price, according to the theory, regardless of time, place, quantity and all the other factors just mentioned. Besides, special cases are special. We may say, therefore, that price for any given state of supply and demand is always uniform price.

Uniform prices are not to be found in reality. They are not facts but fictions. The price of ships or string or sealing-wax for given market conditions is nowhere to be found in the market. Different grades command different prices. Bulk-orders, delivery dates, first lots or fag-end lots affect pricing. Special buyers or categories of buyer receive special terms. Price quoted may differ from price paid, because of means and timing of payment, bargaining abilities and liquidity positions of the parties and so forth. The variations in practice could be listed indefinitely. The functional relations of economic theory, however, demand uniform prices. Consider the Law of Demand in its simplest form, 'When the price of a good falls, quantity demanded rises'. 'The price' here cannot be the price of a particular *item* and the quantities demanded must be quantities of the same quality of the same good. The Law is not falsified, if buyers pay less, without demanding more, because they pay cash and the seller is short of liquidity for some extraneous reason. The Law asserts that a relation holds *ceteris paribus*.

Another example is the equilibrium condition, that output will be adjusted until marginal cost equals price. This must be taken to mean uniform, common, adjusted price, a fiction constructed out of the raw data of the market. For different items normally have different prices and whether a given level of output is in equilibrium would otherwise depend on which item or range of items or which transaction is chosen as the one to compare with marginal cost.[5] The choice would fix the price, while total quantity determined the marginal cost, expressed as the slope of the cost curve at the point corresponding to that level of output. For some choices of items, price might equal marginal cost whereas for others it would be above or below, thus making nonsense of the equilibrium condition. Again, it is uniform price which has to be in question.

Similar reasoning shows that 'true' values are needed for 'quantity', 'income', 'cost' and all other such variables. Thus the 'quantity demanded' corresponding to a given uniform price must be quantity of a standard, uniform good, supplied to anyone regardless of other transactions or of the time of year, or of the state of the trade-cycle and so forth. Unless we have a method for finding the true values of such idealised variables, we cannot test the output of an economic theory. It is not enough to know roughly what sort of facts and data are relevant. We also need criteria for adjusting observed values to true, since otherwise theoretical terms like 'price', 'cost' and 'output' will remain at best semi-interpreted. We argued earlier that Positive economists were hard put to it to decide even roughly what is relevant to the test of a prediction. We now point out that, without exact criteria of application, terms for variables are empirically senseless as well as useless.

The infinite regress of particular influences

The method needed is one to eliminate effects of particular situations. For instance, we know that functions containing the theoretical term 'price' are tested against transactions involving payment of one sort or another

---

[5] Where prices vary in response to some economically relevant and independently measurable factor, like transport costs, by which items can be ranked, the factor can be allowed for, but on the supply side. Such differential costs will appear in the 'marginal costs', defining the *extensive* margin. Output is then determined by two parallel conditions, one on the intensive margin and one on the extensive. Cf. Joan Robinson, *Exercises in Economic Analysis* (Macmillan, 1960).

for goods or services delivered within a definite time. But each particular transaction is influenced by its particular setting and so actual exchange ratios vary. To eliminate particularities, we need a measure of their influence. Thus having discounted all local influences, we then calculate the idealised, uniform price. To put the point formally, we have as data actual relationships of the form:

$$p(x_i) = f(m, a, b, t \ldots), i = 1, \ldots, n$$

where i ranges over items of x, m is the means of payment, a and b are particular buyers and sellers, t the stage of the time period and so forth. From the data we are to derive a function:

$$p(x_i) = h$$

where h is a constant for the given state of supply and demand in the market. This involves knowing $\delta p/\delta m$, $\delta p/\delta a$, $\delta p/\delta b$, $\delta p/\delta t$, ... for all relevant variables. The exercise raises several problems.

Even granted a list of relevant variables, we cannot proceed further without establishing hypotheses about their typical effect on price. For instance, we might propose that 'the more liquid the means of payment, the lower the price of the item' (i.e. $\delta p/\delta m < 0$). To test this, we must know what we mean by some term like 'the degree of liquidity of the means of payment'. But that term is itself a theoretical one, involving an ideal variable. In deciding that cash is more liquid than anything else, for example, we ignore the fact that postage stamps are more acceptable than notes of high denomination for some tiny transactions or that cash is not acceptable at all for massive transactions between large corporations or during extreme inflation. So we now have the same problem all over again and now need to establish further hypotheses about the influence of particular situations on liquidity. Besides, we are faced with the difficulties of testing and establishing these further hypotheses, which may serve to remind us that the problems of our previous chapters are still unresolved.

Nor is liquidity a special case. To eliminate the influence of the particular buyer, we might propose that 'price is higher to a small and powerless buyer'. This gives us a new variable, which we might call 'size'. How is size to be determined? By total sales, by total capital at book value, by total capital at market value of shares, by capitalising current net earnings at current rates of interest, by size of total net profits before (or after?) taxes, by share of the market, by rate of change of share of the market, by rate of growth? None of these measures is self-evidently the right one. Some register previous success, others indicate present resources or fighting strength. The one we choose will need adjusting to allow for some influences better measured by those we reject. That means establishing further hypotheses and, in general, whatever we choose involves a further ideal variable.

We seem faced with an infinite regress. We take a theoretical term or ideal variable. In stating its criteria of application, we relate it to another. The other turns out to involve yet another. At each stage, we need to establish hypotheses which eliminate particularities and these hypotheses again assert relations between ideal variables. Unless we can stop the regress, no theoretical terms will have any criteria of application, and all economic theory will stultify for want of a way to find true values for its variables.

It may be worth emphasising that two points are involved here. There is a general need to stop a regress which leaves the theorist unable to find true values for his variables; and there is a particular need for the positivist to do so with a theory-free stopper. In our own view (to be advanced later) there are no theory-free stoppers but, with a suitable epistemology, a theory-laden stopper will serve. But at this stage the problem is one for Positivism and we shall next consider, in quest for a theory-free stopper, the well-tried doctrine that there are some brute atomic facts. This accords well with Positivism and with Empiricism in general. Before applying the idea to economics, we shall give a brief epistemological account of it.

Atomic facts

Empiricists hold that all knowledge of the world comes from experience. If S is a statement about the world and I know S to be true, then either I know S without any evidence at all or I have empirical evidence e that S is true. If I know S to be true without evidence, then S is a statement of an observation I am now making. If S rests on e, then I need to know that e is true, before I can use it to show that I know S to be true. Either I know e directly or I have evidence e' for e in its turn. Either I know e' directly, or I have evidence e'' for it. The argument repeats itself until I settle for a final statement e^n, which I do know directly. The final statements, known without further evidence, are all statements of observed data. All knowledge thus rests in the end on observation; all statements of the final evidence for which no further evidence is needed can be expressed in a data-language referring to what is observed without interpretation.

Empirical knowledge is thus like a building with foundations. There have to be foundations, it has often been held, because an infinite regress of evidence for evidence for evidence is vicious. The man who believes in fairies can always produce further evidence; and his claims come to nothing, only because fairies are never an incontrovertible part of our perceptual field. Not all empiricists accept this argument, although positivists have usually done so, but they do all accept that observation is centrally important to empirical knowledge. If there are foundations, they must be perceptual. The foundations support the rest by being evidence for the truth of more complex and general statements. Theoretical terms can be fully interpreted and have application only insofar as empirical statements containing them can in principle be justified by statements of evidence, which can be supported in the end by true statements from the data language. All rests in the end on brute atomic facts.[6]

When this idea is applied to a particular science, the notion of atomic fact becomes relative. The data-language of economics does not contain seminal utterances like 'this is a red patch'. But, to be a science, economics needs a data-language of statements, which can be treated as certainly true for economic purposes. In other words, the economist needs data for which, as an economist, he need provide no evidence. These data are his foundations, to be used as evidence for everything more general or complex. They must be stateable in terms free of all economic interpretation, since, if they were interpreted statements, whose interpretation he had to justify, he would be landed with an infinite regress. Being the 'foundations' merely of an upper floor of the building, they are in ultimate need of justification from below. But that does not concern the economist. For example, he need not remove his economist's hat and justify a statement of the form 'a paid $£x$ to b for y at t'. So long as the statement could be known true and known without appeal to economic theorising, he can take it as given.

This epistemology fits naturally with the methodological individualism characteristic of neo-Classical economics. Complex statements rest on simpler observational reports; complex concepts are constructs out of observables by means of theory. Thus concepts like 'capital', being constructed by abstraction from individual market responses, can be expected to be open-ended and ambiguous. This is no weakness, however. There is no such thing as *the* meaning of the term 'capital' nor can there be any such absolute error as that alleged by Joan Robinson when she complains that the neo-Classical concept of capital conflates 'machinery' with its value. The only valid question is whether the conflation is useful in deducing testable hypotheses. There is no other sense, provided the logical steps are formally valid, in which the construction of a theoretical concept can be right or wrong.

For a statement to belong in the economist's data-language, then, it must be capable of being known true without appeal to economic theory. By this criterion, terms like 'liquidity' or 'size of the firm' are not applied to brute economic facts. Ideal variables take true values and these, as we have

---

[6] This doctrine owes much to Logical Atomism but is nevertheless a Logical Positivist one. E.g. Ayer, *Language, Truth and Logic*; R. Carnap, *Der Logische Aufbau der Welt. The Logical Structure of the World and Pseudoproblems in Philosophy*, tr. by R. A. George (University of California Press, 1967).

argued, differ from observed values of what are therefore different variables. The atomic facts are the unadjusted, uninterpreted, observed correlates of statements in which ideal variables do not occur. So how are ideal variables introduced? It will have to be done by abstraction from patterns and regularities observed among atomic facts. We notice, for example, that variations in the price paid for similar items are systematic. Then, by familiar techniques, we calculate a notional price under specified conditions and treat all the actual prices as explicable departures from the notional price. The notional price, got by mathematical abstraction from systematic observed regularities, is then the true value of the ideal variable. We can thus give empirical significance to theoretical terms involving ideal variables.

The strategy is Bacon's second way, rising by gradual and unbroken ascent from the senses and particulars and arriving at the most general axioms last of all. It is also an application of the hypothetico-deductive method, working from tentative hypotheses to true values of idealised variables by a series of tests without ever using terms devoid of empirical significance. It is the task of theory so to define the variables that their true values can in principle be assessed and the task of practice to find the true values. The analytic statements of the theory define the conditions of truth and application; the synthetic statements assembled in practice decide whether the conditions are satisfied. Theory and practice go on honeymoon, showered with philosophical blessings.

The marriage is, alas, unstable. Our earlier line was intended to show that theoretical terms containing ideal variables cannot be fully interpreted and applied, because the statement of the criteria of their application contains further ideal variables and so *ad infinitum*. On the positivist's behalf we then suggested stopping the regress with a data-language and atomic facts. But, we shall argue next, the process of abstraction cannot be justified. We shall do so by reflecting on another central tenet of positivism, that facts are independent of theories.

The regress cannot be stopped, if facts are independent of theories

This doctrine is to the effect that facts are what they are with or without their labels. No actual cube exists or has six faces *because* we define a cube as we do. Conversely, we are always free to change the meanings of our terms without thereby affecting the facts. We shall not go into the epistemology of the doctrine here,[7] but it is plausibly put as a consequence of

---

[7] More is said about analytic truths in Chapter 6 and the nature of definitions is examined in Chapter 7.

the analytic-synthetic distinction. Theoretical statements are analytic; factual statements synthetic. The truth of each is therefore independent of the truth of the other. The actual state of the facts cannot affect the meaning (although it may determine the truth) of any statement whatever.

This view is, we contend, incoherent, in that atomic economic facts will do the work assigned to them, only if they determine the interpretation (as well as of the truth) of some economic statements. The regress, generated by trying to give criteria of application to theoretical terms containing ideal variables, stops with a statement of the form '$V \equiv O$', where no term occurring in O is theory-laden. All economic terms are therefore to be divisible into those which do and those which do not apply directly to atomic facts. 'The price of string' is of the latter kind but perhaps 'the price paid by George to Henry for five yards of grade B string last Tuesday' might be of the former. The statement of the form '$V \equiv O$' is itself to be analytic, for reasons already given. The true value of 'V' is an empirical matter, since it is an empirical matter what George and others have actually paid for string. That still leaves an earlier difficulty unresolved, since it is still impossible to doubt whether O is a good or reliable indicator of V and still impossible to propose an alternative to O without *eodem ipso* proposing an alternative to V. But we have, since stating that snag, acquired another. Between the atomic facts and the true values we have inserted established hypotheses linking the facts. An example was 'the more liquid the means of payment, the lower the price of the item'. The terms in these hypotheses must belong either to type V or to type O or indissolubly to both. If they belong to type V, they are no use in stopping the regress and it is more promising to assign them to type O (even though we have yet to find an example which does not link ideal variables). So the intermediate hypotheses are generalisations related to economic facts as 'All ravens are black' is related to 'Raven no. 1 is black and raven no. 2 is black and raven no. 3 is black ... and so on'. The question is then whether they can be coherently so regarded and whether they can give economic theory the basis in empirical justification which we require.

A crucial difficulty is seen, when we notice that key economic concepts like 'capacity', 'liquidity' or 'resources' can be applied, only if we can estimate what would happen if ... A firm's capacity, for instance, is what the firm would produce, if it ran at full stretch. Statements of atomic facts are statements of what has happened or is happening. To know what would happen, if ..., we need already to have established hypotheses from which we can derive these conditional statements. Terms like 'capacity' therefore cannot occur in these latter hypotheses, without generating a regress. By parity of reasoning, terms like 'cost', which at first look more basic, turn out also to involve conditionals, since their application involves estimates of opportunities forgone. The more we attempt to lay bare the atomic level of particular facts, the more obstructive such general 'counter-factual' relationships become. For instance, mention of 'the price paid by George to Henry for five yards of grade B string last Tuesday' sounded quite specific. Yet a definite numerical value could only be given for the price insofar as there is some specific means of payment of known purchasing power. This purchasing power depends on law-like relationships and can be delineated only with the help of counter-factual conditionals. We shall next try to show that this feature of economic concepts is general and endemic.

Let us first dispose of the objection that it is enough to say, 'George paid sixpence for the string and that's that.' After all, no one has asked after the *value* of the string, any more than they have asked, 'What is string?' or 'Who is George?' and enquiry must stop somewhere, in the name of sanity. We do not dispute the need for a stopping point and we propose to supply one in Chapters 6 and 7. But we deny that positivists can have one. Their criterion for stopping is always that the level of observation has been reached, where there is no need to interpret observation by appeal to theory. Yet a sale for money differs from a barter of mutually useful items, such as string for flint, as is noted in the first chapter of any text book on money. Money is money precisely because it is generalised purchasing power. It is 'generally acceptable in exchange' – a phrase which implies the existence of underlying general laws. So the case cannot be presented as one merely involving unvarnished observation.

Some terms, then, like 'capacity' evidently involve the idea of what would happen, if ...; and so it cannot be a brute atomic fact that an object has a capacity. But why is this true in general of essential economic concepts like 'production', 'consumption' or 'exchange'? The reason, we contend, is that the terms range over the activities of economic agents – producers, consumers and traders. These activities are interconnected both in the practical sense that their performance depends upon expectations about and reaction to other related activities and in the conceptual sense that description of them presupposes a certain allocation of social roles. A producer intends to sell; a buyer intends to consume; a labourer has the ability to work; there is no money where there is no command over resources and no cost where no opportunity is forgone. Conceptually and practically the idea of systematic relationships is always involved, the idea of law-like conditionals. Basic economic terms apply to agents who would not be agents unless they had dispositions and, furthermore, dispositions which can be described only by reference to the surrounding system. Even if 'Raven no. 1 is black' can claim to be theory-free, 'George paid £1 for string' cannot. In short, the more precisely we specify economic observation statements, the more clearly they will depend on lawlike relationships. Any observation statement containing a term designating a value-relationship, price, capacity, cost, income, capital holding and so forth must be regarded as depending on theoretical laws. Since economic intentions are formulated and acts done by reference to value concepts, there cannot be the sort of level of brute atomic economic facts which Positivism requires.

To summarise, the intermediate hypotheses connect theoretical variables. Nor is this surprising, when we reflect that they are to establish the true values of variables and recall that true values are determined only after the data of observation have been adjusted. The arguments given earlier to show that correct adjustment presupposes theory still stand. A brute economic fact would nevertheless be an interpreted fact and intermediate hypotheses are needed in order to arrive at the very facts from which they were supposed to be derived. Operational definitions of economic terms do not serve to introduce terms of type 'O' nor do they allow the economist to isolate brute atomic economic facts.

Ostensive definitions

Before drawing the moral that even ultimate economic facts are theory-laden, we must dispose of the suggestion that ostensive definitions might resolve the difficulty. Perhaps we can give criteria of application for low-level variables simply by acts of pointing. 'That is a transaction', we say, pointing into the bazaar; 'this is cash'; 'that is a consumption good'. That suggestion, however, simply leads straight back to the start of the maze. The function of an ostensive definition is to pick out for future reference. When the tutor says, 'This is cash', his pupil is to pick out only those features of the scene which are relevant. To cut the story short, he is to recognise cash in future not by its appearance but by its powers. He must grasp some of the counter-factual conditionals which his tutor has in mind. Cows are cash in some places but there is no similarity between a cow and a bank note which can be ostensively defined. The similarity has to do with the applicability of laws of monetary circulation.

Economists need to know that their colleagues all use some simple terms in the same way. Knowing that two economists are picking out the same feature when they point takes more than looking disingenuously to see what they are pointing at. When economists disagree, it must be possible to decide whether their dispute is about language or about empirical fact. Pointing is noncommittal until interpreted with the help of theory, especially so when there are rival theories at work. But there is no need to labour the point, since applied economists are well aware that economic data must be lavishly spread with interpretation and treated gently. Data cannot be captured with stabs of the index finger.

We conclude, then, that all economic descriptions are 'theory-laden', and that atomic economic facts, if there are any, are 'visible' only to a man with suitable economic concepts. We can put this by saying either that what some statements mean determines what some of the facts are or that facts determine what some statements mean. There are no economic terms which function merely as self-adhesive labels.

Analytic—synthetic again

To reinforce our findings, let us now revert to philosophy and generate some puzzles by recalling the analytic-synthetic distinction. We have considered several positivist theses, three of which can be stated thus:

S1 'To know the empirical sense of a theoretical term one must have criteria for its application.'

S2 'Basic economic terms can be ostensively defined.'

S3 'Facts are independent of theories.'

Since every significant statement is, for a positivist, analytic or synthetic and none is both, we can ask for a classification of S1, S2 and S3. Perhaps we may be excused from arguing that they are synthetic. We know of no positivist who has tried to produce empirical evidence for statements of this sort. Nor can we see how to do so, unless by arguing that this is a matter of fact now people use terms like 'theoretical term', 'basic economic term' and 'fact', which would prompt us to ask simply 'So what?'. S1, S2 and S3 will have to be analytic. That means, according to the brief account we gave earlier that they record our determination to use words in a certain way and are devoid of all factual content. All theorising consists in the end of making decisions about how to use terms. And, since the statement made by the last sentence will be analytic, we have just recorded someone's determination to use the term 'theorising' in that way. So, if we add to S1, S2, S3 two more statements, one (S4) of what 'theorising' is to mean and the other (S5) of the analytic-synthetic distinction itself, we have five statements which between them make all economic theory fatuous. For there is nothing in Positivism to tell us what makes one use of terms more rational than another and, if there was, it could in turn be cast as an analytic statement no less optional than any other. So if anyone objects that the puzzles of this chapter have arisen from taking the notion of 'theoretical terms' and 'ideal variables' more seriously than is consistent with Positivism, we reply that positivists themselves have to take statements of their own position more seriously than the position allows.

This line of attack admittedly depends on applying a thesis to itself. Weighty authorities have maintained that such moves are illicit, since they result in the famous self-referential paradoxes of mathematical logic.[8] We do not agree,[9] but do not have the space here to try to argue the matter to a finish. So we shall end with a brief general diagnosis of the cause of our present troubles.

Diagnosis and summary

The doctrine that facts and theories are independent makes it hard to know how to treat theoretical terms containing ideal variables. They must have criteria of application, which requires that they be introduced by abstraction from observed behaviour with the help of theory-free hypotheses. At the same time, statements of the criteria of application of a theoretical term are analytic. Operationalism is an attempt to run these ideas in harness. It breaks down, because, firstly, it can no longer be asked whether the tests for the value of a variable are good tests and, secondly, the hypotheses cannot be purged of theoretical terms. Our diagnosis is that we have been trying to bridge the unbridgeable. The analytic-synthetic distinction requires that we simply decide what is to count as an instance of what term. The idea that ideal variables have true values requires that the indicators of an index be good indicators. There is no room within Positivism for both theses.

Faced with a choice of which thesis to reject, we suggest dropping the first. We do not, we believe, simply decide what is to count as an instance of what term. If we did, we would have no rational criteria for selecting facts to adjust or proposing adjustments to make. We must choose the right facts and make the right adjustments. But we are in no position to say so, until we have deployed a new account in later chapters for the methodology of economic science.

Having failed to escape from the charmed circle of theoretical terms, we are now worse off than Evans-Pritchard's Azande. They at least had a king's oracle to guarantee their theory-laden facts. The king's oracle of positive economics, however, is an organ issuing only stipulations, after the manner of all positivist *a priori* authorities. Econometricians are now found to be relying on a poison oracle, which collapses without the back-

---

[8] See B. Russell, Mathematical logic as based on the theory of types, *American Journal of Mathematics*, vol. 30, 1908, reprinted in *Logic and Knowledge*, ed. R. C. March (George Allen and Unwin, 1956).

[9] See E. J. Nell, No proposition can describe itself, *Analysis*, vol. 26, no. 4 (March 1966).

ing of the king's oracle. But, before we look for a new and true king's oracle, we owe the reader a reckoning.

We began in Chapter 1 by reflecting that, if the test of a theory is the success of its predictions, then neo-Classical economics must issue testable predictions. Testing, however, is no casual affair. The theory at stake must include criteria of application for its terms, *ceteris paribus* clauses and rules for interpreting the data of observation. These latter two requirements import a circularity into the process of testing, since failure of prediction becomes a sufficient condition of their not being satisfied. Theorising results in statements not of what will happen but of what would happen, if certain conditions were fulfilled; and whether the conditions are fulfilled depends on the success of the predictions. In other words predictions are no more than the logical implications of assumptions predicated on *ceteris paribus* clauses. Given the analytic-synthetic distinction, hypotheses turn out to be covert tautologies and the Positivist notion of scientific explanation collapses.

This embarrassment was compounded in Chapter 2 by the addition of rationality assumptions. Neo-Classical economics is the study of Rational Economic Man, who is not an actual man but, rather, any actual man who conforms to the model. So, instead of providing the missing occasions when tests are decisive, he reinforces the previous circularity. Nor can assumptions about rationality be dispensed with. Behavioural assumptions and revealed preference theory do not yield a sufficient account of maximising behaviour and a more ambitious notion of rational economic agency is needed. Positivism cannot supply it.

The riddle of Induction arose again in Chapter 3, when we asked about the role of theory in economics. If theoretical statements are analytic, they have no validating role. If they are synthetic, then it has to be possible to decide which correlations are causal and which generalisations are projectible, without appeal to prior or *a priori* theorising. Yet this turned out impossible, especially since theory is involved in the very identification and specification of data. Moreover the effect of construing laws, in Positivist spirit, as correlations between variables, is to conjure the objects and agents which bear the variables out of existence. Theoretical statements are then neither justifiable nor applicable.

Finally in the present chapter we have found related difficulties in the status of the criterial statements mentioned in Chapter 1 and have rejected the claim that all can rest on theory-free, brute, atomic facts. The bulk of our case against Positivism is now complete, although some further objections will be raised in the course of constructing our own view.

The case is so far strictly against Positivism (even though we shall generalise parts of it later in order to reject Pragmatism). Theorising in economics imports a circularity which positivists must regard as vicious. This is not to say, however, that neo–Classical economists can, if they are convinced by the case, simply drop Positivism and otherwise proceed as usual. We shall continue to argue that neo–Classical theory falls without Positivist support; that a fresh epistemology will demand a different economic theory. When we have finally made out our own view of the role of theory in economics, we shall look again at neo–Classical economics and still find it wanting.

Meanwhile, we have acquired debts in these opening chapters, whenever we found discussion of methodological issues blocked by difficulties peculiar to Positivism. In particular, we promised to revert to the topic of behaviourism. This debt we pay in the next chapter.

5

BEHAVIOUR AND PREDICTION

Rational Economic Man took the stage in Chapter 2, where we presented him as the embodiment of maximising models. He failed to steal the show, however, partly because he fell foul of the analytic-synthetic distinction and partly because behaviourism turned all models trivially into maximising models. We concluded that, if we could dispense with behaviourism, we could rescue much orthodox economic theory. In this chapter we shall press home our objections to behaviourism but the prospective rescue of orthodox theory will prove illusory. Even after shedding behaviourism, neo-Classicists still turn out to have a wrong notion of what an economic action is.

We shall begin by assessing the attraction of behaviourism for a Positivist science of prediction, based on regularities in nature. The existence of fallible human agents acting according to their idiosyncratic beliefs and intentions seems a threat to such a science and behaviourism removes the threat. Nevertheless we repeat that maximising models are distinguishable from others, only if economic behaviour is construed as a species of action proceeding from inner reflection. So the question will then become whether this notion of action can be squared with revealed preference theory, which is the Positive economist's version of demand theory. We shall contend first that optimising models are not straightforwardly predictive, although revealed preference theory would require them to be, and secondly that there is, in any case, no way of knowing what preferences are revealed by observable behaviour. Economic actions, we shall find, are to be explained in terms of inner preferences, thus casting doubt on the neo-Classical concept of preference. Can we then restate neo-Classical economics as a theory of economic action? No, we argue, neo-Classical actions are timeless fictions, so abstract that they ignore many crucially relevant features of actual economic processes. This shows the need for a richer notion of action, to clarify the part played by law-like relationships in economic activity. Finally, postponing our own account of economic agents and institutions to Chapters 8 and 9, we shall end by discussing the role of prediction in linear programming models and in economics generally.

Behavioural and programming models contrasted

Neo-Classical models of their essence concern economic *behaviour*. They require that consumers and producers be identifiable agents. Consumers, being households, and producers, being firms, are, strictly speaking, organisations rather than persons. But institutional distinctions are ignored. The theory of the firm, for instance, is indifferent between single or multiple partnerships, limited liability joint stock companies, trusts and holding companies. These are simply forms of producing or marketing agency, whose particular impact on the market is no part of the theory.[1] There are assumed to be agents who decide and execute regardless of institutional form. Were this not so, the theory would have to allow for legal variations, unwritten customs and other sociological factors (as American Institutionalist critics have often urged it should). The result would be different theories for different forms.

The theory is to predict the decisions and actions of ideal agents in ideal (and ideally abstract) conditions, where minimal organisational details are given. Its variables range over specific acts by specifiable agents. In adjusting observed values to true values, the theory reflects the original choice of fictional agents over actual institutions.

Is there any other approach? Well, consider the difference between an equilibrium price in the conventional simple theory of the firm, interpreted as a Positive economist must, and a 'shadow price' derived from a linear programme. The former need, no doubt, never actually be paid; but, if the model is to be testable, the conditions under which it would be paid need to be empirically specifiable. The latter, by contrast, reflects relationships between resources and depends on no behavioural assumptions. A shadow price expresses the contribution of certain resources at the margin to the optimum programme, given the technical constraints and the objective function. It is derived from the data by a standard mathematical procedure. So linear-programme variables need not take as values specific acts by specifiable agents. (When they do not, the model cannot be used to predict behaviour, although it may be used to recommend.) It is no objection to linear programming, although it would be to neo-Classical theory, that

---

[1] In neo-Classical thinking, 'supply' covers both producing and marketing activities. These are often separated in modern models of the firm, as critics and protagonists alike have often urged that they should be, but are not separated in most general equilibrium models. It is tantamount to assuming Say's Law to use the same symbol for both 'volume of output produced' and 'volume of sales recorded'. Unfortunately this happens in even the most reputable circles; cf., for instance, Allen, *Mathematical Economics*, pp. 320–3 or Henderson and Quandt, *Microeconomic Theory*, Ch. 7.

firms are not wont to choose the linear programming optimum before they consciously adopt the linear programming techniques of calculating it.

A possible retort here is neo-Classical theories can be treated as programming models, when so desired. For instance, the conventional theory of the firm can be taken to say, 'if you wish to maximise profits, act so as to equate marginal cost with marginal revenue'. This would make neo-Classical theory instrumental in Lowe's sense and it could then be converted to a descriptive theory by showing that those who maximise profits tend to supplant those who do not. To this retort we reply, first, that, since the truth of the theory needs to be assumed *a priori* in order to show that profit-maximisers fare best in practice, the interpretation concedes the force of our argument about the relation of theory to hypothesis in the previous chapter; and, secondly, that not even profit-conscious firms set themselves to equate marginal cost with marginal revenue, since the statement of the equation is not an instruction in this context but a logical consequence of describing a competitive market in which a firm has satisfied the conditions for maximising profits.

In general, then we seem to be invited to compare neo-Classical models, which are behavioural, with programming models, which are not. Accordingly it seems plausible to say that the former presuppose behaviourism, whereas the latter do not. There is something in this view, we shall contend, but it needs to be put with caution. Neo-Classicism has behaviourist tendencies but does not entail behaviourism. To see how strong the tendencies are, we must first define behaviourism.

The great Amphibium

Each man claims to know of at least one consumer (namely himself), who thinks before he consumes. If he has been educated in the main Western cultural tradition, he tends to picture himself as an *Anschluss* of two elements, mind and body. His body belongs to the world of matter, physical energy and such organic life as is explicable by natural science alone. His mind is the seat of his personality and faculties, the place of emotion, reflection and decision. As Sir Thomas Browne puts it, 'Thus is Man that great and true Amphibium, whose nature is disposed to live, not only like other creatures in divers elements, but in divided and distinguished worlds.'

The voluntary behaviour of a 'great Amphibium' is the effect of non-physical causes. It is caused by mental acts of will which follow mental deliberation. If 'understand' is taken to mean 'identify the cause of', then the Amphibium's behaviour can be understood only after reckoning with his mental states. Unless those mental states themselves have physical causes, there is no reason to suppose that the same physical stimulus will always produce the same physical response. For, at any rate in the complex world of economic stimuli, response depends on what the Amphibium decides upon reflection.

This has sometimes been thought to entail a radical distinction between social and natural sciences. If a 'natural law' is a law connecting states of nature, and if the Amphibium's headquarters are not part of nature at all, there will be few natural laws of social behaviour. Equally predictions of one natural state from another will be endemically liable to upset by the idiosyncracies of the great Amphibia who cause the later states. The evidence on which the prediction is based will differ in kind from the cause of the behaviour predicted. Hence prediction and explanation will certainly not be two sides of the same coin, and prediction will always be at the mercy of factors which play no part in natural science. That will raise an awkward version of the Inductive problem – when can generalisations which do not mention the cause of the phenomena be projected?

What is an enquirer, who is determined that natural and social sciences do not differ in kind, to do about the great Amphibium? The least committal answer is to make his models probabilistic. But, as we argued in Chapter 3, probability is a derivative notion, depending on a solution to the Inductive problem. In the present context, using a probabilistic model would merely be issuing the same predictions with one's fingers crossed. Some more definite strategy is needed to align prediction with explanation.

Less non-committal would be to make assumptions about the rationality of the Amphibium which would allow the model to apply, provided the Amphibium was sensible. This device is standard in utility theory and also in the liberal Utilitarianism with which it has historical and intellectual connections. By crediting the Amphibium with a few very general and simple wants, it is apparently possible to predict with the aid of maximising models, without having automatically to retract, when predictions fail.[2] The behaviour of 'Rational Economic Man' is an ideal variable and predictions of his behaviour are to be tested only when the assumptions about wants hold. But, as we objected in Chapter 2, any model can be seen as a maximising model, unless the agent's intentions and reflections are taken into account. Besides, if the assumptions are bland and the motivation general then the 'predictions' are empty, since 'rational' comes to mean 'conforming to the model'. The model will be the yardstick by which we judge real behaviour. If the assumptions are specific and institutionally definite, then more than natural phenomena are being included in the model.

---

[2] Cf. Robbins' use of this stratagem, discussed in the appendix to Chapter 7.

It may be worth emphasising that the last paragraph, with its tendentious use of the term 'natural phenomena' is addressed to behaviourism and not to Positivism in general. For instance, Weber's notion of *Verstehen* can be treated either as a simple plea for the importance of mental states in the explanation of behaviour or as a claim that actions viewed from inside are explicable only with a new model of what counts as an explanation. Both versions conflict with behaviourism; but only the latter conflicts with Positivism. At this stage we leave open the question of whether mental events form repeatable patterns of association, as Positivism requires, or whether the workings of reason and imagination explain action without being lawlike.

A bolder thesis is that it simply does not matter what the Amphibium thinks. The laws of behaviour hold, either rigidly or statistically, whatever anyone believes or tries to do. This line is recognisably behaviourist. It says in effect that mental states can be effects of physical states but can never be causes. Prediction and explanation are thus realigned, since it is now denied that economic behaviour is explained by the mental deliberations of economic agents. If so, we have a good case for working with revealed preference. But what amounts to determinism will also need to be postulated. We shall say more about revealed preference presently.

Finally the original picture of the great Amphibium may be rejected. The clearest riposte is materialism or the doctrine that there are no mental events at all. (We are not here speaking of dialectical or historical materialism but of the older doctrine summed up by Hobbes in the slogan 'whatever is real is material'.) All is included in a single world of nature, where everything belongs to whatever categories are admitted by physics and chemistry. Materialism is stronger than Behaviourism but implies it. If all is material, then the observable behaviour of men is, together with the $1.00 worth of chemicals which are their bodies, all they consist of. Behaviourism, as usually conceived however, is less crude. It is not committed to saying, for instance, that psychology is ultimately a branch of bio-physics. It claims, more modestly, that actions are movements of the body and that predicates of persons, like emotions, desires and abilities, can always be fully expressed, for the purposes of explanation, as dispositions of bodies to respond in certain ways to suitable stimuli. This provides a stronger rationale for revealed preference theory, although it is a step further removed from the liberal assumptions of utility theory.

By 'behaviourism', then, we mean the thesis that all behaviour has a 'natural' explanation and by a 'natural explanation' we mean an explanation in which everything mentioned is publicly observable. A behaviourist need not maintain that there is no 'ghost-in-the-machine' but he cannot regard anything ghostly as explanatory. The nearer he draws to materialism, the clearer his position becomes. But there are many subtle intermediate positions and it would be rash to suppose that behaviourists were men with a single, simple manifesto.[3]

Varieties of behaviourism

If that is 'behaviourism', then what is 'behaviour'? Some include activity in the brain; some restrict a man's behaviour to his grosser actions. Some speak of linguistic behaviour as including statements as well as sentences, while others insist that the semantic properties of speech are unobservable. Some place behaviour and actions in different categories: others take action as a species of behaviour. For the economist, however, 'behaviour' is basically market behaviour, directly or indirectly affecting market variables. Market variables are taken to be objectively measurable and so observable and economic behaviour is whatever causes changes in their values.

Economists have been most tempted by the version of behaviourism which denies that economic actions need psychological explanations. If 'utility' is to be defined as an inner flow of subjective satisfaction (recalling Irving Fisher's account), psychologists or social psychologists seem the right people to study it. That suggests a three-fold division of expertise; engineers estimate the production function, psychologists map the utility functions and economists process these data to find the shape of supply and demand curves and to predict equilibrium prices and outputs. Admittedly some economists have favoured such a troika. But it is feasible, only if the psychologists can dispense with all economic variables in explaining the formation of satisfactions and preferences and if their results lend themselves to the economist's methods of extrapolation. These conditions are not normally met. The formation of preferences often seems to be a function of economic variables like price, income and output; family size and patterns of family consumption depend on wage levels and on work-patterns, and the latter depend in turn on what is produced and how. The relevance of the method of production points to an important argument which we shall meet again. Utility functions describe preferences, which are formed by family consumption patterns, which depend in part on work

---

[3] For instance Jonathan Bennett, discussing rational behaviour, writes, 'When I speak of behaviour as manifesting rationality, or as showing that the behaver is capable of reasoning processes, I am not — *pace* Descartes—saying that the behaviour in question is an outward manifestation of a secret something called 'thought' or 'reasoning' ... I do not deny that there are private mental states and philosophical problems about them'— *Rationality* (Routledge and Kegan Paul, 1964), p. 10. Bennett rejects dualism and contends that 'rational' is a predicate of behaviour and not of its ghostly causes; but he is wholly opposed to a Hobbesian view that men are solely matter in motion.

habits, which are largely dictated by the organisation of production and so ultimately by the technology in use. Hence utility functions will shift with movements *along* the production function, that is with changes in the ratio of labour to machinery and equipment. But this ratio is supposed to be determined on the basis of given preferences. If neo-Classical models are to be adapted to allow for such interaction, it will mean dropping or modifying the doctrine of Consumer Sovereignty and most central propositions of welfare economics. The formation of preferences is not a topic upon which conventional economists can afford to dwell.

Moreover the psychologist's picture of preference seems quite unrelated to the economist's. For example, the choices summarised in a utility or preference function all represent potential equilibrium situations. With suitable production and income data, any point might represent a price-quantity-preference choice which would be repeated indefinitely while *ceteris* remained *paribus*. This permits both prediction before the action and explanation after it; but only if all the satisfactions expected or foreseen are identical with those realised.[4] Otherwise the *ex ante* utility function will not predict equilibrium in the required sense of 'equilibrium'. Neither psychologists nor economists accept that this condition is normally met, or even capable of being normally met. People learn about the goods they consume and about themselves. They learn what they can do and what they want. Experience and experiment count. No one starts life with a complete ready-drawn utility function. Experience not only reveals our preferences to us but also changes them, as we grow older, wiser or merely bored.

Psychologists are therefore not related to the utility function as engineers are (or are held to be) to the production function.[5] Hence there is advantage in confining the utility function to economics, constructing it from purely economic data. The actual choices made, the actual actions observed to occur are the data, regardless of intentions or inner satisfactions. 'Revealed preference theory', in short, is an economist's version of behaviourism which frees him from dependence on psychology, social psychology or sociology.

We do not wish to put this point too strongly. Neo-Classical theories do not formally entail behaviourism and the flirtations, which are common in

---

[4] As Marshall saw clearly. Cf. *Principles*, 9th edition, p. 78.

[5] To be perfectly honest, neither are the engineers in fact related as they are supposed to be. There have been many good empirical studies of production, but few, if any, have found it possible to construct a smooth neo-Classical production function directly from engineering data. Our general aspersions on neo-Classical doctrines about production will be cast later. Cf. Walters, *Introduction to Econometrics*; R. B. Sutcliffe, *Industry and Underdevelopment* (Addison-Wesley, 1971), Ch. 5.

the theory of the firm and especially in the analysis of consumer behaviour, have never amounted to a promise of marriage. Attraction is there but there is also a counter-attraction. As we argued earlier in Chapter 2, maximising models can be distinguished from others, only if 'economic behaviour' is construed in terms of 'action proceeding from inner reflection'. So, if we want to argue that a generalisation about economic behaviour is projectible, only if it can be derived from a maximising model, we shall need to reject at least the stronger versions of behaviourism.

Behaviourism, maximising and rule-following

Paradoxically there are Positive economists among the strongest champions of the view that generalisations are projectible only when grounded in maximising behaviour. For example, Friedman's concept of 'permanent income' has gained support from a (sometimes unstated) discomfort with the Keynesian consumption function, since the latter is not founded in utility theory nor, indeed, upon any economic maximising model. The neo-Classical economist faces a dilemma. If he adopts behaviourism, he can avoid the charge that utility theory does not square with what social psychologists and others say about people's wants and desires but he must also give up the most plausible and theoretically satisfying underpinning for neo-Classical generalisations. If he opts for maximising, he gains his underpinning but is open to the social psychologist again. However, independently of the apparent findings of social psychology, a case can be made for dispensing with optimising models in descriptive economics. For example, the simplest Keynesian model determines equilibrium output at the point where savings equals investment (Figure 16). Only at that point will the total output be exactly sold. No assumption of maximising is involved. Stability analysis takes the model a step further. If $Y < Y_e$, spending tends to exceed output, since $I > S$; if $Y > Y_e$, then $S > I$ and spending falls short of output. Producers tend to raise output in the first case and to lower it in the second. They are assumed to respond to incentives, but that does not imply maximising, since satisficers also respond to incentives. Indeed it is enough if production departments adjust their rate of output to maintain some target level of inventories. Incentives then become irrelevant, as production and sales departments simply follow rules.

There is much evidence to support such a picture of rule-following, even though it conflicts directly with the central vision of neo-Classicism. This is not surprising, in that the dilemma above sprang from the desire of neo-Classicists to explain household demand in terms of maximising behaviour, thus overworking and distorting the concept of preference and so coming into conflict with social psychology. 'Rule-following' is a more plausible

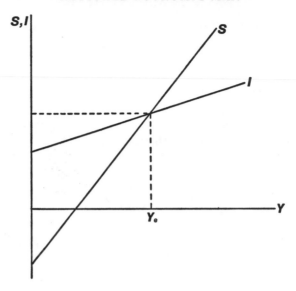

Figure 16

analytical concept and its use avoids clashing with social psychology. But it is no more compatible with behaviourism than was the optimising paradigm, since it makes a pattern of behaviour projectible only if it represents deliberate following of rules. Any number of functions can be generated from a given set of points, and the one chosen must be the best approximation to the actual rule (or mixture of rules and informal conventions) followed.[6] So, even if behaviourism is rejected, we cannot assume that optimising models are therefore what we want.

Yet many neo-Classical economists would still like to derive macro consumption and investment functions from micro models of optimising behaviour. They argue that, even though firms and households do adopt rules of thumb, the economic question remains, since one must still ask how those rules are determined. 'Optimising' here has to be defined in terms of 'rational intentions'. Economic laws will have to represent something like 'rational choice under conditions of scarcity'. The notion that actions are a function of intentions seems to concede something to the great Amphibium and we shall ask next whether the concession can be squared with revealed preference theory.

---

[6] Suppose the six observations show changes in inventory and in rate of output, where the origin is normal output and standard inventory. The regression line (see Figure 17) is surely a better fit than either of the two curves drawn, yet the curves predict all the points and the regression line only once. Any number of curves can be drawn through the given points and we must have a reason for choosing one.

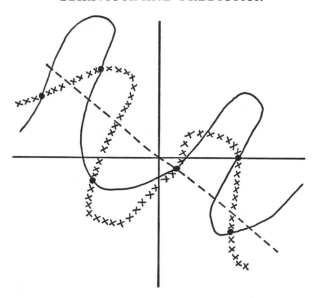

Figure 17

Optimising models are not straight-forwardly predictive. They contain the *best* solution to a problem and do not guarantee that actual agents do in fact produce the best solution. Similarly, when a doctor predicts another ten years for his patient, in spite of heart trouble, he does not guarantee that the patient will not suddenly rush up a long flight of stairs and drop dead. Optimising models offer advice and are predictive only insofar as the advice is followed. The economist who knows what is best for General Motors does not know *eodem ipso* what General Motors will do.

The same applies to models which analyse rule-following. They show the effect of following given rules from given initial conditions. We cannot predict that the resulting path of development will be followed, however, until we know that everyone is 'dutiful'. The development path is what would happen, if all acted as they should. So, if we are to use either sort of model for predicting, we must know how far actual agents deviate from being ideally rational or consistent. That seems to imply that we must know about the intentions, motives and beliefs of the agents and so must eschew all forms of behaviourism. Yet, as we have seen, economists have good reasons for excluding psychology and for sticking to market behaviour. Positivists, indeed, we shall find later cannot admit a full-blooded concept of intentional action even if they wanted to.

At this point the argument threatens to drive a wedge between natural and social sciences. Molecules are never to blame for being less clear-sighted than the physicist. Molecules can never fail to obey the rules governing their behaviour. So it seems that both optimising and rule-based models are peculiar to the world of intentional action and are inappropriate to the non-rational world of matter. This is tricky ground, however, and we shall not rush into it here. In general, we judge that if economic actions are to be represented correctly, indeed 'realistically', account must be taken of reasons, intentions, motives and desires. This point, which is a conceptual one about the form of the representation rather than a practical one about the details, will be developed later. But we do not see that, in itself, it need create a root difference in kinds of explanation between natural and social sciences. There is as yet nothing to suggest more than a difference in subject matter.

A Positive economist, however, must be more committal. He must adhere to the doctrines that sciences differ only in subject matter and that predictive success is the only criterion for judging the truth of a theory. (The grounds were given in our introduction.) So, in dropping behaviourism, he faces an apparent threat to his notion of objectivity. The threat has been parried by some economists with the Large Numbers Argument, that a model predicts for the aggregate and not for the particular case. Perhaps the idea here is that, since an aggregate has no collective mind, questions of its rationality do not arise. But it would be rash to stake a reputation on the Large Numbers Argument, since macro models fare no better in practice than micro. For instance the Klein-Goldberger model did not predict even the *direction* of crucial changes in the British balance of payments in the 1960s. Very few forecasting models have scored well on actual events and most have failed splendidly. If these failures are the fault of the model, that is, if prediction is the criterion for the validity of a model, then economic science is in sad disarray.[7]

Difficulties in Behaviourism

But, if we reject Behaviourism and demote prediction from criterion to desired objective, we can sometimes blame divergence between model and actual events on the agents responsible for the events. There need be no fault in the model, if the agents have not done their 'duty'. This creates an

---

[7] See Sidney Schoeffler, *The Failures of Economics: A Diagnostic Study* (Harvard University Press, 1955) for a fairly complete catalogue of failures up to 1954. Schoeffler blames the failures on artificial attempts to close an essentially 'open system' (one with infinitely many variables and kinds of variable and including a dash of randomness). Although methodologically sophisticated, he remains unrepentently positivist in outlook and we ourselves disagree both with his diagnosis and with his recipe for improved economic thinking. Since 1955 the failure rate has improved little.

apparent demand for a criteria for judging the performance of economic agents (criteria which, we shall argue later, the model itself can supply) but it also gives a needed flexibility in assessing the merits of models. However, we must now meet the social psychologists on their home ground and, in general, having decided that we can sometimes save the model by blaming the facts, we must give conditions for those other occasions when the model is at fault. (That this task is so difficult is one reason why the textbooks hang on grimly to Positivism.) So let us start with a particular case.

Suppose we have a theory from which we derive the specific statement, 'George will order 25 bushels of pears at 5p per lb.'; and suppose that George does not, even though conditions seem appropriate. We must either reject the theory or deny that *ceteris* are *paribus*. The question is (and this is one way of putting the issue of Behaviourism) what, if anything, is included in the *ceteris paribus* clauses about George's mental state. We contend that, if George fails to order the pears because he forgot, missed a bus, quarrelled with the supplier, misaddressed an envelope, misjudged the future price of pears, developed a phobia for fruit, did his sums wrong or was sacked, then 'other things' were not 'equal'. Since that is unlikely to be disputed, the question becomes whether behaviourism can allow for human fallibility.

Forgetting is not simply not remembering. Making a mistake is not simply not doing. Failing to do x is not simply doing not-x. The Pope perhaps bought no pears last week but it does not follow that he forgot or failed to buy any. General Motors does not fail to respond to changes in the demand for cocoa and the British Treasury does not forget to restrict the travel allowance of Eskimos. 'Failure' is a concept presupposing and getting its sense from a variety of others like 'trying', 'intending', 'hoping', 'having a duty', 'being empowered', 'deciding'. When a man fails to reach a goal, the goal has to be *his* goal and his not reaching it has to be *his* fault.

At first sight, there is no behavioural difference between not doing and failing to do. For, as far as what actually happens is concerned, there is simply no difference at all. Failure is a matter of the explanation for events which did not happen and not of the events themselves. So Behaviourism seems ruled out on two counts, first that failures and mistakes are not observably distinct from simple non-occurrences and secondly, that, even if they were, they would need 'mentalistic' explanations. If either difficulty cannot be met, no economist can afford Behaviourism.

To bring out the first difficulty, suppose we predict, 'George will forget to order 25 bushels of pears'. Here his not ordering the pears is not a sufficient condition of truth (indeed it may not even be necessary, if he can order them by mistake). What is sufficient? Roughly, George must have intended earlier to order them but then not have done so at later times when he could have, without there being any sufficient reason for not doing so. In other words forgetting in this context is explained by reference to what he would have done, had he remembered. Forgetting is thus a case where the nature of the behaviour observed depended on the true explanation of it. We identify a failure, as opposed to a simple non-occurrence, by its explanation. We know by observation perhaps that George ordered no pears, but we do not know that George's behaviour counts as 'forgetting to order the pears', until we know what he *would* have done.

The behaviourist presumably proceeds by stating behavioural observations which, together with general laws, would enable him to verify or falsify statements like 'George remembered to order pears'. The problem is to determine which cases of not ordering pears are cases of forgetting (or failing in other ways) and which are cases of not wanting to order them after all. Whether the distinction can be made is a question in the philosophy of mind and in psychology too subtle to tackle here. So we shall content ourselves with arguing that revealed preference theory cannot take account either of human failure or of human development and that genuinely maximising models are not available to a behaviourist.

What preferences are revealed?

Utility theory is meant to deal with recurrent decisions and regular buying habits. Non-recurrent decisions are difficult for any consumption theory and, we shall argue, especially for revealed preference theory. Many major purchases cannot be repeated. Cars and furniture, for instance, are bought only every few years and their design changes constantly. A household's economy also changes over a few years. With shopper and goods both evolving, we cannot easily base predictions on experience. Nor can we predict by generalising, since changes in technique and fashion do not happen at a constant rate. Unique and initial choices are tricky to accommodate but practically important. But this is more of a limit on the scope of behaviourist models than a radical objection to them and we must now dig deeper.

Revealed preference models can be tested only on the assumption that choices actually made are equilibrium choices, i.e. ones which, *ceteris paribus*, will be repeated in similar price-quantity-income circumstances. Actual behaviour must, in other words, be deliberate and not the product of error or forgetfulness. Otherwise the agent's preference-map will be wrongly drawn and so a poor guide later, when he does indeed do what he intended. (The agent, who acts inadvertently on Monday but deliberately on Tuesday, is not necessarily blessed with inconsistent preferences nor have his preferences necessarily changed.) To test revealed preference theory, we need some way of knowing when actual behaviour does reveal preference and is not merely misleading.

Shall we therefore take an agent's typical choices over a period rather than those he makes on one particular occasion? A map drawn in this way will include a measure of error and forgetfulness, which seems a positive merit, if we want to predict what he will actually do, rather than what he would really like to do, when fully alert. The proposal is plausible and, as Little and Graaff have argued[8], seems the best way to interpret revealed preference theory. But, we argue next, it is disastrous.

An agent, who sometimes forgets or makes mistakes, also tries to improve his performance. He learns from experience. The first time he faces a given market situation, he may not know what he wants. Or, if he does, he may not know his best strategy. Or he may approach in an experimental mood, in order to decide on his priorities. Later, with experience, his habits will stabilise. So, if 'typical choice' is to be his mean choice, it will be too heavily weighted towards his earlier attempts to express the true value. Diagrammatically, a likely result is as shown in Figure 18, where he buys 1 unit at the first trial, 2 at the second and so on until he buys 5 units at the fifth and does so contentedly three times running. Here his mean purchase is $3\frac{4}{7}$ units, his median purchase 4 units and his modal, and true, purchase 5 units. Which is 'typical'? The example is constructed to make the modal purchase the right one. But other examples could be contrived to make the mean or median nearer the truth.

Suppose we allow for ageing. In time a household passes through different stages of life, which must be taken into account, if preference maps are to be useful for long-run analysis or for deriving consumption functions based on a life-time's expected income. Now successive trials reflect two distinct factors, the effects of experience in arriving at a true value and a shift in those true values, as the household undergoes rites of passage. Since the point of the exercise was to discover true values by observation, these shifts are disastrous. At the least, we shall need to know the direction of shift in advance; in order to make sense of our observations, and, even so, we shall be unable to decide what best measures 'typical' behaviour. (For instance, if the true value will shift down, then the mean or median may be the best measure in our diagram.)

Three replies suggest themselves. One is that the assumption of 'perfect information' serves to remove any snags arising from the agent's indecisions. But, we retort, revealed preference maps can hardly be thought of as recording the 'actual choices' of consumers ideally blessed with 'perfect informa-

[8] I. M. D. Little, *A Critique of Welfare Economics*, 2nd ed. (Clarendon Press, 1957); J. de V. Graaff, *Theoretical Welfare Economics* (Cambridge University Press, 1963).

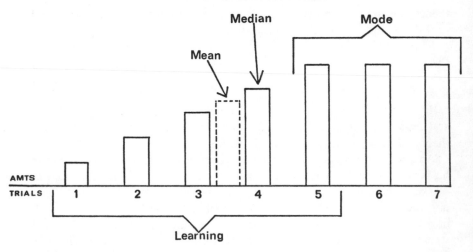

Figure 18

tion'. Besides even a consumer with perfect market information may still not know his own wants or may still be ready to experiment; and a household is even less likely to plan its whole history in its early stages.

A second reply is that the economist may know the direction of shift in advance from some other source. But, we retort, a behaviourist has no other sources of information. It is not open to him to ask the household what they plan to do about events like the arrival of children, since the object of taking a behaviourist stance is to get away from notions like plans and intentions. Nor can he ask psychologists, sociologists or other professionals to tell him how economic agents arrive at true values, without assuming that they can solve an economic problem, which he cannot solve himself. And, even if they did give him answers, he would still have to decide whether they applied to economic and market circumstances.

Thirdly, there remains a renewed appeal to the Law of Large Numbers. If the theory applies to consumers not as individuals but in the mass, then with luck individual idiosyncracies which lead to deviations between actual and true values will cancel out. But, we retort, this reply is a simple *ignoratio elenchi*. Granted that the theory is intended to apply to Large Numbers (in that its object is to construct a *market* demand curve), we still need to know the distribution of deviations. There is no reason to think it random. On the contrary, factors just mentioned like learning, from experience, ageing or changes in family structure are likely to affect a population systematically; so much so, indeed, that they are already topics for research. Here is one case where individual differences do not cancel out and we thus reject all three replies.

What would an econometrician do? He would probably work with two sets of roughly similar data. On one he would ignore any adjustments for error, forgetfulness and learning and look for a shift in the values of the variables over time. Then he would apply his findings to the other set of data, in order to discover which measure of the central tendency best expressed the true value and how large the effect of error, forgetfulness and learning was. In doing so, he would be assuming that changes in consumption patterns produce a larger shift than do the effects of error, forgetfulness and learning.

Such assumptions are not testable within econometrics, since, as we saw earlier, the interpretation given to the econometrician's findings depends on them. Nor, by the previous argument, are they empirical truths borrowed from other social scientists. So they have to be *a priori* deliverances of economic theory. They are not, in our view, therefore objectionable. On the contrary, we shall repeatedly insist that econometrics needs a stock of *a priori* truths, whose justification belongs to economic theory. Our point is simply that the behaviourist as we presented him, rashly undertook to test such 'hypotheses' against observed fact. We thus find him in the by now familiar difficulty that yardsticks cannot be tested against themselves.

We contend, therefore, that the 'true values' we seek in demand theory are the actual preferences of agents or households and that the behaviourist does not succeed in capturing them with his revealed data. He must rely on theory; hence, by the argument of the previous chapter, he cannot test his theory against the facts. That completes our case against Behaviourism and for holding that economists should be at least as interested in inner preferences as in their external manifestations. If the case is granted, the conventional economist will do well to reject Behaviourism, in order to be able to use the notion of maximising, when trying to arrive at sound predictions. For he will then apparently be free to claim that there are 'general laws' about maximising behaviour. Once again, however, there are difficulties and we turn next to the role of action in maximising models.

Programming models and characteristics of goods

If we treat action as the deliberate doing of what was intended, our difficulties seem to vanish. A purchase becomes genuine only when deliberate. The agent's own avowals become a, and indeed the only, reliable account of what he is doing. Mistakes and failures can be allowed for in the light of the agent's own answers. (This is not to say that agents cannot be mistaken or deliberately misleading – there are well-known ways of checking up on this.) Moreover, we can now say whether his decisions are arrived at by maximising or through following certain rules and whether any emerging pattern is projectible, because demonstrably the best for his situation, or his avowed duty.

Neo-Classical calculations of this sort admittedly wear an air of fantasy. Indifference maps always look more pretentious than practical. When, for instance, a black Aid to Dependent Children mother in Harlem asks an officer in a brigade fighting the War on Poverty how she is to get the most for her money, is he to counsel her to equate price-ratios, pair-wise, to her marginal rates of substitution? There would be no fantasy in her reply![9] Yet the trouble is not that the neo-Classical concepts are technical and abstract but that they do not fit. For equally technical and abstract answers have been given in these circumstances with success.[10]

The point must be put with care, as maximising models all have similarities, arising from their common concern with maximising. Our claim is that some specifically neo-Classical features of such models are objectionable and they rely on a general defence by Positivism. As we remove their Positivist supports, we must see what becomes of them. Let us consider linear programming, a maximising model not in the neo-Classical style.

Suppose we wished to help a poverty warrior find the cheapest adequate budget for a poor family. Take a very simple case, adapted from a well-known text.[11] Suppose there are only two nutrients, calories and vitamins, but five available foodstuffs, containing various combinations of the nutrients. The foods have prices and the problem is to find the cheapest diet meeting an adequate standard of nutrition.

The problem seems straightforward but the conventional economist should find it unsettling. For it is a *demand* problem with all the earmarks of a *production* problem. Commodities are to be chosen not for the 'utility' or satisfaction they yield but for their contribution to the further end, nutrition. Foods are desired for their nutritional content (and we could readily expand the problem to include other characteristics like taste, digestibility or religious significance). So the revealed preferences of agents need not be accepted but may be criticised, for instance for paying more than necessary to reach the desired minimum standard, or for setting a standard beyond available resources. Moreover some standards, like nutritional ones, must rest on scientific knowledge rather than on preferences, in which case one will contribute to welfare by meeting them, only if the standard is scientifically correct. Hence, in general, revealed preference is no guide to economic welfare. Both market choices and standards can be rationally criticised. With this in mind, let us continue with the example.

[9] Cf. Sol Yurick, *The Bag* (Trident Press, 1968), pp. 21–37.
[10] E. Durbin, Oscar Ornati, NYC Rand.
[11] R. Dorfman, P. A. Samuelson and R. M. Solow, *Linear Programming and Economic Theory* (McGraw-Hill, 1958), Ch. 2, p. 13.

The minimum standard of calorie intake is 700 units, of vitamin intake, 400 units. Prices and the nutritional content of the foodstuffs are given in the following table.

Foodstuff	1	2	3	4	5	Standard
Calories	1	0	1	1	2	700
Vitamins	0	1	0	1	1	400
Prices	2	20	3	11	12	

The graphical method provides a systematic answer for a limited number of cases. When there are two constraints they are taken as two axes, and the objective function is measured along the third, and contour-mapped onto the constraint plane. When there are two variables they are measured along two axes, and the objective function along the third. Taking the example above, we construct a table showing the amounts of C and V obtained per $1000 spent on each food.

	1	2	3	4	5	Standard
C	500	0	333.33	91.91	166.67	700
V	0	50	0	91.91	83.33	400

Foods 2 and 3 clearly will not figure in an optimum; 3 is inferior to 1 in C and equal in V, and 2 is inferior to 4 and 5 in both. From this information a diagram is drawn (Figure 19). Each point is marked by a number, indicating which food it represents. Lines are then drawn connecting 1 and 5, and 5 and 4, representing combinations of these foods on which a given amount of money is spent. Lines further out represent larger sums, i.e. are the contour-lines of the objective function mapped onto this plane. The points where the contour lines change slope are joined by rays from the origin. The corner point of the feasible region (the shaded area) falls between these rays, hence the optimal solution will consist of a combination of foods 4 and 5. The solution can be read from the graph, or determined by setting the coefficients of goods 4 and 5, multiplied by their amounts, equal to the nutritional requirements.
Thus:

$$1x_4 + 2x_5 = 700$$
$$1x_4 + 1x_5 = 400$$

So $x_4 = 100$, $x_5 = 300$. Putting in prices, we see that the whole budget comes to $4,700. A little arithmetic will persuade the sceptic that no other combination meets the nutritional conditions so cheaply. But it was not obvious at a glance where the best solution lay.

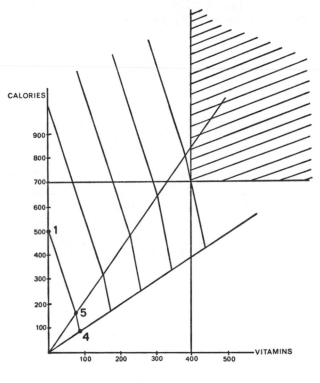

Figure 19

This is certainly technical and abstract, but it clearly makes sense, dollars and cents. A reply couched in the language of 'shadow prices' and 'matrix inversions' will not be understood but the essentials of the problem can be put simply enough, and, anyway, the resulting budgets can be compared directly. The linear programming optimal budget is demonstrably the best, provided that all the constraints have been listed. The agent, who wants the cheapest diet, subject to stated constraints, who is clear about the constraints and right about what nutrients he needs, will, barring mistakes, buy in confirmity with the linear-programming solution. His pattern of purchases will be projectible.

This projectibility can give no comfort to the Positive economist (nor to any neo-Classicist, as we shall see), since the projectibility of the purchasing pattern rests not on revealed but on *calculated* preference. The pattern of purchases is *demonstrably* best. Moreover, nutrition is not a matter of preference; what is good for a man is notoriously not always what he likes. So (to foreshadow a later point) it is important to know whether market transactions reflect judgements of what is best (for instance for growth or survival) or merely reflect preferences and likings. Only the former are projectible, we shall maintain later; although, where judgement and desire conflict and desire wins, we may be able to predict disaster with all the certitude of a Victorian pulpit.

That may be obvious but it is not trivial, as the serious medical problem of obesity in America witnesses.[12] Since obesity shortens life, lowers productivity and costs work time through illness (thus lowering the return on investment of education and training in 'human capital') it is an economic problem too. So a positive economist might be tempted to decry the linear-programming solution, on the ground that it is a poor predicter of what agents actually do. But that would mistake the force of the solution. If the agent does not confirm to the solution but still sticks to what he said about the constraints, then he is irrational. The model is a test of his rationality and his actual behaviour is not a test of the predictive power of the model. This again illustrates one of our main themes, that an important task of economics is to demonstrate how to succeed.

This brings us to a point we can only touch on now. One can succeed in accomplishing a task and one can also succeed by winning a competition. So far we have followed the neo-Classical tradition in assimilating 'winning' to 'accomplishing a task'. Nevertheless, the winning of competitions is important in economics and has its own features, notably when it comes to prediction. Where the economic process is competitive, in the sense that we need to pick the winners, then neo-Classical predictions of what will happen *ceteris paribus* become suspect. And competition-for-victory is indeed endemic, not least in the world of monopolies. Conventional thinking tends to stress competition within sides of the market (between seller and seller, for instance) rather than across the market (between seller and buyer). Yet the latter kind exists in all market structures and matters to prediction, whenever each party can gain only at the expense of the other.

Linear programming, on the other hand, is formally analogous to game theory. Picking the best budget is like picking the best strategy mix and our interpretation recalls the game of chess discussed in the appendix to Chapter 3. There we held that the role of a theory was not so much to predict a series of winning moves (which might never occur) as to contribute to victory by giving lessons in tactics and strategy. Even where there is no victory to be had, theory can serve to distinguish better from worse strategy. Linear programming thus embodies a notion of 'competition'

---

[12] See the Surgeon General's report, Obesity and fad diets, *The Congressional Record* (12 April 1973) and cf. the Senate Committee report on hunger (U.S. Congress, Senate, Committee of Labor and Public Welfare, Subcommittee on Employment, Manpower and Poverty, *Hungr and Malnutrition in the United States*, Hearings, 90th Congr., 2nd Sess., U.S. Government Printing Office, 1968).

which accords both with the accomplishing of tasks and with the gaining of victories.

A technical point deserves mention. In our programming example a change in the price of good z leads to a dropping of 4 and 5 and a new budget consisting of 1, 2 and 3. A change in the price of a good (even a small change) can cause the elimination or addition not only of it but also of other goods. A small price change, in other words, can cause large and discontinuous changes in consumption patterns involving several goods. It can, for that matter, have no effect at all. Text book demand curves, by contrast, are drawn on the assumption that small changes in price will lead to correspondingly small and continuous changes in demand. This orthodoxy conflicts with realistic consumer choice.

Furthermore, we (implicitly) assumed that households would seek to cost-minimise in their consumption of necessities, which implies the maximising of their 'surplus income'. This is sensible enough, since such households will have more to spend on hobbies, holidays or improvement of status, and so requires no unnatural abstraction from reality. But it draws attention to the source of a household's requirements, which are dictated by its social life, including the jobs held by its members. So, contrary to the neo-Classical scheme of things, demand depends, at least in large part, on the social relations developed in production.

These and earlier points are devastating for orthodox demand theory. In sum, behaviourism cannot rescue Positive economics, because we cannot tell behaviourally what preferences are being revealed. To gauge preferences, we must reckon with inner reflection, which also lends itself to the projection of hypotheses based on maximising calculations. But this involves a clash with positivist methodology. If that methodology falls, there is no longer any way to deflect the challenge that neo-Classical assumptions are unrealistic and neo-Classical questions misdirected. Accordingly we have taken a small step towards realism in this section. Instead of wishing abstract 'preferences' for goods on households, we asked how they would in actual practice best set about getting the cheapest diet consistent with adequate nutrition. Similarly we could envisage households buying the cheapest combination of clothes consistent with expected standards of dress on the job, the cheapest method of transport to get to work on time and so on. Such simple enquiries seem at first merely somewhat more practical than those made by a neo-Classical approach but are soon seen to cause chaos in orthodox demand theory.

Performances and productions

Abandoning Behaviourism in order to take into account inward features of action therefore gives scope to linear programming without comforting the neo-Classical economist. The reason will become clearer, if we reflect further on the notion of action. We shall argue next that when everyday actions are translated into neo-Classical models, they lose certain dimensions of time, with fatal results for predictions.

Neo-Classical verbs, if we may be permitted this stroke of grammatical daring, lack a continuous-present tense. To 'buy' is to become the proper owner at some legal instant of time. To 'sell' is to cease to own at some legal instant. Neo-Classical transactions are completed in a flash. Such verbs can be used in the continuous present but, we claim, then lose their neo-Classical sense. 'He buys' is neo-Classical; 'he is buying' refers to a protracted ritual of enquiry, debate, dalliance, decision and fumbling for change. What the agent 'buys' at a legal instant, he 'is buying' long before and even after. The process of buying is begun in order to be duly finished; the fact of having bought, which is all that appears in the neo-Classical model, has no beginning. The former is an activity, the latter a statistic.

Let us call typically neo-Classical actions 'performances' and protracted activities 'productions'. Unlike performances, productions have a beginning and an ending, take time and can succeed or fail, can arrive at other outcomes or be reorganised in the middle.[13] Productions of goods and services or the construction and installation of durable capital equipment are prime examples (as we shall point out again in Chapter 7, when we discuss this full-bodied sense of 'Production' further). As we have already seen, the prediction of performances suffers from the snag that, where it is done with a maximising model, the 'prediction' functions as a test of the rationality of the agent and not as a test of the soundness of the model. We have argued already that this is a snag only for Positive economics. Let us now consider the prediction of productions.[14]

The story of a production is the story of three different decisions, each taken in the light of different data. The first is the decision to begin the process or to go ahead with the investment project. It depends on expected future prices, current technology and present assessments of competitors' responses and often hinges on experienced guesswork and a feeling that the project should be tried. Expected returns must be at least equal to the general average rate of return – the rate of interest – on the entire capital invested. The second decision is whether, having begun, to continue. In

---

[13] For an examination of different kinds of verb and a philosophical account of the differences in the kinds of action they describe cf. A. Kenny, *Action, Emotion and Will* (Routledge and Kegan Paul, 1963).

[14] This should also help to elucidate the points at the end of Chapter 4, where we held in effect that economic facts could not be treated as isolated atoms in a constructed molecule. The basic decisions which determine whether an economic production takes place are elements in a complex network of logical interdependences.

addition to the initial data, corrected by emerging experience,[15] it depends on whatever competitors are by now in fact doing about the project. Moreover, there is now a new criterion for whether the project is worthwhile. Sunk costs are by now sunk and only fresh expenses are to be reckoned against the needed rate of return. The project continues, even if its total earnings are likely to be below the general average rate of return, provided that additional expenditure will earn at least the general average rate. The third decision taken when the project is installed and ready, is whether to launch into production. There is again more information by now. Also the criterion of an acceptable rate of return has again changed. What now matters is whether current expenses can just be covered. No return at all need be earned on capital to make production just worthwhile.

To predict whether installation will start, will continue and will be completed, the economist needs three sets of data and must issue three separate predictions. He can also attempt a fourth prediction, whether the project will in fact work successfully. The firm may take its three decisions after sound calculation but then fail in production. Competitors may prove too subtle or ruthless. Engineering specifications may not be met, machines may break down, plant lay-out may prove inconvenient, power sources may fail, water and sewage systems may refuse to take the strain. Such obstacles may prove so expensive, that the project breaks the neo-Classical economist's predictive rules of profitability, even though it is carried through to the bitter end for sound economic reasons.

Neo-Classical theory does not so much dispute this picture of production activity as ignore it. Postulates of perfect information, perfect foresight and perfect skill remove most of the questions, at least as regards prediction, from consideration. Such postulates, we contend, are neither wise nor legitimate. If, in Friedman's words, economics 'is to provide a system of generalisations that can be used to make correct predictions about the consequences of any change in circumstances' then failing to take account of influential facts will result in incorrect predictions. Nor is it 'as if' the postulates were true. Information, foresight and skill have costs and improvements in any of them can be made only at extra cost, which in turn influences decisions. Perfect information, foresight and skill are present, only when no further improvement in profit or production is possible, only when the marginal product of information is zero. This would conflict with economic rationality. Expenditure on information and skill stops, when marginal product equals marginal cost, which is positive. Hence there cannot be perfect information and skill. Hence there must be room for

---

[15] K. J. Arrow, The economic implications of learning by doing, *Review of Economic Studies*, vol. 29, no. 3 (June 1962); N. Kaldor, Capital accumulation and economic growth.

mistakes, failures and learning. Hence it is not only practically wise but also theoretically required that this appear in the model.

(It may be objected that the costs of acquiring and processing extra information and of providing extra skills are included in overheads and that their marginal cost is accordingly zero. If this is supposed to be an account of what actually happens, we find it implausible. If it is a theoretical point, then the problem is merely shifted from the short to the long run. But, as we discuss the matter more deeply in Chapters 8 and 9, we shall not take it further here.)

To summarise the point, we are here concerned with a conceptual question about the theoretical shape of economic actions. Neo-Classical models represent actions as instantaneous, logically simple and complete – what we have called 'performances'. But actual economic actions, which we have called 'productions', are protracted, complex and require completion. They take time, instruments and materials and they can succeed or fail, be abandoned or continued. Descriptions of 'performances' telescope all the stages of 'productions'. So, in as much as a model is to be judged by whether it predicts well, which stage of the 'production' should be taken as the test of a prediction of a 'performance'? The question is unanswerable, since 'productions' do not feature in neo-Classical economics.

Our general moral is that neo-Classical models do not yield the sort of predictions required by Positive science. The reason is not that prediction is impossible but that it is decisive only in conditions not allowed for by neo-Classicists. The official positivist position is that, if a theory implies that in given conditions x will happen, and if the conditions hold but x does not happen, then the theory is to be rejected. This scheme ranged over 'timeless' performances, whereas, we contend, productions take time and skill. Consequently, if the conditions held but, because of further information and learning during the process, x does not happen, then the theory is not to be rejected. The point is not met by bland talk of expanding the *ceteris paribus* clauses. The results of learning, setbacks and unforeseen interruptions are very much part of the process and, as every consultant economist knows, need to be allowed for when predicting. But there is no room for them in a world of performances.

This is not to say that neo-Classical predictions are bound always to fail. The later decisions in a production (those to continue and complete installation and to go into operation) involve successively lower 'cut-off' rates of return. So a kind of inertia is involved – sunk costs can be disregarded and only the opportunity costs of extra expenditure considered. At these stages small setbacks will not upset neo-Classical predictions. Nevertheless there is still a threat from larger incidents not mentioned in the neo-Classical account and, in general, there is still no case for giving prediction pride of place in economics. We have argued here that the economist is as much concerned with providing recipes for achieving whatever is wanted and shall argue in Chapters 8 and 9 that he must also explain how the material side of society works. Diagnoses and remedies matter no less than forecasts.

Summary

We can best draw the threads of the chapter together by a closing look at the relation of prediction to explanation. In speaking of 'action' in terms of 'inner reflection' and 'actual preference', we have not intended to pre-empt any issues in the philosophy of mind. In particular we have neither asserted nor denied that the explanation of behaviour in terms of mental states is law-like in the Positivist sense. But we have claimed that, to predict actual behaviour in actual cases, the forecaster needs to know more than falls within economics. This is no snag for a linear programming model, which gives advice but does not predict whether the advice will be followed. Positive economists, however, would judge neo-Classical models by their predictive success and, as we have urged repeatedly, their 'predictions' are rendered vacuous by their subjunctive conditionals.

Similarly, a programming model does not explain why economic agents act as they do, except insofar as they consciously follow the advice. Positive economists, by contrast, purport to base neo-Classical models on empirical generalisations, which explain what they predict. But there is a distinction to be drawn between the economist's model rules and the rules which agents actually follow. Prediction and explanation being, for a positivist, allegedly two sides of the only coin, whatever renders 'predictions' vacuous renders 'explanations' vacuous also. Since neo-Classical models range over 'performances' and ignore 'productions', this point has to be met by padding out the *ceteris paribus* clauses. But padding the *ceteris paribus* clauses simply reinforces the vacuity.

Once again we do not wish to claim too much. We neither assert nor deny that the distinction between model rules and agent's rules is one of principle between natural and social sciences. But the positivist must deny it and we can at least say what has to be true, if he is to be right. There will have to be, in principle, a unified super-science without *ceteris paribus* clauses. Economic irrationality, in other words, will have to be non-economic rationality, in that minimal sense of 'rational' which brings out that only an orderly subject matter is amenable to science. So, for instance, the border between economics and psychology has to be authoritatively drawn in the super science; otherwise economist and psychologist simply preserve their pet theories against refutation by blaming apparent exceptions on factors in the other's domain. This is viciously circular, unless the two domains are marked out absolutely from above. Since there will be a similar boundary to be marked out between natural and social sciences, the project is an ambitious one. In the ultimate model there will no more be a distinction between economist's model rules and agent's rules than there is between physicist's rules and molecules' rules.

Meanwhile optimising models also are so far threatened with the circularity which afflicts neo-Classical models. When the best advice fails to result in the best solution, is it to follow logically that the conditions were mistaken or the advice not strictly adhered to? If so, it again seems that the model is untestable and we are no further forward. Our reply here is only that, by dethroning prediction, we have created a needed scope for optimising models. Our final reply, however, will be to reject Empiricism in favour of rationalism and neo-Classicism in favour of Classical or Marxian theories. We set to work next with an account of the problem of *a priori* knowledge.

6

'A PRIORI' KNOWLEDGE

Truths of mathematics have been compared to the gelid peaks of distant mountains, which cause the climber a shiver of excitement. On the other hand they are often regarded as moves in a game, whose rules we invent and discard at will. Rationalists have more sympathy for the former view; empiricists for the latter. As we have already seen, empiricists cannot accept that a generalisation is projectible, only if deduced from a sound theory whose range of application is known. For this would imply that theory has its own truth, in the sense that the laws of, for instance, logic, number theory or the differential calculus are as much part of our knowledge of how things are as is the law of gravity. Empiricists are bound to reject any such view of theory on the ground that statements which are true *a priori* cannot also be synthetic. Rationalists disagree, arguing that there can be *a priori* knowledge of matters of fact and that this alone provides a coherent role for theory. In this chapter we shall look for chinks in the armour of Empiricism and, in the next, shall deploy a brand of Rationalism which we judge better accoutred. Of the various empiricisms, we shall discuss only Logical Positivism and Conceptual Pragmatism in any detail and so offer our apologies in advance to any others unjustly neglected.

The separation of the 'a priori' and matters of fact in Empiricism

If empiricists have a slogan, it is that 'all knowledge comes from experience'. This seems at first evidently true. Babies are born knowing nothing – or at least nothing which they can state as a proposition – and so evidently learn about everything from their own names to Keynesian economics in the course of experience. But this is not what the slogan means. The point is not that we learn what we know by experience but that all claims to knowledge of the world can be justified only by appeal to experience. The slogan belongs not to genetic psychology but to epistemology. In positivist idiom, if a statement is about the world, then it is synthetic and can be justified only by observation and induction. (Rationalists, for their part, can agree that, without experience, babies would learn nothing and adults know nothing, without accepting any Empiricist epistemology.)

No one has ever disputed the old scholastic tag that 'the senses reveal no necessities'. Observation shows how the world is, and (with the help of induction) how it was, will be and always is in given conditions. But that X is so never implies that X must be so and claims that a statement is necessarily (as opposed to contingently) true cannot be justified by observation or induction. So the more tempted an empiricist is to say that all genuine knowledge is empirical, the more embarrassing he finds the truths of logic, mathematics and other *a priori* systems. We know, for instance, because we can prove it *a priori*, that profits are at maximum under perfect competition when $MC = MR = AC = AR$, that the maximum revenue-earning product mix imputes the minimum rental value to fixed resources and that the multiplier is the reciprocal of the marginal propensity to save. The layman, once he has seen the difference between *a priori* proof and empirical evidence, is likely to suppose that these theoretical truths state relations between variables which *must* hold in practice. He will be surprised to hear perhaps that they are not genuine knowledge and, in any case, that they are not about matters of fact. The empiricist will have to convince him and cannot rely merely on the good will empiricism has won by its scientific triumphs.

After all, why not allow *a priori* knowledge of matters of fact? For that matter, why bother whether a truth is established by logical reasoning or by empirical observation? Indeed, if, as is often said, 'philosophy leaves everything as it is', what possible difference can it make? Epistemology, at least of the grand or systematic variety, is today suspect even among philosophers. The epistemologist can perhaps usefully tidy and codify the economist's methods and remove from economics philosophic litter deposited by other philosophers. But what entitles him to impose his view of economic theory? In answer, we hope to have shown already that Positivism has done more than package what economists would have thought in any case. It provides neo-Classicism not only with crucial defences but also with methodological ammunition against such basic Classical-Marxian notions as the distinction between productive and unproductive labour (for violating the fact-value distinction), the labour theory of value (for failure to predict), or the analysis of capital into fixed and circulating, constant and variable (for offending against the Verification theory of meaning, by apparently resulting in no behavioural propositions). Defence and attack both rely ultimately on the analytic-synthetic distinction. So do the Positivist interpretations of the hypothetico-deductive method and its attendant idols of prediction and confirmation; they are not simply a neutral solution to a scientific problem about criteria of progress. Nor is the analytic-synthetic distinction itself a neutral solution to a philosophical problem. We have argued already that it is tendentious; but we have still to give philosophical reasons for rejecting the epistemology it supports.

The empiricist is bound to deny that there can be *a priori* knowledge of matters of fact. This is a consequence of holding that all claims to knowledge of the world can be justified only by experience and that whatever is known by experience could have been otherwise. (We used these two theses to define Empiricism on pp. 3–10 of our introduction.) He cannot allow that experience must have any particular character, if he is to insist that our world is in every way only one of many possible worlds and so discoverable only by empirical study. Faced with what look like necessary truths about the world, he can respond in three ways. He can deny either that they are necessary or that they are truths or that they are about the world. He can make more than one of these moves but he must make at least one. Otherwise he has no further reason to insist either that his picture of the world as a series of contingently connected states is correct or that experience is the only way to justify claims to empirical knowledge. If he gave way here, there would at once be further implications for the methodology of the sciences and, in particular, for the scope and strategy of theorising, of just the kind which we are trying to establish. He must deny that they are necessary or that they are truths or that they are about the world. He can make more than one of these moves but he has to make at least one, lest his theory of knowledge collapse at once.

There is a perverse heroism about denying flatly that the truths of logic and mathematics are necessary, if that is to mean they are contingent.[1] It strikes most enquirers as a wildly implausible line but is nevertheless oddly hard to refute. The usual riposte is to distinguish two 'directions of fit'. When a hypothesis fails to fit the facts, it is too bad for the hypothesis. When a mathematical truth fails to fit the facts, it is too bad for the facts. (If the addition of two eggs to two eggs resulted in three eggs, that would show one egg to have vanished.) This distinction is analogous to one drawn earlier when discussing economic rationality – when a model provides a correct account of what it is rational to do, we judge the agent's behaviour by the model; when the model is simply predictive, we judge the model by the agent's behaviour. Another riposte is to argue that the statement 'It is possible for a contradictory statement to be true' necessarily involves misuse of language. Although these ripostes can probably be parried, we shall take them as sufficient for the moment, but reopen the question presently, when we discuss and reject the pragmatist thesis that even the truths of logic can be revised.

---

[1] J. S. Mill espoused this view (although not whole-heartedly) in his *A System of Logic*. Herbert Spencer also favoured it. Otherwise it has had few defenders, but can still be found occasionally, for instance in Herbert Marcuse's *One-Dimensional Man* (Beacon Press, 1964), Ch. 9.

Nor shall we discuss directly the suggestion that logic, mathematics and other *a priori* systems contain no truths at all. According to this line, what look like truths are really rules or instructions or, as it is sometimes put, parts of a social 'grammar'.[2] The idea has never been applied to economic theory and we hope to be excused pioneering it, by advancing general arguments in favour of treating axioms and theorems as truths.

That brings us to the third line mentioned above, that there are *a priori* truths but not about matters of fact. This is the Positivist position. (To avoid confusion, let us say here that it is not the Pragmatist position but that we regard pragmatists too as empiricists.) *A priori* truths, in a positivist's view, 'record our determination to use words in a certain way'.[3] They are, in the famous phrase, 'true by convention'. Our question is 'what makes some truths necessary?' and the positivists' answer is that invention is the mother of necessity. Negatively, this allows them to admit the existence of necessary truths, which surely become harmless, when it is seen that they are necessary only because we make them up, and so cannot provide a source of knowledge which rivals experience. Positively, it underpins the doctrine that only experience can justify claims to knowledge of the world. 'Analytic', as the term has so far been used in this book, is to be tied to the idea of convention.

What is meant by saying that necessary truths are true by convention? There are many formulations but the crucial element in all of them is that necessary truths are optional, that they might have been otherwise. If P is a necessary truth in a system S, it is always possible either to revise the rules of S, or to construct another system S', so that either not-P is a theorem or there is no way of deriving P and also no way of deriving not-P. In other words *every* necessity is optional and *any* rule can be changed. Schematically, if Q implies P, then there is a rule R, such that $(Q \rightarrow P)$ and R can be revised in favour of R', such that not-$(Q \rightarrow P)$. We decide what rules to have, which includes deciding what is to count as applying each rule. For we do not do by convention what we cannot avoid doing. (The sense of 'convention' here is a loose one and implies no ceremony, referendum or occasion at which the rules were adopted. As with the social contract theory of political obligation, there need not have been a conven-

---

[2] See, for example, F. Waismann, *The Principles of Linguistic Philosophy* (Macmillan, 1965), Part I, esp. Ch. 2. For criticisms see Martin Hollis' review in *Foundations of Language*, vol. 5 (1969), pp. 128–34.

[3] See Ayer, *Language, Truth and Logic*, Ch. 4 (whence this phrase is stolen) for a pellucid exposition. He is to be classed, like Carnap, Schlick and all scions of the Vienna circle, as a *logical* positivist, to distinguish him from Comte and nineteenth-century positivists, who had the spirit but not the sophistication of modern positivism.

tion, provided that it is as if there had been one. What can be changed is as if agreed by convention.)

This approach is not intended to make economic theorising either empty or useless. Subtle calculation is often needed to detect an implication, as the enigma of Fermat's Last Theorem bears witness. Calculation is evidently an aid in engineering. Nevertheless theory cannot extend to matters of fact. Factual conclusions can be got only from factual premises. Analytic statements serve only to introduce terms and transform statements.

It is all too easy to state the theory incoherently. We are not to say, for instance, that logic and mathematics give us a set of conditional assertions, like 'If Keynes' axioms apply, then so do his theorems' for which no justification is needed beyond a proof of validity. For that would mischievously suggest that sound conditional statements were absolutely true, whereas we have explicitly said that *all* necessities are to be optional. Whenever an axiom has an unwanted implication, it ought in principle to be possible to shed the implication by changing the rules. Equally it ought to be possible to combine any axiom with any theorem whatever by choosing suitable rules. Unless every necessity is optional, not all necessary truths are true by convention.

Keynes' General Theory, for instance, according to this view, is got by working out the consequences of combining optional definitions of economic terms with optional rules of logic and mathematics. Its theorems have internal but not external support. That is why they can be held to lack all factual content and also why we argued earlier that, from the Positivist stand-point, *a priori* theories do not render hypotheses more probable. Any such system is in principle axiomatic, its theorems being got by deductive inference. Both the axioms and the rules of inference are, in the Positivist view, at human discretion. However, if synthetic extra premisses are added, it will be possible to derive conclusions with probability or predictive power but these conclusions are essentially only transformations of the synthetic premisses and acquire no extra empirical support or probability in their passage through the theoretical transformations.

Analytic and synthetic elements in macro-economic theory

Let us see what this comes to, with the help of a standard Keynsian model, fairly simple but rich enough to contain examples of most kinds of common macro-economic terms and propositions. We shall try to show that, in echo of Chapter 4, a positivist cannot coherently distinguish the empirical and theoretical elements in the model and that, insofar as he attempts to, treating the latter as optional either results in complete nonsense or transforms the model into one of a recognisably different kind.

So let Y = National Income = National Product; D = Disposable Income; T = Taxes; C = Consumption; I = Investment; M = Imports; G = Government Spending; X = Exports.

$T = tY$, where t is the rate of taxation, all levels
of government combined. (1)

$C = a + bY$, where a is autonomous consumption
and b is the marginal propensity to
consume out of disposable income. (2)

$M = mY$, where M is the propensity to import. (3)

$D = Y - T$ (4)

Then, assuming government spending and exports are given exogenously, we set total output produced and imported equal to total demand originating at home and abroad:

$$Y + M = C + I + G + X \qquad (5)$$

Hence, by substitution:

$$Y = \left[\frac{1}{1 + m - b(1 - t)} \right] (a + I + G + X) \qquad (6)$$

where the expression in square brackets is the multiplier. So, if there is a change in, say, X, the corresponding change in Y (i.e. ΔY) would be:

$$\Delta Y = \left[\frac{1}{1 + m - b(1 - t)} \right] \Delta X, \textit{ceteris paribus.} \qquad (7)$$

This looks like an empirical generalisation derived as a theorem; and is commonly treated as one by economists. At first sight it seems that (1), (2), (3) are empirical, (4), (5) are tautologies and (6), (7) are further empirical propositions deduced from (1), (2), (3) with the aid of (4), (5) and the tautologies of algebra and the calculus.

But, on closer inspection, the division into analytic and synthetic is not easy to make. In general the first three equations resemble what logicians call propositional functions containing, so to speak, dummy variables, which need to be given values if they are to count as propositions. (Thus $T = \frac{1}{2}Y$ would be a proposition, whereas $T = tY$ is a propositional function.) As propositions, (1), (2), (3) would be synthetic. But their status as propositional functions is more doubtful. Moreover they differ in important ways.

Let us look more closely, bearing in mind that economists mean to refer with each of the variables T, C and M to a stream of payment which can be maintained indefinitely and so can be an equilibrium. (Thus, although consumption could be financed out of capital or borrowing for a time, equilibrium consumption must come out of income.) Now consider whether these statements can indeed be separated into analytic and synthetic elements. For instance '(2) $C = a + D$' states a relation of the form '$C = f(D)$', which latter could be taken as analytic, given economists' practice of using 'consumption' to refer to a stream which can be indefinitely maintained. Insofar as $C = a + D$ can be regarded in the context of the whole set of interdefined concepts as simply a way of rendering the meaning of $C = f(D)$ precise, then it should be separable into analytic and synthetic components. By the same token $T = tY$ is an instance of $T = f(Y)$ and $M = mY$ of $M = f(Y)$ for which similar claims can be made. Moreover (1) and (2) can be treated as explanations of the truth of (4), which is assuredly analytic.

The problem now appears two-fold. First it is not easy to decide the status of the proposition 'Consumption spending comes out of personal disposable income', which underlies $C = f(D)$. It differs significantly both from (4) $D = Y - T$, which is presumably analytic, and from a proposition like 'imports vary with national income', which is presumably synthetic. It cannot plausibly be said to embody or depend on a definition of its terms and it is not an arbitrary or optional posit, since, without it, the whole picture of the circular flow of income and spending would have to be revised. The best we can say is that it is so integral to the theory as to be protected against all possible refutation yet cannot be classified analytic; and functions as a substantive and well grounded hypothesis yet cannot be classified synthetic.

The difficulty arises because, from a Positivist view-point, whatever states a possible fact cannot be an analytic truth. So it is tempting to escape the difficulty either, as pragmatists do, by refusing to operate an analytic-synthetic litmus test in the first place or, as we ourselves shall propose, by allowing that synthetic statements can be *a priori*. But the positivist must persevere. He must insist that every statement is analytic or synthetic and that none is both, on pain of having his theory of knowledge collapse. He has to maintain that the difficulty occurs because the statements are ambiguous and that it can be resolved by identifying the various senses of each, in such a way that all the resulting clarifications can be classified as analytic or synthetic. The reader must be left to judge whether (1), (2), (3) will yield to this treatment.

Now consider (5) $Y + M = C + I + G + X$. It is not an empirical generalisation that in equilibrium output plus imports exactly equal demand generated at home and abroad. Nor is it a mere consequence of what we choose to mean by 'equilibrium', as can be seen by comparing this Keynesian model with the one examined in the last chapter, whose equilibrium condition was that savings equal investment. (The reader who sets out to discover whether savings equals investment in the present Keynesian model will not find himself deciding what to choose to mean by 'equilibrium'.) In general, moreover, in a range of neo-Classical and Classical-Marxian macro and micro models, we note that, for equilibrium, a set of variables representing supply (for instance production, offers to sell, ownership rights) is equated to a set representing demand (for instance offers to buy, propensities to spend) and that the equation must be made *correctly*. 'Correctness' here is a matter neither for generalisation nor for stipulation; but we have as yet no hint what it does depend on.

This leads us back to the claim that analytic propositions depend on options, in some sense. Could we define a possible short-run situation in which aggregate demand need not equal aggregate supply? Well, if we were to leave the divergence unaccounted for, we could not then solve the model for (6) and (7), since (5) is needed in the chain of substitution. Yet, if we were to account for the divergence by describing exactly what happens to unsold inventories and unfilled orders, so that substitutions in the equations remain possible, then we would have a different kind of model, one of disequilibrium dynamics. (Suppose, for example that aggregate demand exceeds aggregate supply, making (5) an inequality. Unfilled orders would be met by expanding production or, if capacity is reached, by raising prices. This response would exactly fill the orders and choke off the excess demand and supply would once again equal demand.) So, if the model is to be solved as it stands, (5) is essential and, if it is to be solved at all, some substitute for (5) is needed, which will change the character of the model, while continuing to rely on an ultimate principle of balance between Supply and Demand. Consequently the 'options' at this stage are limited to a range of models, one and only one of which is our Keynesian model. There is no alternative to relying on a principle of balance between supply and demand, if any coherent model is to result from changing (5); nor is there anything to suggest that all coherent models are epistemologically equal. In short, if there are options of the sort required by the doctrine of 'truth by convention', they must be very much deeper than we have yet gone.

We are thus left with a need to make equations *correctly* when expressing conceptual connections between economic terms. The need shows up two difficulties in the analytic-synthetic classification, one being that some crucial equations cannot be readily classified in either way and the other that some equations which are surely to be classified as analytic nevertheless cannot be rationally treated as optional. So the moment has come to criticise the distinction itself. Two separate questions are at issue, whether all cognitively meaningful propositions are analytic or synthetic and whether the Positivist way of characterising analytic truths is correct. (Not all those who have accepted an analytic-synthetic distinction have been positivists or even empiricists; not all empiricists accept an analytic-synthetic distinction). We shall argue that the truths of logic and mathematics are not 'analytic' in all senses of the term; that they are in no sense optional or empty of factual content; that nevertheless Pragmatism only makes matters worse by dropping the analytic-synthetic distinction altogether; and (in the next chapter) that a Rationalist restatement of the nature of necessity will resolve our present epistemological difficulties.

'Analytic' analysed

When we first introduced the notion of analyticity in our introduction, we said that a true statement is analytic if it cannot be denied without contradiction, or if it is a consequence of the meanings of its terms. It is important firstly that these criteria do not come to the same thing and secondly that neither is enough to show that analytic statements lack factual content. (The term 'analytic' has appeared in the works of philosophers of many schools and Positivism cannot monopolise it without an argument.)

To say that a statement cannot be denied without contradiction is usually to say that its truth is guaranteed by logic alone. By 'logic' is meant the whole apparatus of formal logic, including set theory but not, at least in the first instance, mathematics or distinct formal systems like kinship algebra, neo-Classical marginal analysis or Classical-Marxian production theory. If necessary truths from these latter systems are intended to be fully covered by the contradiction criterion it has next to be shown that all systems are reducible to logic. We shall argue briefly in the next chapter that this cannot be done. For the present, we shall be content to argue that even if it can be done, it does not give Positivism enough.

Let us suppose then that all analytic truths are truths of what is recognisably logic. Why are truths of logic true? The Positivist answer will have to be that they are true because we make the laws of logic up. The answer presupposes that we could in principle invent alternatives to any and all laws of logic. But could we? It is at first sight plausible to think so, because it seems to be merely a convention of English that the little word 'not' means what it does. So if we changed its meaning, analytic statements at present containing it would no longer be analytic truths. For instance the truth of 'if marginal cost does not equal marginal revenue, then profits are not at maximum' seems to depend partly on the meaning of 'not', which depends in turn on our regarding statements like 'a statement and its negation are not both true' as true. A different notion of negation would generate a different logic.

But would it? We are speaking not of sentences but of the statements they express. Let us agree that we decide by convention what sentences mean, in that we decide which sentence shall express which statement. Thus the different sentences 'The sky is blue' and 'Der Himmel ist blau' both express the same statement. The single sentence 'He ran into the bank' expresses different statements, depending on whether the context is money or motoring. Agreeing that we decide how to interpret a sentence does not mean having to agree that we invent statements. We invent names for babies but we do not invent babies for names. A language in which one could truly say 'two and two are not four' differs from English at least in that this sentence cannot express the statement expressed by the English sentence 'two and two are not four'. If one knew that 'two' 'and' 'are' and 'four' meant the same in both languages, it would follow that 'not' had different meanings. For the meaning of the English word 'not' is given by statements like 'a statement is not both true and false', 'if two numbers are equal, they are not unequal' and so forth.

To generate a different logic, we need to have true *statements* like 'some statements are both true and false'. At the same time we need to know when the same statement recurs in an argument, when an inference is to count as valid and when an argument results in a contradiction. A logic which replaced *all* our logical truths with others would be one where, insofar as we can understand the proposal at all, any conclusion whatever was derivable by any inference whatever. In other words, the term 'inference' neither would nor could mean what we mean by it. For its present meaning is given by statements like 'Q can be validly inferred from P only if it is impossible for P to be true and Q false.'

It may be objected here that mathematics proves the contrary. Non-Euclidean geometries suggest that what is true in one system may be false in another. Mathematicians sometimes speak as if the apparent fact that the only final constraint is the need to be consistent showed that mathematics was an invention. If there is 'play' in mathematics, where the same distinction holds between sentence and statement, are we not pitching our case too strong?

Our answer is twofold. Firstly, that Euclid's parallel postulate can be replaced does not show that all his axioms are at our discretion. The object of theorising in this area is to delineate a geometry and not every formal system is a geometry. The minimal axioms needed to ensure that the system is a geometry are not proved conventional by showing that other axioms can be replaced. (This reply is taken further in the next chapter.) Secondly, whatever is dispensable, the mathematician does need to be consistent. This indicates that all mathematical truths can be written in absolute form by prefacing them with 'in our logic'. For instance theorems of Euclidean geometry depending on the parallel postulate become 'absolute' when written in the form, 'Our logic and Euclid's axioms being given, T is a theorem.' In general, no argument starting from the premiss that theorems of a system S are optional, where S is not itself a logic, can soundly conclude that our logic is optional, if our logic has been presupposed in deriving the theorems of S.

'Our logic' is a vague term, which may prompt another objection. There are disputes among logicians about what 'our logic' comprises. Intuitionists and classicists, for example, are divided on whether the Law of the Excluded Middle, that every statement is true or false, is part of an irreducible corpus or whether it is optional. Gödel's results threaten any claim that the nature of logic is fully understood. So is there not 'play' in logic, as there is in mathematics?

In reply, we modestly disclaim a divine grasp of the nature of logic and cannot pronounce on the Excluded Middle or Gödel. We do contend, however, that logic is an activity with a point to it, namely the stating of truths in conditional form, and that whatever defines the nature of logical truth forms a set of irreplaceable truths.[4] No apparent system without consistent rules for arriving at conditional truths by inference can be a logic. No doubt axioms can be distinguished from theorems and no doubt some axioms can be questioned. But not all axioms and rules can be introduced from scratch, as there must already be axioms and rules for introducing them. Steering well clear of the advanced researches of logicians, therefore, we maintain that, even if all analytic truths are logical truths, this does not support the claim that they are optional.

A further objection may be that there are uninterpreted logics, which allow a free choice of symbols and rules and so are conventional in the sense required. Consequently, it may be said, our previous answer shows only that we covertly presuppose existing conventions when interpreting a logic and not that the basis of our logic is immutable. Our reply is that there is no such thing as a wholly uninterpreted logic. A man cannot invent a logic just by making marks at random on a piece of paper and exclaiming 'Here is an uninterpreted logic!'. He has to explain why the marks are to count as logical marks, which involves him in explaining which further strings of marks would count as well-formed and what manipulations are or are not licit. He must distinguish at least one logical constant and one rule of transformation. To that extent he is interpreting his marks and we can now repeat our previous answer.[5]

---

[4] Cf. Michael Dummett, Truth (*Proc. Arist. Soc.*, 1968–9), reprinted in G. Pitcher (ed.), *Truth* (Prentice-Hall, 1964).

[5] A less curt and more technical case for denying that logical constants are minted by convention is brilliantly put by Arthur Pap in *Semantics and Necessary Truth* (Yale University Press, 1958), Chs. 5–7.

We therefore have reason enough to deny that logical truths are all true by convention and so turn to the second definition of 'analytic'. Our point will again be that even if all necessary truths are analytic in this second sense, they are not therefore either vacuous or conventional.

By the other criterion given earlier, a statement is analytic, if it is a consequence of the meanings of its terms. This differs from the last in not presupposing that the rules of logic are enough. In popular form, 'it all depends what you mean by . . .' whether a truth is necessarily true. Whether patriotism is a virtue 'depends on what you mean by "patriotism"'. Whether savings must equal investment, whether demand equals supply in equilibrium depends on what you mean by 'savings', 'investment,' 'equilibrium' and so on. So, even if it turns out that not all analytic truths are logical truths, it is still on the cards that all analytic truths are true in virtue of the meanings of the terms they contain.

Stated thus, the thesis is non-committal between Rationalism and Empiricism. Plato, too, when pursuing the nature of absolute justice or beauty, thought the answer depended on the meanings of the terms in key sentences. But Plato, unlike positivists, held that meanings were real and immutable; that there is one right answer to the question 'What is it to act justly?' Putting the thesis in this form does not in itself help the view that necessary truths are optional or empty. Moreover the previous argument shows, we hope, that, although we invent words for meanings, we do not invent meanings for words like 'truth' and 'inference'. So what further move can a positivist make?

To show meanings optional, there will have to be a purely philosophical thesis about definition, to the effect that only lexical or stipulative definitions are licit. We defer discussion of the nature of definition as we see it to the next chapter, where we claim the existence of true axioms and real definitions. We can dispose of the positivist's case in short order. By his own account the definition a positivist gives us of 'definition', his definition will be either lexical or stipulative. So why should we accept it? He cannot reply that his definition is 'true', since he does not believe in true definitions. Nor, if the difficulties raised throughout this book come to anything, can he claim it is useful. We have so far found no argument to suggest that whether there are necessary truths depends solely on what we mean by 'necessary truth', any more than whether there are inveterate hoarders depends solely on what we mean by 'inveterate hoarder'.

We have also failed to find a strong enough philosophical case for saying that necessary truths lack all factual content to offset the objections raised in interpreting our Keynesian model just now. We have seen why a positivist wants to maintain it. But his line seems to depend on begging the question by simply asserting that all actual events and laws are contingent. Moreover, when he says 'No analytic truth has any factual content', he is presumably uttering an analytic truth (one both empty and optional). His own account of analyticity prevents his arguing for his view of facts and laws *a priori*. And his attempts to argue inductively have run persistently into trouble.

He therefore still owes us a reason why we should accept his theory of knowledge in general or his approach to economic theory in particular. What sort of reason would do? To offer logical or mathematical reasons for agreeing that logic and mathematics are optional and empty is to hold one-self up by one's own bootstraps. (There is always a further bit of fairy-lore to justify a belief in fairies.) So it looks as if the reason will have to be empirical. He will have to maintain that his proposals are, like the tauto-logies of Keynesian economics, a useful base of operation.

Unfortunately he has already sawn through this branch and so can no longer sit on it. The choice of a set of analytic statements is useful only insofar as there are inductive grounds to expect that it will continue to be useful. In choosing, he decides, epistemologically speaking, not only which set to apply but also which set to create. The choice is idle, unless some sets are more useful than others, as endorsed by inductive reasoning. So the creation of analytic truths becomes the advancing of a hypothesis for testing. Equally, when two sets apply to the same cases, he will advise us to pick the simpler. But why should we do that, unless the simpler is, on inductive grounds, more likely to be useful tomorrow? As soon as a choice between sets of analytic statements is made rational, the statements cease abruptly to be vacuous. (The same rejoinder deals with the view that some choices have a biological value; but we defer the point as it applies rather to pragmatists, who would not be embarrassed by the rejoinder.)

We conclude then that the doctrine of Truth by Convention contains *a priori* elements which contradict it and that, when it is asked to explain what makes one theory better than another, synthetic elements appear also. This is the philosophical reason why we failed to make Positivist sense of our Keynesian equations. Necessary truths are not all optional and our stock of knowlege cannot be cleanly divided into what we invent and what we discover.

Pragmatism: 'no statement is immune to revision'

Empiricism thus loses some of its heaviest guns. But it has other batteries and we cannot yet claim the field for rationalism, in order to deploy our own account of economic theory and the nature of economic science. First we must deal briefly with Pragmatism, or rather with the Conceptual Pragmatism championed by W.v.O. Quine.[6] We pick on Quine, because he would agree with many of the objections raised against Positivism and, in particular, against the analytic-synthetic distinction but nevertheless concludes in favour of Empiricism. Theory and fact are, he contends, interwoven and the Inductive and Deductive problems are inseparable. He rejects the usual Empiricist strategy of erecting empirical knowledge on a foundation of brute fact and argues for a single theory-laden world. The implications for economics have not yet been drawn and no one has written a manifesto of Pragmatist economics, as Milton Friedman has for Positive economics. But a half-articulated pragmatism unquestionably pervades much contemporary economics[7] and we shall try to suggest where it might lead.

Quine's position is made more appealing and also more difficult by being stated in a riot of metaphors. He invites us to think of human knowledge as forming 'a seamless web', 'a field of force, which touches experience only at the edges'. Our beliefs stand as a single body, which 'face the tribunal of experience together'. Positivists maintain that only synthetic statements ever face the tribunal of experience and that the separate class of analytic statements are of their nature exempt from testing. Quine denies this. Any belief, he holds, can be put in the dock and rejected in the light of experience. Admittedly some are more 'deeply entrenched in our conceptual scheme' than others and we would be more reluctant to part with them. But even laws of logic and simple theorems of mathematics do not differ in ultimate kind from reports of the day's news or of the findings of direct observation.

This account might seem merely a revival of the idea that what look like necessary truths are really very well-confirmed and very general empirical hypotheses. But it is not, since Quine has also rejected the synthetic half of the analytic-synthetic distinction. Truths are neither analytic nor synthetic. Instead they are all part of the web, all open to revision and all, if we choose

---

[6] W.v.O. Quine: Truth by convention, in *The Ways of Paradox* (Random House, 1966); *idem*, Two dogmas of empiricism, in *From a Logical Point of View* (Harvard University Press, 1961); *idem*, *Word and Object* (M.I.T. Press, 1960); H. Putnam, The analytic and the synthetic, in *Minnesota Studies in the Philosophy of Science*, vol. III), ed. by H. Feigl and G. Maxwell, (University of Minnesota Press, 1962); Goodman, *Fact, Fiction and Forecast*; C. G. Hempel's later writings contain much relevant matter and there is a general conceptual pragmatist epistemology (although still wedded to conventionalism) in C. I. Lewis, *Mind and the World-Order* (Charles Scribner's Sons, 1929).

[7] It is perhaps especially evident in the writings of R. M. Solow. See, for instance, *Capital Theory and the Rate of Return* (North-Holland, 1963).

to grant them immunity, capable of retention. The difference between our reaction in mathematics and our reaction in botany, when experience conflicts with what we expect, reflects a difference in our habits of thought and not a difference in the nature of those subjects. The whole scheme forms, so to speak, a mobile, with the laws of logic at the centre, reports of observation at the periphery and the beliefs of commonsense and science ranged in between according to generality and importance. Experience impinges only on the periphery but a fierce enough buffeting there will cause the whole contraption to move, laws of logic and all.

The effects of the buffeting are partly up to us. We choose what is to move and what is to stay fixed. When experiments in physics show that something must give, we choose whether to amend the law of entropy, revise the principles of optics, countenance the reversal of time or admit the existence of anti-matter. Each choice has its price elsewhere in the system and we have to pay the bill. Provided we pay, the choice is ours. The nearest we come to finding a necessary truth is with those beliefs (like the basic principles of our Keynesian model) whose revision is too expensive to contemplate. 'Come what may', we would hang on to the laws of logic. But this is a fact about us and even the laws of logic could be revised. Conversely any belief can be preserved. If we insist that the earth is flat, the bill will be high but we could meet it by scrapping much of optics and mathematics. There is no ultimate reason for present relative degrees of 'entrenchment'.

To put it more formally, there are no truths devoid of all factual content and no truths with only factual content. There is no external reason for treating some statements as more basic than others. No statement is immune from revision. No distinction can finally be drawn between truths which serve to order experience and truths which merely describe it.

Faced with this masterly piece of philosophical conjuring, our attack seems to vanish and, with it, our hopes of turning our critique of Positive economics into an assault on Empiricism in general. The pragmatist is unruffled by finding himself unable to distinguish a failure of *ceteris paribus* conditions from a refutation of the theory. If every hypothesis can justifiably be maintained in the teeth of experience by making suitable adjustments, then there are no independent and unconditional criteria of falsity. The positivist had to decide whether the world judged his models or his models the world — whether his models of rational economic behaviour were descriptive or prescriptive — but he fell foul of the analytic-synthetic distinction at every turn. By contrast the pragmatist need not worry. He is free to project hypotheses based on maximising or not to project them, depending on whether he finds them useful and elegant. What look like *a priori* indispensable theorems about rationality are, for him, simply notions entrenched by time and our biological make-up in our conceptual scheme. No doubt it is less trouble to accept the notions we inherit but we can scrap them if they prove tiresome. A theory can support a hypothesis, from a pragmatist stand-point, in the sense that it is better entrenched than the hypotheses derived from it and contains a summary of the reasons for its entrenchment. There are no snags arising from failure to separate theory and fact, since all data in the pragmatist's world are theory-laden and all theories determine facts. Positivist vices are pragmatist virtues and our attack has apparently faded away.

The implications for economics itself are also striking. Let us glance at some of them, starting with the interpretation of our earlier Keynesian equations. Whereas the positivist must regard statements which cannot be classified wholly analytic or wholly synthetic as compound or ambiguous, the pragmatist is happy to use them to rebut the analytic-synthetic distinction. So (4) $D = Y - T$ is merely 'more analytic' than (2) $C = a + bD$, which in turn is deeper entrenched than (1) $T = tY$ and (3) $M = mY$ but less well entrenched than (5) $Y + M = C + I + G + X$, insofar as (4) $D = Y - T$ can be replaced without incoherence but replacement of (5) $Y + M = C + I + G + X$ would change the whole character of the model and replacement of the underlying principle behind (5) would call for a still more basic revision, perhaps in the laws of logic. Thus the difficulties found earlier for the positivist in microeconomics illustrate the pragmatist's position. In general he has no reason to hold that entrenched statements are vacuous – indeed they express the structure of a theory-laden world – and no difficulty can arise from that quarter. So his account of macro-economics will avoid the problems raised so far.

Other implications have the same charm. For instance, micro-economics is often introduced to students, as if it were more basic than macro-economics. The economic world is composed of economies, composed of firms and markets, composed of individuals. So it seems natural to start with atoms and work up to the more complex structures. This strategy accords well with Positivist epistemology, since all empirical knowledge is thought of as a hierarchy in which each level is supported from below until a foundation of simple observation statements is reached. (We applied this idea to economics in the last chapter, where it fared ill.) So it would be not only natural but also obligatory to reduce macro to micro. Conceptual Pragmatism simply removes the pillars of the temple. Micro is not more basic than macro and, unless there are pedagogic gains, there is no reason to start with it. The only question is what produces the most elegant and convenient whole.

Similarly a pragmatist would regard neither perfect competition nor any other conception of the market as the irreducibly basic one. Models are conjectures in the search for simplicity, coherence and elegance and are to be judged in those terms. Full-cost pricing, oligopoly, monopoly, perfect and imperfect competition models enter the lists on equal terms, none is to be preferred in advance and any or all can be used to analyse the same facts or be discarded as it suits. Much the same goes for macro-economic concepts. The pragmatic economist has no *a priori* reason either to agree or to disagree with those (like Joan Robinson) who take 'capital' to refer to the value of a set of disparate factories, inventories of miscellaneous inputs and outputs, goods in process and so forth, with the result, that, because of price changes among the components, the same set of physical goods can represent different 'amounts of capital' in different circumstances and different physical sets can represent the same 'amount of capital'. This concept of capital may be closer to actual usage in some ways but, in a pragmatic view, this is no merit. The question is only whether it works better than the orthodox economists' notion, which has the great merit of simplicity. If it yields a better measure of the contribution over time of education or of technical progress to growth, using the 'amount of capital' as a 'factor of production', well and good. The case may be complex (with Cambridge, England, for instance, on one side and Cambridge, Mass. on the other) but it is not, apparently, at all philosophical.

The pragmatist treatment of interdefined terms

The gains from dropping the analytic-synthetic distinction also seem large, when we turn once more to the problem of criteria. We found that, within positivist canons, no theory is usable until its terms have criteria of application. Where terms are interdefined, at least one of them needs to be given empirical sense. Where there is a circle of interdefined terms without an exit, none of them is an *economic* term, as the meaning of each is exhausted by stating its formal relation to the others. To illustrate the shift from Positivism to Pragmatism, we shall next present an example of such a circle, arguing that Positivism can do nothing about it but that Pragmatism seems to offer an exit.

Consider the economic terms which are basic in all micro-economic models: utility, cost, revenue, output, price, profit, income. Following Wicksteed, let us give them their pure neo-Classical marginalist definitions. 'Cost' is opportunity cost; the 'cost of a good' is the opportunities forgone by diverting those resources from other production; the 'cost of an extra unit of a good *A*' is the amount of the next most highly desired good forgone. Hence 'cost' is defined in terms of sacrifices of desired goods, that is in terms of utility. 'Revenue' is simply price times output. 'Price' is equal to marginal utility, adjusted for income effects; hence 'price' measures what would be sacrificed at the margin for an extra unit. 'Output' is output of goods, the output of a producing unit. Any production process has a number of results. (Cutting timber yields sawdust as well as planks; mining produces holes as well as gold.) A result is 'output', if and only if it is wanted. The defining characteristic of output is that it yields utility not to the producing units but to the consuming units. 'Price' and 'output' both being defined in terms of utility, 'revenue' is also so defined. 'Profit', being revenue minus cost, is also defined in terms of utility. 'Income' is payment for services, compensating wage-earners for the disutility, at the margin, of work and compensating providers of capital services for the disutility of postponing consumption. Hence 'income' is command over utilities paid as compensation for incurring disutilities. All the terms can thus be defined by reference to 'utility' (although 'utility' need not be the only concept used) and must be so defined, if their economic significance is to be understood. Each denotes a form of utility.[8]

Now consider 'utility' itself. By modern reckoning, it refers not to a 'flow of satisfaction' or to a feeling of well-being but to preference or willingness to choose. A consumer's preference for good A over good B is measured by the amount of B he would give up for an extra unit of A. We know a consumer's preference for A over B at the margin, if we know the sacrifice of B he is willing to make for an extra unit of A in terms of B. 'Utility' is thus defined nowadays in terms of acceptable opportunity cost.[9]

The circle is complete. The basic terms of marginalist micro-economics can all be defined by reference to 'utility', which is defined in its turn by reference to 'cost'. They make up a formal family and none so far has any empirical significance. How do we break out of the circle?

We could try defining 'utility' by reference to the consumer. 'Preference' is whatever leads a consumer to choose one bundle of goods A and B over another. Marginal rates of substitution between A and B are got by extrapolation from choices actually made. So actual choices become the observed

---

[8] It might be objected that we have mixed definitions with equilibrium relations; and so wrongly denied that cost can be measured in money terms, whereas it equals sacrificed opportunities only in equilibrium. We disagree. Only in equilibrium is cost determined by *marginal* relations. Nonetheless the cost of a good is always a matter of opportunities sacrificed, even if out of equilibrium the wrong sacrifices may have been made. Money is an adequate measure according to Marshall, only if the marginal utility of money is constant; and, according to modern theory, only because the value of money is determined through the price mechanism, like all other exchange relationships.

[9] Strictly speaking, 'utility' is defined in terms of 'extent of preference' which is defined in terms of 'acceptable cost'. But the exact order of definition need not trouble us as an 'acceptable cost' is one the consumer would not 'reject'; and 'rejection' is explicated in turn in terms of 'preference'.

data needed to give empirical significance to one of the terms in the family circle.

But who is 'the consumer'? Consumers are no doubt 'those who make this sort of choice', which includes firms, middlemen and retailers. In competitive markets, however, these categories should only reflect the pressures of final demand, without revealing their own preferences. So 'the consumer' is 'the final consumer'. But who is he? He must be whoever chooses in the light of his preferences alone and not in hope of gain from further transactions. Thus 'preference' is the choice of the final consumer and 'the final consumer' is the consumer who reveals his own preferences. The circle is still complete.

Other tries are also circular. For instance 'the firm' and 'the production function' are inseparable. 'The firm' is what has a production function; 'the production function' is what a firm has. But, since readers who found some force in our argument of Chapter 4 about ideal variables will not be surprised by the circularity, we do not propose to labour the point with other examples.

The circle is generated by the distinction drawn between formal and empirical significance. The distinction drawn, empirical criteria for applying one term can be given only to someone who already understands how to apply another. Since he understands how to apply the other, only if he understands how to apply yet another and since the regress is infinite, empirical criteria can never be given at all. Equally, if to understand a statement of the form 'A has greater marginal utility than B for consumer C' one must know its truth conditions and if knowing its truth conditions depends on understanding another statement with a term from the family circle and if the regress is infinite, then no statement of that form can be understood.

The example of 'utility' also illustrates Quine's reasons for rejecting the analytic-synthetic distinction. In explaining what it was for a statement to be 'analytic', we used a family of terms like 'contradictory', 'impossible' or 'meaning'. Schematically we might have said

(1) '"P implies Q" is an analytic truth' = df '"Not-(P implies Q)" is contradictory'

(2) '"Not-(P implies Q)" is contradictory' = df 'Q is part of the meaning of P'

(3) 'Q is part of the meaning of P' = df 'It is impossible for P to be true and Q false'

(4) 'It is impossible for P to be true and Q false' = df '"P implies Q" is a necessary truth'

(5) '"P implies Q" is a necessary truth' = df '"P implies Q" is an analytic truth'

Again, to understand any of these terms, one would have already to understand another. The relationships are more tightly knit and more schematically expressed but there is the same regress and the same result that none can be understood at all.

There are two ways out. One, which we shall ourselves defend, is to pin the blame on empiricism, by claiming that there can be *a priori* knowledge of matter of fact. If there are necessary truths stating relations which are bound to hold among whatever in fact falls under certain concepts which can be understood *a priori*, then we can break out of the circle by appeal to *a priori* foundations for all knowledge. The other, which is Quine's, is to pin the blame on the analytic-synthetic distinction and the strict dichotomy between formal and empirical significance. If all statements can be revised in the light of experience, then, in principle, whatever allows the understanding of any allows the understanding of all. Without the analytic-synthetic distinction, it becomes possible to hold both that theory determines the order found in experience and that theory is always open to revision. Complete pragmatism thus seems to offer an exit.

Pragmatism and truths independent of coherence

Conceptual Pragmatism is therefore attractive to empiricists, whether they be philosophers or social scientists. A causal law becomes simply a general statement which it suits us for the moment to hold on to. The testing of predictions becomes the occasion for deciding which parts of our theory we are most attached to. 'Brute atomic facts' are abolished and sleight of professional hand when abstracting from data becomes legitimate. The Definitions, Hypotheses, Assumptions, Deductions, Predictions, Implications, Observations and Theories mentioned in our beginners' diagram (Figure 1) of the Hypothetico-deductive method in our introductory chapter collapse into one another. We can base ourselves on a new diagram, looking something like Figure 20.

Science thus sheds its philosophical corsets. But, before we find ourselves wholly undone, let us ask where we are. Science is usually thought of as the application of brute logic to brute fact with the help of elaborate theory. Traditionally, empiricists have construed this to imply that there is a world independent of human thought about it, which is not the only possible world. Logic tells what we need not bother to look for; experience tells us what we have found. Positivism civilised logic, making it a human invention, but only in order to insist on the utter bruteness of the independent facts. Pragmatism civilises the facts too. Nothing remains independent of our thought. A true belief is true only insofar as it coheres with all others we choose to believe at the time. In a sense, we have plunged into a romantic unreason, where only myths are real.

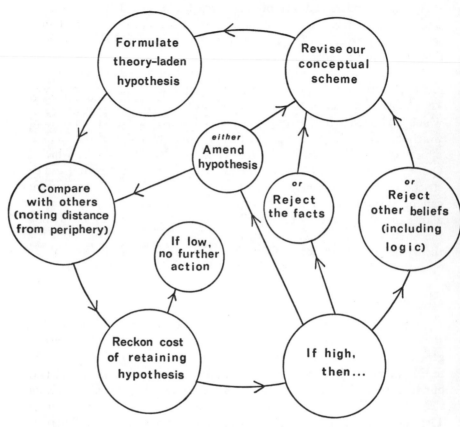

Figure 20

Now, it is unclear how much of these last remarks a pragmatist would choose to believe. Quine appears to dissent at two points. He speaks of 'experience', which acts as boundary to our conceptual field of force and whose tribunal our beliefs face. He speaks also of prices which we must pay for changes in our scheme of belief. So, if we conceive of choice among beliefs on the analogy of a marginal utility model of a consumer's indifference curves, then it seems not to be true after all that the consumer is utterly sovereign. There are two constraints, one in the buffetings of experience and one in the logic of opportunity cost of beliefs forgone. It looks therefore as though a pragmatist does, after all, want some brute facts and some brute logic.

He may want them; but he cannot have them. If there are any given elements, then they are not to be accounted for by an epistemology, whose central tenet is universal choice. Where something is fixed, the fact that we can choose what to say about it is trivial beside the fact that we cannot choose whether what we say is true. Either there are these fixed elements or there are not. If there are not, then we appoint the tribunal of experience, arrange its evidence, decide its verdicts and set its penalties. In this case there is no further reason why all verdicts should not be favourable and all fines zero. On the other hand, if there are fixed elements, then there are truths whose truth depends on more than their stipulated coherence with other statements. To accept the first horn of the dilemma is unscientific; to accept the second unpragmatic.

To put it formally, let E be a statement to the effect that experience shows that a revision is needed in our scheme of beliefs; and let L be a statement to the effect that we cannot retain both belief P and belief Q. Can we or can we not revise E and L? If we can, then it is true neither that our beliefs face the tribunal of experience nor that action is needed when they do. If we cannot, then it is false that 'no statement is immune to revision'. (This, we believe, is enough to refute pragmatism, without even having to urge the seemingly damning results of taking the statement that 'no statement is immune to revision' and asking whether it is immune to revision. There are also snags in the whole notion of conceptual revision,[10] which we shall take up in an appendix to the present chapter.) We therefore contend that pragmatism cures the patient of analyticitis, only by cutting his head off.

The point can be reinforced by referring again to our Keynesian model, which so embarrassed the positivist. The pragmatist fares much better, until confronted with (5) $Y + M = C + I + G + X$. No doubt he passes it off blandly as 'deeply entrenched' but revisable at a price. But, as we saw earlier, the price is, for a limited revision, a different sort of model and, for a radical revision, complete incoherence. Without (5), there is no solution to the model as it stands and, unless supply and demand tend to balance in reality, the system cannot function properly. These constraints and the general economic significance of (5) are not accounted for by Pragmatism, just as the immutability of the law of non-contradiction cannot be explained away by noting that, if we are content to babble, we can always do without it. We can always abandon economics but renunciation is not a daring kind of radical revision.

Summary

With these objections to Logical Positivism and Conceptual Pragmatism, we rest our case against Empiricism. The case is not formally complete, since our discussion has not exhausted all existing variants and we have not

---

[10] Cf. E. J. Nell, No statement is immune to revision, unpublished paper, 1969.

proved that no fresh ones are possible. But Positivism and Pragmatism between them command the field and we have been content to campaign in the central area. Even so we may be charged with ignoring some distinguished contributions to recent debate on the nature of science, notably perhaps by Collingwood, T. S. Kuhn, Popper, Wittgenstein or Peter Winch. The reason for their absence is not that we deem them uninteresting or unimportant but that they do not offer empiricist solutions to the problem of *a priori* knowledge. Our own concern is strictly epistemological and, since we are trying to carry the argument some distance into economic theory, we do not have space to range further afield. Positivism and Pragmatism are, we suggest, the two main modern heirs to an Empiricist tradition, which rejects Cartesianism while retaining an ambivalent sympathy with Kant.

The moral we wish to draw is that necessary truths are no less part of our stock of knowledge of the world than contingent truths. This is more than we have yet shown and, indeed, more than the minimal claim needed for rationalism. The minimal claim is that there are necessary truths which can be known but not according to empiricist criteria of knowledge. (Plato, for instance, combined a belief in eternal verities with a denial that anything can be known about the world of sense-experience.) But that leaves the function of necessary truths too mysterious for comfort and, in any case, those empiricists, who accept a distinction between necessary and contingent truths, may not think the minimal claim worth disputing. We ourselves still wish to hold that a generalisation is projectible, only if deducible from a sound theory, whose range of application is known. We also want to regard the statements of a sound theory as necessarily true. So we shall have to claim more than the minimum needed for rationalism; and, in doing so, shall have almost all rationalists for company.

In upshot, Pragmatism is finally more absurd than Positivism. It grants independence neither to facts nor to theories and so plunges the scientist into romantic unreason. Positivism at least insists on the independence of facts. Nevertheless we reckon Pragmatism right to argue that scientific data are theory-laden. Unromantic reason then demands that theories be independent and this is the thesis to be explained and defended in the next chapter. First, however, we shall pursue the pragmatist notion of intellectual revision to its, we maintain, incoherent conclusion.

APPENDIX TO CHAPTER 6

ON THE PRICE OF CHOOSING TRUTH

A conflict with experience at the periphery occasions readjustments in the interior of the field. Truth values have to be redistributed over some of our statements. Re-evaluation of some statements entails re-evaluation of others, because of their logical interconnections – the logical laws being in turn simply certain further statements of the system, certain further elements of the field ... But the total field is so underdetermined by its boundary conditions, experience, that there is much latitude of choice as to what statements to re-evaluate in the light of any single contrary experience.

W.v.O. Quine, Two dogmas of empiricism

When experience conflicts with expectation, pragmatism always offers the scientist a choice of how to pay the bill. Our objection was that universal choice includes choice of whether to pay the bill at all and that statements of the 'price' of revisions should, for the sake of consistency, themselves be revisable. This absurd consequence excused us from considering how choices might in fact be made. Lest we be charged with underestimating the merits of seeing science in terms of consumer choice, we propose here to give Pragmatism more rope. After all, scientists do often weigh the effects of different ways of dealing with recalcitrant experience. Let us see what might be involved.

A choice needs a chooser. The chooser needs authority, otherwise the same scientific statement can be true for you and false for me. To preserve 'objectivity' (or at least consensus), someone has to be entitled to choose for all of us. Who? The obvious answer is that the right to choose lies with the scientific community in question or with its accredited representatives. But, although many pragmatists commonly give this answer, it conflicts with a central tenet of pragmatism. As Quine says, knowledge forms a seamless whole and 'boundaries of disiplines are matters for deans'. Even if the existing fabric is more densely knit in some places than in others, lines of demarcation are finally arbitrary. So there is, in principle, no 'scientific community in question' with the right to decide matters which are everybody's business. Besides, an expert within a field is not automatically entitled to umpire interdisciplinary disputes, and plenty of important questions transcend the boundaries of disciplines.

So how are umpires best chosen? As in the Supreme Court, different umpires have different tendencies and the choice of the 'best' ones cannot be wholly dispassionate. So 'best' is presumably to be defined pragmatically in terms of our goals. Hence some have argued that science and, indeed, epistemology rest finally on ethics, since selection of goals necessarily involves ethics.[11] But, whether the final test is ethical or merely expedient, there has to be some choice of goals, otherwise the statement that human beings have specified goals will not be revisable. Nor can one of our ultimate goals be the pursuit of objective truth, since according to Pragmatism, truth is not objective and cannot be objectively pursued. Besides different groups have different ends and to speak of 'our' goals, without first deciding who 'we' are would beg the question at issue. Also different methods of voting will produce different umpires or even (granted the existence of familiar voting paradoxes) none at all. So the choice of umpires must be finally irrational.

Let us assume, however, for purposes of argument, that the preferences of the intellectual community are given and that we have umpires, who are to apply those preferences and produce optimal revisions with the help of modern decision theory. (The assumption seems to us mischievous and wholly illegitimate both here and in political theory and economics generally but it is commonly made on weighty authority.) Although no one has ever tried to draw an indifference map for an intellectual community, Pragmatists are committed to believing it possible, with the usual proviso that the map need not show how choices are actually made, so long as it shows the results. The question then becomes whether decision theory can provide a method of determining what revisions to make when experience conflicts with expectation.

There are many models of choice and they do not give the same answers or even the same kinds of answer. We shall next examine three different ways of interpreting pragmatists' talk of choice, in order to show that, like so much in modern Pragmatism, it is little more than metaphor. The image shatters when it is rendered precise.

Neo-Classical consumer choice

Suppose that there are only two options in a particular test situation, revision of logic and revision of physics. To achieve a set level of explanatory satisfaction, we give up a mixture of logic and physics, with the restriction that logic is very dear to us and a great deal of physics should go first. The neo-Classical indifference curves might look as shown in Figure 21, where each curve represents a different level of explanatory satisfaction and the

---

[11] Cf. Morton White, *Toward Reunion in Philosophy* (Harvard University Press, 1956), where this view is explicit.

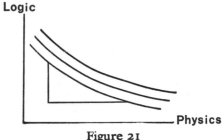

Figure 21

higher curves represent a higher level. The curves fall from left to right, are relatively flat and convex to the origin, showing that increasingly large advances in physics are needed to compensate for increasingly small sacrifices of logic. (We accept for the moment that the idea of comparison makes sense, appealing to the economist's stock defence that only ordinal comparisons are required.)

When experience and expectation conflict, revision occurs of logic or physics or both. If only logic is revised, the initial position in physics is preserved and *vice versa*. We can thus draw a line to represent the relation between logic and physics, assuming them logically independent (see Figure 22). The slope of the line shows the 'price' of physics in terms of logic, as determined in the particular test.

Next we bring prices and preferences together, superimposing the price line on the preference diagram (Figure 23). The optimal revision is determined by the point of tangency between the experimental price line and the highest explanatory satisfaction curve. A slightly different mixture would yield a lower level of satisfaction, in that it would mean shifting to a lower curve. The point of tangency uniquely determines the change in the accepted body of scientific doctrine following an unexpected experimental result. Its position will depend on the 'price' of P in terms of L for that experiment; the flatter the price line, the greater the cost of L and so the larger the element of P in the revision.

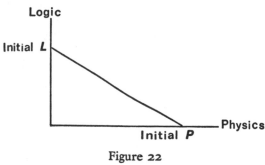

Figure 22

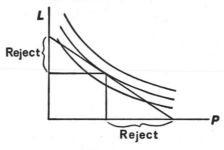

Figure 23

Readers, who are still following this exposition with straight faces, will have noted how sensitive the conclusions are to the assumptions. Suppose the assumption of convexity in the preference maps were dropped. Logic would be given up less readily than physics but at a constant rate, regardless of how much had been sacrificed already. There would be only three possibilities. If price and preference lines had the same slope, the result would be indeterminable; if the price line was steeper, only physics would be rejected; if it was flatter, only logic. In other words, very wide 'price' changes reflecting very different experimental results will have no effect on the revisions in the structure of knowledge. That would not accord with observation.

The consumer-choice model does at least yield a determinate result, given the community's preferences, and so frees us from any quirks of the umpire. But it would cease to do so, if the preference map and the price line are discontinuous or coincide over a relevant range. Neither convexity nor continuity is likely.

Other neo-Classical models

Alternatively, we can focus on the contribution in explanatory power made by various inputs, for example logic and physics, and construct a suitable 'explanation function'. As each input is increased, the contribution of a further addition tends to decline. Their prices are determined, as before, by experimentation. Sentences of each input will be revised in the light of experience up to the point where the marginal contribution, in terms of explanatory power, is just equal to its price, in terms of the explanatory power which the best alternative input would have produced.

Alternatively, we could try maximising explanatory power directly. When a revision is needed, we make the theory more general, so as to accommodate the new result, but giving up some simplicity and convenience,

166

for instance by allowing chance or exceptions or by altering boundaries between disciplines. We increase the generality of the entire structure of knowledge to the point where the additional explanatory power from the increased generality is just offset by the additional cost from the sacrifice of simplicity and convenience.

These ways of making the Pragmatist notion of choice precise are borrowed from the standard economists' tool chest. If they have an air of fantasy, it is because their assumptions are far-fetched and because there is no practical way of measuring 'more physics', 'explanatory power', 'increase in generality', 'loss of simplicity' and so forth. These common phrases do not lend themselves to measurement, even as far as a linear transformation. Nevertheless pragmatists should be willing to try.

Programming models

If the pragmatist goal is to maximise the generality of our structure of knowledge, subject to the multiple constraints of experience, we must be able to deal with more than one result at a time. Logic and physics contribute, but in different degrees, perhaps as shown in Figure 24, where a given amount of logic contributes as much generality as a much greater amount of physics. (The 'objective function' need not be linear – the lines could as well curve inwards.) Suppose there have been three major tests, each of whose results can be accommodated by some revision of logic or physics or both. The effects of the tests will normally overlap in part, in which case only the severest constraint on generality will be operative (Figure 25). The shaded region in Figure 25 represents the feasible set of combinations of logic and physics and the most generality will be achieved somewhere on its boundary. To find it, we put the two diagrams together (Figure 26): The maximum will be where a corner of the feasible region touches the highest line of the objective function. Hence the combination of logic and physics which meets the constraints of experience and achieves the highest level of generality is that shown as (P_m, L_m).

This interpretation is more promising. Convexity and continuity need not be assumed (although we shall not illustrate integer programming). Constraints can be multiple and there can be more than the two dimensions of logic and physics. But it does demand that logic and physics be measurable and it does assume that theorising has a single objective, like generality. (Other desiderata, like elegance, simplicity or teachability, can be added as constraints but cannot be treated as goals.)

Whatever the merits of borrowing models of neo-Classical consumer choice, producer choice or programming, we remain in the dark until told how to measure whatever we are talking about. Pragmatists especially can-

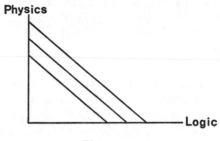

Figure 24

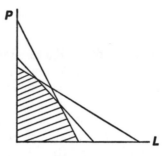

Figure 25

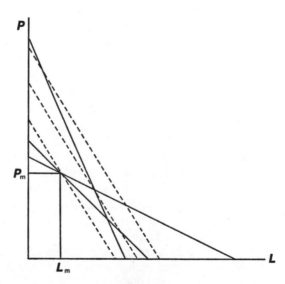

Figure 26

not depend on a theory which does not work in practice. Meanwhile, it is hardly likely that theoretical developments in intellectual fields can often be compared in terms of greater or less advance. To change a theory is not necessarily to add to it or subtract from it. As often as not, theories are replaced, refined, deepened, elaborated or reformulated in unquantifiable ways. Even if we waive these objections, however, a fatal dilemma still remains. Which of the various optimising models is the right one? If all are equally valid, then, since they give different results, the revisions validly made will depend on the model preferred. If only one is right, then how do we know which? To reply that one model is necessarily best is to establish a fixed point in the pragmatist world of universal choice and so to abandon Pragmatism. To reply that one model is most useful is to invite a query about the criteria of usefulness, which leads to a circle or a vicious regress. An appeal to some kind of scientific or humanist ethics shares the same fate. To hold that all models are equally valid is to generate all the original troubles afresh. Once again Pragmatism leads to romantic unreason.

We hope we have now paid out enough rope and that the pragmatist has duly hanged himself. Choice which includes choice of its own guidelines is the negation of science and of all systematic thought.

7

DEDUCTIVE EXPLANATION

Those who have handled sciences have been either men of experiment or men of dogmas. The men of experiment are like the ant, they only collect and use; the reasoners resemble spiders, who make cobwebs out of their substance. But the bee takes a middle course: it gathers the material from the flowers of the garden and of the field but transforms and digests it by a power of its own.

Francis Bacon, *First Book of Aphorisms*

Having failed to learn wisdom from the ant, we now turn to the spider and the bee. Bacon's bee is a charismatic insect and no doubt everybody's paradigm. But it must not be the excuse for begging the question and we do not yet know what the digestive 'power of its own' is, nor how it differs from 'making cobwebs out of their own substance'. Our suggestion is that its power comes from access to necessary truths, which pragmatists cannot abolish nor positivists explain away. These necessary truths are not purely logical. They introduce central concepts which define the subject and scope of theories and state equilibrium conditions which enable models to be solved. This is what we had in mind when proposing that explanation takes place when a conclusion is deduced from a sound and independent theory. So we shall start the present chapter by reflecting further on the nature of necessity and its role in rationalist theories of knowledge. Then we shall put forward our axiomatic model of explanation, claiming that it resolves the persistent puzzle of which generalisations are projectible. Then we shall focus on the application of theory to the world, arguing that economic variables need particular kinds of bearers. For neo-Classical economics, the bearers are households and firms and there are restrictions on how they can be characterised, arising from their need to be able to remain in existence over time. These restrictions will suggest a rudimentary production model, in which exchange is a logical consequence of interdependence in productive activities. The model will turn out to conflict with some basic neo-Classical assumptions and so prepare the ground for our Classical and Marxian rumblings in the final chapters.

Rationalist necessity

Our own view is that economic laws are 'necessities to which human action is subject' and we shall now present a rationalist interpretation of this ambiguous phrase.[1] Four senses of 'necessity' suggest themselves — mechanical, psychological, logical and conceptual — and we shall briefly distinguish the first three, in order to arrive at the fourth. Seventeenth-century rationalists were wont to think of the natural world as a perfectly programmed machine. Each state was the only possible outcome of the previous one, being brought about by the operation of iron causal laws in the previous conditions. These causal laws were determining and determinate *ab initio* and the course of history from the initial state of the universe was inevitable. To the scientist who understood all, each minute detail revealed the working of what later thinkers termed the Unseen Hand. Even if the initial state of the universe was not the only possible one and even if there might initially have been other laws (for instance an inverse cube law instead of an inverse square law), nevertheless, the machine once set in motion, only one continuation was possible. This is the mechanical thesis of iron determinism but, since no economist has held it (certainly not Marx, who is sometimes wilfully misunderstood to have done so), we hope to be excused from debating its merits.

The idea that economic laws state psychological necessities of human action has found more favour among economists. Indeed Utility Theory can be regarded as an expression of it, either as a quasi-empirical theory of basic human motives and drives or as an epistemological claim that economics rest on ultimate self-knowledge of human desires. Whether this sense of necessity is a rationalist one is a moot point, which we shall not pursue here, although more will be said in the appendix to the chapter. As has been made clear already, we do not believe that there can be a psychological solution to the problem of *a priori* knowledge.

Human action is, we agree, subject to logical necessities, since there is no way of actualising the impossible. But this commits us to little. If it is taken to mean that the course of history is not merely the only mechanically possible one but also the only logically possible one, then we disclaim all interest in any such Spinozist version of iron determinism. If it is taken to mean that our *a priori* knowledge is confined to knowledge of logical relations, then we reject that also, for reasons to be given presently. We

---

[1] The phrase is taken from Lionel Robbins' *Essay on the Nature and Significance of Economic Science*. Robbins' view will be discussed, in relation to Milton Friedman's, in the appendix to this chapter.

accept, however, that *ab imposse ad non esse valet consequentia*, a principle with implications to be exploited later.

Mechanical necessities are concrete; logical necessities are abstract. There is no defying the law of gravity and no escaping the law of non-contradiction but most will feel these laws to be inexorable in different ways. As it has sometimes been put, one is a law of nature, the other a law of thought. The distinction between nature and thought is easy to accept, even though hard to define or ultimately to justify, and we are content to rely on it in introducing conceptual necessity. By a conceptually necessary truth we mean a necessary truth in which some constants which do not belong to formal logic occur essentially. For instance it is necessarily true that 'if the elasticity of demand is greater than unity, then a reduction in the price of a good will lead to an increase in total expenditure on the good' and, *prima facie* at least, constants like 'price' occur essentially in it, without being logical constants. Such truths are analytic in the alternative sense of our previous chapter, namely true in consequence of the meanings of their terms, but, as we remarked then, calling them analytic is non-committal between rationalism and empiricism. For reasons to emerge in a moment, we shall call them conceptual, in that they rely on basic concepts under which an activity must fall, if it is to be correctly identified as theoretically significant activity. It is in this sense, we shall argue, that economic laws are necessities to which human action is subject.

Rationalism is often and too hastily equated with a strong form of determinism. This is a mistake. Spinoza is unusual among rationalists in maintaining that nothing in the past, present or future of the universe is contingent and most others have held, like Descartes or Leibniz, that the initial conditions and perhaps the laws of nature could have been otherwise, with a resulting rejection of fatalism or predestination. Admittedly it can be objected that these exceptions are either insufficient or inconsistent. But the objection, even if it holds (which Leibnizian scholars will recognise to be a tricky question), does not apply to conceptual necessities. Our own view is that there are genuinely contingent truths which cannot be proved (except with the aid of contingent premises) in a complete theory of phenomena. We shall contend that a sound theory is a system of necessary truths, whose application is a contingent matter. For example, there do not have to be households and firms but, if there are, they must have certain properties in order to be bearers of certain economic variables. Statements of the conditions of application for economic theories are necessary, as are statements of compatibility and incompatibility among economic predicates. But statements of what economic agents there are and of what they will in fact do are contingent. We are thus not committed to a strong form of determinism. Indeed we are less committed than those many empiricists who have held that everything happens predictably according to a pattern of cause and effect, hoping that substitution of regularity for necessity in the analysis of cause will allow free choice to coexist with order in the natural and social world.

It is not always easy to determine whether a truth is necessary or contingent and one task of logic and theory is to reveal latent implications. Consequently truths which look contingent may turn out to be necessary — a fact which will be important when we discuss the application of theory. Rationalists have sometimes expressed this by distinguishing contingent knowledge from contingent truth, in order to point out that one can have contingent knowledge of a necessary truth. For instance, if a man happens to know two Greeks with the same number of Greek relatives, then he happens to know that at least two Greeks have the same number of Greek relatives. But so far he knows it only contingently or *a posteriori*. When he can prove that at least two Greeks have the same number of Greek relatives, however, he knows it *a priori*.[2] Similarly mathematics is rich in conjectures some of which have yet to be proved. We shall contend that the theoretician's task of finding latent proofs for apparently contingent connections is an exercise in scientific explanation.

We now owe the reader a definition of 'necessary', as it occurs in terms like 'necessary truth' or 'conceptually necessary truth'. But, although the last chapter has shown what we do not mean by it, the term cannot be defined, for the reasons Quine uses against conventionalism. For instance '"P" is necessarily true $=$ *df* "Not-P" is contradictory' leaves 'contradictory' undefined and an excursion into the family circle in order to define 'contradictory' will lead us finally back to 'necessary' again. Besides, it is misleading to define a necessary truth as one whose denial is contradictory as this suggests that the truth is necessary *because* its denial is contradictory. In fact, however, the relation is the other way and the denial is contradictory because the truth is necessary. Similarly a theorem is not true *because* it can be proved: it can be proved because it is true. Proof is a heuristic device and not a statement of the grounds of truth. Quine's own conclusion is that no term from the circle makes sense, unless 'necessary' and 'contingent' truths differ only in their degree of 'entrenchment' in our conceptual scheme' but this doctrine has already turned out to reduce all enquiry to chaos. We ourselves conclude that some term needs to be understood *a priori* without definition, agreeing with Quine that this conclusion is not

---

[2] Let there be n Greeks. If all are to have a different number of Greek relatives, then they have 0, 1, 2, ..., $n - 2$, $n - 1$ respectively. But if any of them has $n - 1$ Greek relatives then no one has 0. Hence at least two Greeks have the same number of Greek relatives.

open to empiricists. We shall take 'necessary' as undefined and define 'impossible as 'necessarily not' and 'contingent' as 'neither necessary nor impossible'.

Faced with our refusal to define a crucial basic term someone may protest that all traditional distinctions between 'necessary' and 'contingent' are incomprehensible. If so, he is certainly wrong! He cannot mean merely that he happens not to understand any, as that shows only his dimness of wit. He cannot mean that no one happens to understand any, since he must be willing to argue with those who think they do. So he must mean and be ready to prove that any distinction is incoherent. His proof would need premisses which entailed its conclusion and so take the form 'Necessarily (if P, then not-Q)'. Consequently it would be self-refuting and the distinction cannot be proved incoherent. To grasp the notion of proof, he must understand the notion of necessity and, indeed, understand it *a priori*. So there are truths, which are necessary in some sense of that term and we must next explore the ground of the necessity, to show how theory contributes to scientific explanation in general and how necessity enters into economic theory in particular.

Our coyness about 'necessity' extends only to defining it. We accept as a criterion that a truth is necessary if its denial is contradictory (or provable from truths whose denial is contradictory) and we accept that logical truths are instances. We are thus content with the usual assortment of examples — truths of logic, of pure mathematics and of other formal systems, like graph theory, kinship algebra or Classical-Marxian economics, and, presumably, of epistemology. But it is important to notice that the exact import of calling such truths 'necessary' is elusive. Theorems of logic are provable, in that their denial contradicts axioms of logic and so may be said to provide the clearest case. But this is sufficient to show the theorems of logic *true* only if the axioms are themselves necessarily true and, as we shall suggest presently, to say that the axioms of logic conform to the axioms of logic is not precisely to say that they are necessary truths. In other words even purely logical truths can be deemed to involve a conceptual element, in the sense that the notion of necessity seems to have to be presupposed in explaining why conformity with the axioms of logic is intellectually significant. A purely logical truth, then, is one whose denial contradicts the axioms of logic and what makes it purely logical is that the only constants occurring essentially in it are logical constants, for instance 'if two statements are not both true and one is true, then the other is false'. There is current dispute about which constants are purely logical constants; but there is at least a *prima facie* case for holding that the theorems of, say, Classical-Marxian economics contain essential constants like 'capital' which are not purely logical constants. In this case proof of their necessity depends partly on the laws of logic and partly on the truth of axioms containing non-logical constants. Having rejected mechanical or psychological accounts of *a priori* necessity and having denied that necessary truths are true by convention, therefore, we are still left with two tasks. One is to show that there are indeed necessary truths in which non-logical constants occur essentially. The other is to show that such truths can be explanatory of actual phenomena. We shall tackle the latter task first, by reminding the reader of how we came to make this claim and then introducing a model which can be deemed explanatory, provided we can perform the former task.

The need for a rationalist account of *a priori* knowledge arose from the snags of empiricist models of explanation. To recapitulate briefly, if any hypothesis is to have any probability whatever, we must know when we are warranted in projecting a correlation and must know when failure of prediction is to be blamed on the hypothesis and not on the *ceteris paribus* conditions or on the adjustments made to observed data. This requires a solution to the riddle of Induction — not merely a philosophers' conundrum, since as we shall show, the exact form of the solution will affect the strategy of economics, where, in any case, direct projections from past experience are unreliable. We expressed what we believe is wanted in the slogan that a hypothesis is strengthened by being deduced from a sound theory, arguing that the soundness of a theory is partly a matter of the truth of its definitions and axioms. It is here, we claim, that necessity comes in. So we shall next outline our model of what we call 'deductive explanation' and then discuss the role of definitions and axioms.

Rationalist explanation

'Black box' problems and exercises in elementary mechanics provide a starting illustration. One way to discover the capacities of a machine is to try all possible stimuli and note the results. If the machine is simple, an exhaustive account of it can be found in this way. If it is complex, the enquirer will have to pause presently and make a logical model, which shows what stimulus is bound to provoke what response, provided the model is accurate. Elementary examples are to be found in school mechanics textbooks, where a problem is set, say about the fate of a fly strolling on a revolving cylinder, and the answer shows what is bound to happen, if the conditions are fulfilled. That those conditions were fulfilled is the cause of the fate of the fly and the proof of the answer explains why. Schematically, the strategy for dealing with complex machines is to find a statement of the form:

$$T \rightarrow ((C \text{ and } \textit{ceteris paribus}) \rightarrow (S \rightarrow R))$$

where T is a statement of the theory or model
C is a statement of the initial conditions (true rather than observed, values of variables being given)
S is a statement of the stimulus (action or event)
R is a statement of the outcome.

The connections are logical and the formula is more than a statement of what has so far been observed. S explains R, in the sense that S can be proved, given T, C and *ceteris paribus*, to imply R. The model is not sound merely because S is regularly connected with R (nor unsound merely because the correlation is imperfect) and theory makes its own contribution by guaranteeing that the connection is significant (and specifying when tests of it are decisive).

The schema just given is very general and holds for several kinds of model, three of which we shall now distinguish. Let us call them 'production models', 'programming models' and 'prediction models'. The function of a *production* model is to assemble all the interrelations and interdependencies among production activities (discussed at the end of Chapter 5) and thence to calculate the conditions which must be met, if the system is to reproduce itself exactly. In terms of our explanatory schema T is the theory of production (including any required mathematics), C is the set of input—output coefficients, S is the activities of producing and using up materials, time and energy and R represents the exchanges and distribution of output needed, if the system is to repeat the process.

Secondly, a *programming* model is designed to guide and improve performance. Our schema again applies, for instance to the diet problem of Chapter 5: T is linear programming theory, C comprises the set of nutritional coefficients and of prices, S is the objective of cheapest diet meeting stated constraints and R is the calculated diet. (Alternatively, the objective can be treated as part of T and S regarded solely as sets of constraints, to give corresponding sets of diets for R.)

Thirdly, a *prediction* model shows what will probably happen, for example the Keynesian one in our previous chapter: T is Keynesian theory, C the set of parameters t, a, n, m, and so on, S represents an exogenous change, say in exports or government spending ΔG and R is then the resulting change in income ΔY. Thus a production model gives conditions for the system to continue, a programming model shows how to improve performance and a prediction model forecasts whether the conditions will in fact be met or the improvement be forthcoming.

Now let us focus attention on the role of T in the schema. Earlier, in order to meet difficulties in the empiricist's accounts of explanation, we promised to make the soundness of theory depend partly on the truth of its definitions and axioms. These definitions and axioms, we shall maintain, serve to state the properties which a thing or activity must have if it is to fall under the essential concepts of the theory and if it is to continue in being as a thing or activity so classified. A production model, from this point of view, defines part of the essence of the social order by stating what has to be true of any system which can maintain itself through production. The 'real definition' of production will turn out to be the basis of a general theory of production and the necessity we have in mind is a conceptual one with actual implications for whatever comes within the scope of the theory. To clear the ground for this thesis, we turn next to the nature of definitions and their place in theories, in an attempt to show that there are indeed necessary truths in which non-logical constants occur essentially.

Real definitions

Honest definitions are, from an empiricist point of view, of two sorts, lexical and stipulative. Lexical definitions report usage, for instance 'Utility = personal convenience or profit', 'Inflation = increase beyond proper limits esp. of prices etc.' (from the *Oxford English Dictionary*) or '*Equilibrium s. das Gleichgewicht*' (from Cassell's *English–German Dictionary*). Stipulative definitions introduce a term by specifying what it will be used to mean. ('When I use a word', Humpty Dumpty said in a rather scornful tone, 'it means just what I choose it to mean — neither more nor less'). These are the only honest kinds, although there are some hybrids, like 'precising definitions', which stipulate an exact sense for a word already in use. Lexical definitions are true or false but only insofar as they correctly report what the usage of a word happens to be. Stipulation is an act of choice and so can seem to create truth, but only insofar as we are willing to accept that truth can arise from convention.

Dishonest definitions are typically 'persuasive', in that empiricists see them as rhetorical tricks for changing descriptive meaning, while preserving emotive force. ('True temperance is a bottle of claret with each meal and three double whiskies after dinner', remarks a character in Huxley's *Eyeless in Gaza*.) However sonorously proclaimed on whatever authority, they are always mischievous. They seem to reveal the true meaning of terms like 'Justice', 'Obligation', 'Utility' or 'Value', whereas, to empiricist eyes, there is no such thing.

This view is less than compelling. We already have reason to doubt that truth can arise from convention or, at least, that conventionalism can account for all necessary truths; and lexical truths are presumably contingent. So there will be some statements which a logical positivist regards as analytic truths, because he can deduce them from definitions used as axioms but which now turn out not to be truths at all, because, to detach an analytic conclusion from an inference, we need analytically true premisses. All mathematical or econometric theorems will be examples. Moreover, when it comes to justifying the view, we are presumably being offered a definition of 'definition'. Whichever category of definition the definition 'All definitions are generically lexical, stipulative or persuasive' falls in, we need not accept it as of any epistemological worth. Indeed, it would not be even a possible epistemological thesis, unless it were neither lexical nor stipulative nor persuasive. The view is both inconvenient and self-refuting.

A contrary opinion with a long pedigree is that there are 'real' definitions, which capture the essence of the thing defined. When Socrates asks what Justice is, or Courage, or Knowledge, he wants a true answer but not a lexical or stipulative one. His method is to reject a series of attempted definitions of the form '$X = \text{df } Y$', on the grounds that 'Courage', for instance, is not to be equated with standing one's ground when attacked, since guerillas are often brave and rarely stand their ground. It is doing what one is afraid to do. A thing's essence is those properties without which the thing could not be the thing it is; or, to anticipate our discussion of production, what it must have, if it is to continue to exist. So, the essence will be the properties a thing has to have if the concept of that kind of thing is to apply to it. A concept's essence is a statement of the predicates which must apply to anything falling under the concept.

Real definitions loom large in the Rationalism sketched earlier, as soon as an attempt is made to express or enlarge our knowledge by means of an axiomatic system. In *Leviathan* Hobbes undertakes to deduce the best way to organise a state from a real definition of Man as a system of matter in motion, driven by a desire for power. In the *Ethics* Spinoza proposes a universal science, resting partly on a real definition of 'Substance' as 'That of which a conception can be formed independently of any other conception'. The need for them is the need for any axiomatic system to have premisses which, although unproved within the system, count as truths, in order to demonstrate that theorems derived not only follow but also are true.[3]

---

[3] Cf. Irving Copi, Essence and accident, in M. J. Loux (ed.), *Universals and Particulars* Doubleday, 1970), for a further account of this view of science.

When (or if) all knowledge and science are finally embodied in a single system, there will have to be premisses which are absolutely unprovable but true. Let us call premisses known without proof or evidence 'self-evident'. The need for self-evident truths is not a rationalist idiosyncracy. As we saw earlier, empiricists too have often insisted on such 'foundations of knowledge' and made some of the same claims for sense-datum statements or protocol sentences, which rationalists make for real definitions. If our objections to Pragmatism are sound, the need for foundations is genuine. If our objections to Positivism are sound, we need rationalist foundations.

This claim would be easily deflated, if the only self-evident necessary truths were logical definitions and axioms. In the last chapter we aired the suggestion that all necessary truths were either logical primitives or deducible from logical primitives by logical rules alone and promised to raise objections, which we shall now do. For, while the existence of some self-evident logical truths is enough to embarrass empiricists, we wish to claim that there are also real definitions of non-logical concepts and that these are significant for empirical enquiry.

What distinguishes one formal system from another? Why do we regard kinship algebra and marginalist micro-economics as different? What makes algebra and geometry different but still both branches of mathematics? We have no quarrel with the usual answer, that distinct systems are got by adding suitable special axioms to logic and basic mathematics, the latter itself being got in the same way from logic. Euclid's axioms, for instance, mark out a geometry by introducing a concept of a plane into basic mathematics. If, as Descartes puts it, 'the whole of philosophy is like a tree whose roots are metaphysics, whose trunk is physics and whose branches are the particular sciences', then real definitions occur at the forks. A geometry, for instance, consists of all implications of a set of axioms, which include real definitions of whatever terms are necessary for the system to be a geometry. Such terms do not belong to logic but, like logical constants, they are essential to the truth of some necessarily true statements.

If all formal systems reduced to logic, there would be no real definitions of non-logical terms. We shall not rehearse here the highly technical reasons which have led to the general rejection of formalism (or logicism); but shall instead rely on a simpler, if less powerful, argument.[4] An axiom is an unproved premiss containing defined or undefined terms and a definition defines one terms by means of others. So, if we take all the terms in the axioms and definitions of a system S, we get a list whose members are un-

---

[4] A. Pap, *Semantics and Necessary Truth*, Ch. 5, to which we referred earlier, contains a masterly discussion of this and related topics and commands our complete assent.

defined or interdefined. We can then ask what system S is. Is it the propositional Calculus, Euclidean geometry or micro-economic theory, for example? To answer, we must know that the terms of S are, say, micro-economic terms. But how do we know that? It cannot be merely because the list contains 'cost', 'revenue', 'output', 'price', 'profit' and 'income'. For these are merely ink marks in the first instance and their claim to express economic concepts depends on their having the sense they bear in micro-economics. Yet inter-definition does not by itself secure them that sense. If we invent the words 'tosc', 'uneever', 'utotup', 'cripe', 'fortip' and 'monice' and then interdefine them with a flourish, we shall not yet have expressed any concept at all. There have to be some key terms, say 'production' or 'exchange', which are understood *a priori* and then introduced in real definitions, which express that *a priori* understanding. They serve to specify what sort of system S is and also state a condition for the applicability of predicates from S to the world. To repeat, we regard Quine's pragmatist 'family circle' objection to Logical Positivism, cited in the previous chapter, as wholly sound and unanswerable within empiricism. Rejecting pragmatism, we turn to rationalism to explain how theoretical understanding is possible. Economics is not what economists do but what they ought to do.

We maintain that there are necessary truths in which non-logical (in this case economic) constants occur essentially. An opponent must retort either that truths of economic theory are, appearances notwithstanding, contingent or that the apparent non-logical constants are eliminable and so not essential or that constants like 'utility' or 'exchange' (depending on the theory deemed to be basic) are after all logical constants. We reject all three lines. We have argued extensively that economic theory cannot consist solely of facts and hypotheses and so that its statements cannot all be contingent. Secondly at the end of Chapter 3 we tried to express the Law of Diminishing Marginal Utility wholly as a functional relationship between variables without success and, even so, found that there were still covert non-logical constants left in the formulation, whose progressive removal would make the formula progressively less usable. The moral of this seems to us a general one. Furthermore, even if a logically pure version were possible (suggesting that the Law of Diminishing Marginal Utility is therefore a substitution instance of some more general logical truth), the statements, stating which economic terms were to be formalised with the aid of which logical terms, would themselves be required premises of complete proofs in economic-cum-logical theory and so be themselves necessary truths in which non-logical constants occurred essentially. Thirdly, an opponent is welcome to say flatly that the constants of economic theory are already logical constants, since this renders his position vacuous.

Waiving the evident snags of treating terms like 'utility' or 'exchange' as on a par with terms like 'not', 'or', 'all', we are happy to have our own view supported under any name. Admittedly these replies do not do justice to the subtleties of formalism but we prefer not to tax the patience of our economist readers by a full-dress discussion.

The need for real definitions to act as unproved premises is a particular case of the need for true axioms. Since inference only transmits truth (or, to be exact, knowledge of truth), without true axioms, theorems cannot be proved true. Without necessarily true axioms, theorems cannot be proved necessarily true. Since true conditional statements of the form 'If axiom A is true, then theorem T is true' are necessarily true, there have to be necessarily true axioms somewhere. This finding is reinforced by our quarrels with Positivism in Chapter 4, where we argued that a system all of whose premises or assumptions were contingent could not be applied to the world, since it could always be asked how we know that a given theoretical term applies to a given particular phenomenon. The positivist retort was to appeal to pure, uninterpreted, indisputable, atomic facts or self-evidently veridical observations. But there turned out to be no suitable atomic facts. Pragmatism, recognising this, tried to manage without any fixed basis at all but intellectual chaos resulted and we now conclude that we need necessary truths as a basis. If economists want to criticise and recommend policies on theoretical grounds, there will have to be necessarily true axioms and definitions in economics.

Are our 'axioms' what are usually called 'assumptions'? In the sense of being unproved premises, they are. But to assume a premiss is to assume it true. Until its truth is established, conclusions from it are conditional. We see a need to be able to justify assumptions (or to 'discharge' them, as logicians term it). *Ex hypothesei* this cannot be done by proof or evidence. So we are at an impasse, unless we take a theory of knowledge which admits the existence of self-evident necessary truths. By a 'sound theory' we mean a set of *true* axioms, including *real* definitions and their logical consequences. What theory it is depends on which concepts are understood *a priori* and expressed in the definitions.

Stipulative definitions can be easily coined and postulates lightly assumed. But real definitions must be right and axioms must be true. 'Self-evidence' is therefore a strictly epistemological and not psychological notion. It is to be construed as 'known without proof or evidence' and not as 'obviously true at a glance'. Axioms come first in the final statement of a sound theory but for heuristic purposes, approximations or conjectures will be needed, until it is finally clear what has been presupposed all along. We have not conjured away the problem of knowing when a theory is sound and must now return to the interpretation of recalcitrant experience.

Testing rationalist theory

Suppose we have assembled a theory, whose implications conflict with the facts. To put it formally suppose we have:

(1) A (i.e. a statement of the axioms)
(2) $A \longrightarrow T$ (i.e. 'If the axioms are true, then so is the theory)
(3) $T \longrightarrow ((C$ and *ceteris paribus*$) \longrightarrow (S_j \longrightarrow R_j))$
(4) C and *ceteris paribus* and S_j
(5) Not-R_j

If any four are true, the other is false; but 'Not R_j' does not disprove any particular one of the others and 'S_j and R_j' does not prove the soundness of the theory. So how do we set about establishing (1)–(4)?

(2) and (3) raise only the problems of checking that an inference is indeed valid. Admittedly this can be tricky but, in principle, any chain of inference can be analysed into simple links and a process of wholly formal and abstract reasoning should suffice. We therefore take the problem to concern (1) and (4). Let us start by recalling the distinction between production, programming and prediction models, for the problem is different in each case. The familiar questions arise only with the last, so let us look at the others first. Consider a production model (we will examine one shortly) showing the conditions which must be met for smooth and exact reproduction of a set of activities. According to the present formula, T represents the theory of production, C the input-output and other coefficients, S the conclusion of production, and R the final exchange ratios. Suppose the theory is sound, the coefficients well-established, and the period of production observably at an end. What then, would 'not-R' mean? If it means that the exchange ratios R are not in fact established, nothing follows, for the theory never said they would be. The theory *proved* that those exchange ratios were *necessary* for exact reproduction, but, of course, reproduction might not take place. But if not-R means either that a different set of exchanges takes place with exact reproduction, or that the computed set is established without reproduction occurring, then either the conditions C or the evidence for not-R must be rejected. For proofs prove; it is impossible for T, C and *cet. par.*, and S to hold without entailing R, as just interpreted.

Now consider the programming model in Chapter 5: given the objective to obtain the cheapest diet satisfying the nutritional constraints, and given those prices, 100 units of number 4 and 300 units of 5 is the best shopping list. Again what could not-R mean? If it means that the agent on whose behalf it was calculated does not, in fact, follow this advice, then so much the worse for the agent. Either he has not given us all the relevant data or he is a fool. But the problem as formulated is completely solved and the calculated budget is necessarily the best. If someone claims empirically to have found a cheaper budget, satisfying the conditions of the problem, either the original data or the claim must be rejected.

In each case the theory, together with the conditions, is unambiguously sufficient to generate the conclusion, which may therefore be used to interpret and criticise reality. The theory is a blueprint, to which reality can be adapted, or by means of which it can be understood and altered or improved. The theory and the conditions together imply *a story in logical time*, namely '*S* implies *R*', which provides a map for the agents to follow through historical time.

This will serve to indicate the problem of predicting. A prediction model is supposed to generate conclusions in historical time from a theory operating in logical time. The difficulty is simple; short of a theory of complete historical determinism, no set of economic conditions and theories can be sufficient to entail any economic conclusion in historical time, at least no conclusion of the sort we ordinarily consider. The reasons are those we gave at the end of Chapter 5. To introduce an activity into a model is to treat it as a 'performance'; the activity must be represented by a variable, whose values are numbers. The activity of buying shoes with all its dithering and indicision is finally reduced to the variable, 'quantity of shoes'. The relations of this variable to others are those and only those specified in the model. But in reality we may forget, change our minds, develop a craze for bare feet, in the middle of carrying out our normal pattern of purchases. History is open, at least until proved closed. Our actual economic activities are 'productions', not 'performances'; they take time, require repeated decisions and must be brought to successful conclusions. 'Performances', in fact, are designations of the successful completions of productions. Thus a model whose variables designate performances begs the issues of perseverance and success.

Yet prediction models are not therefore worthless. For instance, suppose that the Keynesian model of Chapter 6 incorrectly predicted the change in Y consequent upon a certain change in G, where it was reliably known that the model applied, that all chains of inference were correct, and that the basic coefficients were right. Faced with the failure of prediction, the theorist must first decide whether the recalcitrance of reality is, so to speak, structural or accidental. (In a changing world this may not be a clear-cut distinction.) If structural, this means that one or more significant variables have been left out, or some key relationships mis-specified. If accidental, some unexpected or non-economic event supervened; for example a major political upset caused panic, the outbreak of war caused hoarding, or some crucially placed individual behaved foolishly. The way to find out is to trace the increment of government spending in detail through the channels of circulation, as it re-appears as income and is respent. It may then emerge that the particular form of additional government spending, say for bombs for Vietnam, required a steep rise in imports. Thus, one of the variables, M, should have been written as a function of the composition of G. The model was mis-specified.[5] Or it may emerge that the increase in G was channelled primarily to one large Texan defence contractor, whose chief financial officer found it convenient to use the proceeds to restore the funds he had rifled from the company's till. Thus, due to somewhat unpredictable though hardly non-economic, human proclivities, liquidity rather than income will be increased. (The example is a caution: one should never conclude that because we are dealing with macro-economic questions individual human error will 'cancel out'.)

We may find that new variables have emerged, we may find changing or developing relationships, or we may find any combination of a myriad idiosyncratic particular and accidental causes. The failure of a prediction is an important occasion for checking the working of a model against the sequence of economic events in historical time. But it does not follow that because a prediction went wrong the model must be changed. Nor does it follow that because the prediction is wrong the corresponding explanation is invalid. If we were asked to explain the observed change in income, the correct explanation would be the increase in G, together with the theory of the multiplier, *modified* by the accidental factors already discussed. But the basic explanation, providing an understanding of the mechanism by which the increase in income takes place, is still the theory of the multiplier. The theory explains *increases in income* and so explains this particular increase in income. But 'increases in income' take place in logical time, whereas any particular increase actually happens in historical time. The explanation of any particular event must therefore be an historical explanation, taking full account of all the irrelevances and peculiarities involved in the specific incident.

The explanation of a kind of event, therefore stands on the same footing with the conditions for reproduction or of optimising, and the formula given above applies to it as well as to them. But prediction and the explanation of specific, historical events both involve the additional step of moving from logical to historical time, from idea to reality.

Chess again

We may develop these points by returning to the analogy with chess we drew in the appendix to Chapter 3. Not only is this analogy of some interest

---

[5] Not necessarily, however. The rise in imports may have been occasioned by a once-for-all shortage, the result of accidental non-economic factors. It would then be wrong to change the model.

in philosophical terms, but it also shows that our approach can deal with the problem of competition, winning and losing. A theory of chess shows how to maximise positional advantage in a situation analysed in terms of concepts like 'force', 'space' and 'time'. Suppose we have a well-articulated theory, which fails to win games for its proponents. Are its concepts at fault or is it being misapplied? To decide, we need some notion, like the power or usefulness of a piece on a given square in a type of situation, which is not defined in terms of the concepts under examination and which can be assigned different values. We then need a rival theory which assigns different values to the pieces in the same situation. We then await the results of playing a large number of games according to each theory. The greater the success, the likelier it is that the value of the pieces is as the successful theory implies. For success justifies the claim that previous moves were played for a good reason and gives us a *prima facie* ground for concluding that the original theory was properly applied but had the wrong concepts. Before passing judgement, however, we compare the two sets of axioms. If the old axioms turn out to entail the new, it then becomes more likely that the old theory was misapplied. Otherwise the other conclusion can stand.

This is an experimental process of seeking the balance of probability. But the sense of 'experiment' is a mathematical one and the probability is a function of ignorance. We have been describing the process of testing a promising conjecture which cannot yet be proved or disproved. For instance, the four-colour theorem, that four colours are enough to colour any map drawn on the surface of a sphere so that no two regions of the same colour are touching, is likely to be true. The evidence is partly systematic failure to find a map needing five colours and partly proofs of simpler related theorems. But 'likely to be true' means 'likely to be finally deducible within a sound theory', presumably an extended topology. The process is an empirical one of testing ahead of an advancing army of proofs and the testing, which made no sense in its earlier Positivist context, is a process of conjecture.

It is important to our account that the models or theories to be tested are standardly programming or maximising ones. The sort of theory of chess we have in mind does not predict what players will play but, rather, tells them how to play better. It is still predictive but only with the extra condition that the model's advice will actually be taken and, even so, does not predict an exact course of events. To illustrate the point from chess once more, let us suppose that in some game white has just reached the position shown in Figure 27. Prospects do not look very bright; if white stops the black pawn from queening, he loses his pawn on g6 and the game. However:

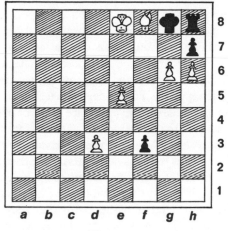

Figure 27

White	*Black*
1. Pawn to *g7*.	1. Pawn to *f2*.
2. Bishop to *e7*.	2. Pawn to *f1* (= Q).
(not 2. P takes R (= Q) ch., K takes Q.	
3. K to *f7*, P to *f1* (= Q) ch., and black wins.)	
3. Bishop to *f6*.	3. Queen takes bishop.
4. Pawn takes rook (= Q) ch.	4. Queen takes queen.
(not 4. P takes Q, stalemate.)	
5. Pawn to *d4* and wins very neatly.[6]	

The analysis guarantees white a win. Even if he spots it and decides to follow it, there is still no prediction of what he will actually play after the first move, since that depends on what black plays. Instead it gives him replies to black's possible moves. It predicts a win but not a particular win. Moreover the statement of the analysis is a set of conditional truths which are necessarily true and also informative about the facts of the situation. Finally it shows why 1. Pawn to *g7* is a good move and explains why white, if he has grasped the point, plays it.

Similarly, in economic policy, a government or firm can in principle know what state or sort of state they will reach, without knowing how they will get there, provided they are ready with replies to intermediate responses.

[6] A pretty study by A. P. Gulayev, 1940. Experienced players will no doubt forgive our invented notation, which is intended to guide the novice.

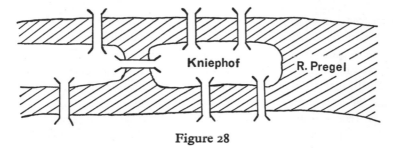

Figure 28

Just as most players would lose or draw the game from the position just given, so the government can fail, if it is short on theory or makes a mistake. But, of necessity, if the theory is sound and applied correctly, the results will be as predicted.

This also illustrates our earlier point that necessary truths are not always known to be necessary and, in the absence of proof, may be taken as contingent. (This contrasts sharply with the, we hope, by now discredited doctrine that analytic truths lack all factual content and are not informative.) From the fact that a man knows a statement on empirical grounds, it does not follow that the statement is not true of necessity. Statements cannot be both necessary and contingent (as defined above) and they cannot be both contingent and provable. But we see no reason why they should not be both known *a posteriori* and necessary. For instance, the inhabitants of Königsberg were not in doubt that there was no way to stroll across each of the town's seven bridges just once (Figure 28). But they did not know that it was logically impossible to do so, until Euler proved it. Euler explained why no stroller had crossed each bridge just once, by producing a theory with that as a consequence.

We contend, then, that to explain an event is to find another to count as its cause, so that, when the two events are described in theoretical terms, that the explanandum occurred is deducible from a statement of theory, conditions, *ceteris paribus* and explanans. As the example of chess and the remarks about prediction show, there is no conflict with the notion of agency or free choice. A rationalist view of *a priori* knowledge does not commit us to any form of iron determinism.

The essential concepts of economics

That completes our suggestion for a deductive model of explanation and so ends the mainly epistemological phase of the argument. We have committed ourselves to the existence of necessary truths in which non-logical constants occur essentially and so to the claim that at least some theories rest on true axioms embodying real definitions. We have argued that the fall of Positivism brings Positive economics down with it, leaving neo-Classicism open to charges of unrealism and distortion. (Two examples were given in Chapter 5 – that a realistic account of consumer choice conflicted with orthodox demand theory and, more generally, that a realistic account of action must concern itself with productions, whereas neo-Classical theory dealt with performances.) Now we have taken a further step. If theories are to rest on true axioms and real definitions, then a charge of unrealism must be taken seriously. When Joan Robinson argues that 'Capital' is being defined incorrectly or Pasinetti claims that the principle of scarcity cannot apply to capital, there is no longer a philosophical reason to evade a direct reply. This is not to say that any complete realism is required (or even possible). Our argument in effect distinguishes between essential and incidental. For example, theories should, in our view, reflect the fact that information is imperfect, not because it happens to be imperfect but because, as we shall show later, no market could function if information were perfect. Theoretical concepts must incorporate the essential aspects of the phenomena they cover; and theories must comprise relations between these essential concepts. But we have yet to say which we take the essential concepts of economic theory to be and, although we shall risk doing so, we foresee an objection that this is none of our philosophical business. If the objection is sound, then the book must rest with what we have said about the roles of production, programming and prediction models and so, indeed, amounts to a kind of back-handed defence of Rational Economic Man as an ideal programmer instead of as the target of prediction.[7] However, it is our hope that our philosophical impetus will carry us further and that what has been said about criteria of application leads on to a realisation that the concept of Production is the essential one. At any rate we still have some unresolved questions about the range of a theory's application which beckon us beyond the analogy with chess and we shall now embark on the promised deployment of a rudimentary production model.

Whereas the terms of chess, like 'bishop' or 'knight' apply to any bit of wood or stone which is made to obey the relevant rules (or to nothing physical at all, when the game is played in one's head), social agents and institutions need material support. Although bishops of the church and knights baronet owe their identity, like chessmen, to observance of rules and roles, they depend also on the maintenance of church or feudal system. The dependence is partly physical but also conceptual. This assertion will

---

[7] Hollis sees more force in the objection than Nell does but, since he takes the relation of epistemology to economic theory to be, in general, what we claim it is, puts any hesitations about the transition down to his lack of economic sophistication.

188

seem trite to some readers and misguided to others and we shall try to show next how the material conditions for the continued existence of a social system provide necessary criteria of application for economic terms. In doing so, we shall explain why we say that economic variables need particular kinds of bearers, and make good our allegation that the conditions of application of any sound economic theory conflict with some crucial assumptions of neo-Classical economics. What, then, is involved in applying a theory to a social and economic system?

To speak more precisely than before, let us agree to take 'law' in its Positivist sense as a functional relation between variables. As, for example, with the Law of Diminishing Returns the relation shows how one variable moves as others vary, without saying anything about whatever the variables apply to. So let us take 'model' as a set of laws, all the values of whose variables are determined, and 'theory' as a model, whose scope and conditions of application are precisely known. A theory is thus a model, the *bearers* of whose variables and the conditions under which they have the variables are precisely specified. (We here recall a distinction drawn in Chapter I and its appendix between assumptions which assign specific values to variables and assumptions which assign characteristics to the bearers of variables.) The scope of a theory is the range of bearers of its variables, expressed as a statement of the properties the bearers need, if the theory is to apply to them. The general statement of what any economic theory requires of the bearers of economic variables will mark out the subject matter of economics.[8]

---

[8] Objection may be taken to the contrast just drawn between statements of laws which say nothing about whatever the variables apply to and statements about bearers of variables and their properties. It is a distinction which most people use readily enough every day but which is alien to the Positivist analysis of scientific language. Positivists (and others) are wont to treat all statements applying a predicate to a subject (or ascribing a property to an object) as being of some such form as $(x) Fx \rightarrow Gx$. In other words 'Businessmen seek to maximise profits' is construed not after the manner of old-fashioned English grammar but as saying that, if anything has one property (that of being a businessman), then it has another (that of seeking to maximise profits). The subject or thing characterised disappears and only a correlation between variables is left. What we are calling 'bearers of variables' become concatenations of properties. We shall not trace the epistemological reasons for making such a move and we also wish to avoid the hugely technical debate still in progress between friends and enemies of the attempt to describe the world without subject terms. But we must say something, to escape a charge of begging the question. So we admit to believing that the attempt fails and that language must budget for things as well as for properties. As far as we know, this is the general view. But, were the general view proved unsound, then we would try to separate kinds of predicate, along the lines of a familiar distinction between sortal and characterising universals. Without supposing that this *nolle prosequi* disposes of the objection, we propose to proceed.

A variable is a collection of characterising possibilities, a set of related positive values which a characterising term could take. Its application is restricted to those bearers which could possibly be so characterised. A college has no colour and the thoughts of even the most forceful thinkers have no accelerating mass. So let us now revert to our remark that social actors depend conceptually as well as physically on the conditions for the material existence of social positions. Positions in the neo-Classical social order are occupied by households and firms, who are the usual bearers of the neo-Classical variables. The relationships postulated by neo-Classical theory define the activities of households and firms and so, within the limits of the model, tell us what it is to be a household or a firm. This presents a version of the problem of application of theoretical terms raised in Chapters 4 and 5 – how we know what in the world corresponds to the entities of theory. For chess, as already noted, the problem solves itself since the players create or designate pieces to conform to the known rules and thus in effect transfer the game from logical time into historical time. It is the players and not the pieces who confer identities and roles and make the moves. In an economic system, by contrast, the players are the pieces. There are no pre-existing, independent beings to assign entities to positions. The list of social entities depends on the social order itself. If a social position is to be filled, the social order must produce what is to fill it. So the connection between terms describing social positions and the actual positions is provided by social decisions and mechanisms to train, induct and sustain incumbents.

So to determine the applicability of a concept in neo-Classical economics, say 'demand-price', we must first identify the bearer of the variable, here a household. The bearer will be assigned various variables and the theory, falls, if the variables are incompatible. Thus those who demand final goods cannot also be, for instance, those who accept savings deposits. There is nothing for conventional economists to object to so far. But, we insist, in setting forth the conditions of applicability, the theory must also show what is necessary and sufficient for households and firms to be able to continue to exist in their present form. It must show how the system can reproduce the bearers of the variables in a regular and continuous way. This is an important matter, if, as we shall contend in the next chapter, neo-Classical theory makes impossible demands on the bearers of its variables and so renders itself inapplicable.

Prices are prices of commodities and, in Classical and Marxian models, commodities are the bearers of price variables. But in neo-Classical models prices are functions of quantities of goods in supply and demand relations. Instead of prices *in se*, there are supply-prices and demand-prices for different amounts of a given commodity and the bearers of these variables are those who propose to pay and those who expect to receive respectively, households and firms. Similarly the rate of interest is the rate of interest on loans, which are its preliminary bearers; but in neo-Classical models variables are behavioural and need agents as bearers. So lenders and borrowers are the bearers and there will again be demand rates and supply rates. The marginal efficiency (marginal productivity) of capital is somewhat different, being defined as the derivative of an investment (production) function. The bearer of this variable in the first instance is the argument of the function for which the derivative is taken; this argument is in turn a variable borne by whatever the function is predicated of, here a firm or an aggregate of firms, which will be, in the final analysis, the bearers of those variables too.

Households and firms are thus the ultimate bearers of neo-Classical variables. If our account in this chapter is accepted, they are to be described, as part of the theory, in real definitions which mark the boundary of economics and give rise to scientific laws expressing essential aspects of economic interaction. Now let us note some further restrictions on the ways in which they can be characterised.

Even variables which can apply to a thing singly may be inapplicable in combination. For example, the consumer who is the bearer of the variables 'quantity of commodity i to be consumed' and 'competitive demand price for i', where $i = 1, \ldots, n$, must be able to maintain both his market and product information and his ability to adjust rapidly to market imperfections, whatever actual pattern of consumption he engages in. As we have seen already, these assumptions are needed, in part, to make it possible to treat prices as uniform to all buyers always and everywhere. Information is itself a commodity, marketed by the communications and publication industries and ability to adjust rapidly to market information depends partly on the absence of complementarities in consumer durables and partly on an effective communications and transport network. So, as we shall argue in a moment, there has to be an underlying pattern of 'infrastructure consumption' whose supply, demand and prices cannot be determined by the model and which restricts the possible combinations of the original variables.

Moreover, even when variables are in general capable of entering into certain functional relationships[9] and their intended bearers are in general

---

[9] For a variable to be part of a functional relation it must discriminate the values in a manner appropriate to the formal operations involved in the relation. A variable whose only values are natural numbers cannot enter into a functional relation involving differentiation and integration (or even unlimited division); one whose values can only be ordered is no use in arithmetical operations. Some of the difficulties this raises for at least one branch of economic theory are discussed by Little in his *Critique of Welfare Economics*, Ch.X, 'Indivisibilities and consumer surplus'.

appropriate, there may be a restriction because the bearers lack suitable mathematical characteristics. For example, utility *functions* present no difficulties but actual consumers seem tiresomely reluctant to order their preferences transitively, let alone convexly, and so fail to act as bearers of the variable 'utility of i to a consumer'. Nor is this surprising, when we reflect that goods are valued for characteristics like taste, warmth, texture or style which cannot be easily compared or ranked.[10]

Putting these restrictions together, we shall next try to develop a primitive infrastructural model showing the conditions for an economic agent's continuing to sustain his existence. It will be a model where exchange is a logical consequence of interdependence in production activities and will illustrate the theme that without such interdependence, there can be no social life.

Any human society, if it is to continue, must secure food and must produce, rear and train a next generation. There must be more food than is needed for the present generation alone. If F is the output of food and N the number of man-days of work which the society can put forth, then

$$F_F \ \& \ N_F \rightarrow F : \text{Raising crops}$$
$$F_N \ \& \ N_N \rightarrow N : \text{Supporting families}$$

indicating that food and labour are both needed both to produce food and to support present labourers and raise the young. (The subscripts show the industry where the input is applied.) Suppose that just enough food is grown to support just enough people to grow food and train their replacements (i.e. $F_F + F_N = F$ and $N_F + N_N = N$). Under these circumstances exchange is fully determined. The exchange ratio between food and, so to speak, labour-power is set by the equations:

$$F_F + WN_F = F$$
$$F_N + WN_N = WN$$

where W is the 'real wage' and price of food in labour-power is taken as unity. The 'real wage', the exchange between food and work, is thus:

$$W = \frac{1}{N} \ F_N + \frac{N_N}{N_F}(F - F_F)$$

If either $F_F + F_N > F$ or $N_F + N_N > N$, the society cannot continue, using its present techniques. If either $F_F + F_N < F$ or $N_F + N_N < N$, the society has a surplus to trade with, invest or spree. But the equations will

---

[10] For an interesting attempt to construct a theory of consumer behaviour on the assumption that utility is derived from the characteristics of goods, see K. Lancaster, *Consumer Demand*, Columbia University Press, 1971.

no longer be determinate. The surplus must be accounted for. Once the disposition of the surplus is determined, so too is the pattern of exchange. Let us see how this works.

Suppose the society is dominated by a warrior caste for whom the rest must work. Industry is arranged so that the surplus consists solely of mandays of labour, levied in proportion to those already worked. Let us call this levy the 'corvée', designated by C, which will be a pure number. Then our formulae become:

$$F_F + (1 + C)WN_F = F$$
$$F_N + (1 + C)WN_N = WN$$

with

$$C = \frac{N}{N_F + N_N} - 1$$

and W the same as before. Many quite complex variations are possible. Suppose, for example, that in addition to the warriors there is a priesthood, who collect part of the annual crop in the form of a sales tax, S. The formulae are now:

$$(1 + S) F_F + (1 + C) WN_F = F$$
$$(1 + S) F_N + (1 + C) WN_N = WN$$

and the equation for S in terms of C will be a rectangular hyperbola, whose shape will depend on the $F:N$ ratios in the two sectors.[11] It is patent that the better-off the priests are, the worse the warriors fare and *vice versa*. Less obvious is that W, the exchange ratio which permits distribution and reproduction, also varies with the relative prosperity of priests to warriors. Writing W as a function of $(1 + C)$, we have

$$\frac{1}{W} = \left[N - (1 + C)\left(N_N + \frac{N_F F_N}{F_F} \right) \right] . \frac{F_F}{F_N F}$$

[11] For notational convenience let $F = N = 1$ (each good is measured in its own units) and express the coefficients accordingly. Then, solving each equation for W:

$$\frac{1 - (1 + S) F_F}{(1 + S) F_N} = \frac{(1 + C) N_F}{1 - (1 + C)N_N}$$

Cross multiplying and, dividing through and rearranging, we get:

$$\frac{[(1/F_F) - (1 + S)] \ [(1/N_N) - (1 + C)]}{(1 + S)(1 + C)} = \frac{F_N \cdot N_F}{F_F \cdot N_N}$$

the meaning of which will be plain from Figure 29.

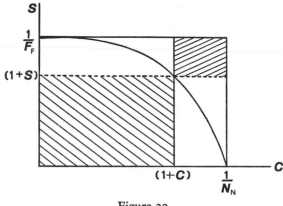

Figure 29

which shows that the exchange ratio is determined, when C is determined. Even in a simple model like this, it takes some calculation to keep track of W and in a serious model the problem can be formidable. However the simple model is enough to illustrate our basic point, that the distribution of the surplus, although accomplished through exchange, is not itself an exchange. The pure numbers C and S are distribution variables, whereas W is the exchange ratio or price. This suggests a marked contrast with neo-Classical theory, which tries to treat the rate of profits (a pure number analogous to S), as the price of capital.

This model is not intended to be plausible as it stands, but, rather, to show how the notion of exchange is connected to the notion of the continued existence of a society. As soon as at least two interdependent activities are agreed necessary, each has to rely on the success of the other for its inputs or replacements. This determines an exchange ratio or at least sets limits to it. The model illustrates the truism that in producing anything one adapts it to specific purposes. Were this not so, production would be not so much pointless as logically impossible. In adapting something, one uses energy and uses up materials and tools. Hence wherever there is production in a continuing system there must be exchange. But there can be no exchange without the fruits of production to exchange and so a theory of exchange requires for its application the existence of a continuing society describable in a prior production model.

We shall exploit this finding in the next chapter, where we argue that economic theories cannot afford to ignore the institutions and interdependences they are supposed to apply to. Neo-Classical theories, indeed, will turn out to make latent assumptions about institutions, which positively render them inapplicable in principle. But that will need a long argument and we shall now draw breath by summarising our moves so far.

The rationalism we propose is conceptual and the necessary truths it relies on are conditional. It is concerned not flatly with what there is or must be nor flatly with what will happen or must happen. Instead it tries to discover what must be true of anything to which a given sort of theory applies and what must happen, if a programme is followed. Nevertheless these are genuine necessities involving real definitions and true axioms. This is the only way we can see of preventing Pragmatism from reducing all hope of knowledge to futility, in the fervour of its attack on Positivism. Rationalism does at least make it possible to entwine the Inductive and Deductive problems, as we argued earlier that they must be entwined.

The upshot is not simply that the hypothetico-deductive method is restored to grace. When hypotheses are treated as concealed conjectures, the role of prediction in the social sciences is changed and programming and production models become the paradigm of explanation. The principle is that what conditionally must be conditionally will be, or, in an older phrase, that what is true of the concept is true of the instance. The problems of determining what is true of the concept are best seen by analogy with mathematics, and, in the process of mathematical experiment, prediction has a limited and diminishing place. As in chess, accuracy is guaranteed finally by reason, which finally explains the success of experience.

The argument is so far apparently neutral between any economic models which can be construed as programming or production models and our final campaign is more ambitious. Conditional necessities become descriptive, when their conditions are fulfilled. We therefore went on to argue that each theory has conditions of application, which include a statement of the sort of bearers its variables need. Economic variables, in particular, can apply only to a continuing system, where there is production and, therefore, exchange. These are the economic concepts which we claim to be understood *a priori* and which have to be instanced, if any economic theory is to apply. That is the point we have reached and our final campaign has thus opened *pianissimo*. Nevertheless we hope it will prove enough not only to overthrow neo-Classical theories but also to give the field to Classical and Marxian analyses.

Before starting this last manoeuvre, however, we shall join in the fight about assumptions and methods, which has enlivened the *American Economic Review* for some years. We do so to show once again that philosophy makes a difference. Since the issue does not concern the transition from this chapter to the next, we have relegated our intervention to the following appendix.

TWO ECONOMISTS

After more than a century of intensive activity in scientific economics, two economists who have made outstanding substantive contributions to our science and whose positions on questions of economic policy are moreover not far apart, seek the ultimate basis of economic knowledge in considerations which (a) contradict each other and (b) are each subject to strong objections. One is led to conclude that economics as a scientific discipline is still somewhat hanging in the air.

T. C. Koopmans wrote these words in 1957,[12] the economists referred to being Milton Friedman and Lionel Robbins. Fifteen years later economics still seems to us to lack visible means of support, which is why we have written this book. In partial 'proof of the pudding', we propose here to show how Friedman and Robbins contradict each other about the answers to our earlier questions and then to argue that the deductive model of explanation just given will meet some of the strong objections mentioned by Koopmans. We shall take as texts Friedman's essay, The methodology of Positive economics,[13] and Robbins' *An Essay on the Nature and Significance of Economic Science*. There is more recent literature, but those works have weathered well and, particularly in the case of Friedman, raise points which have not been met. Indeed, we shall argue that Friedman, though in our view wholly wrong, has seen the issues far more clearly than most of his critics.

Friedman writes as an empiricist in general and as a positivist in particular. Robbins is harder to classify. His original version of 1932 is, on the whole Rationalist but by 1935 he was readier to think of economics in empiricist terms by playing up its psychological content. We shall argue that his earlier line is preferable. Both authors confront what we have called the Inductive and Deductive problems, arriving at very different solutions. Ignoring the historical order of writing, we shall first follow Friedman from Positivism, through Pragmatism, to an impasse and then trace the interplay of Empiricism and Rationalism in Robbins. We shall read rather more philosophy into the texts than is made explicit there and our account of them will be selective; but we hope to have been true to their epistemological intent.

[12] Koopmans, *Three Essays*, p. 141.
[13] Part I of *Essays in Positive Economics*. Our page references are to the Phoenix edition of 1966.

The task of Positive economics, Friedman opens, 'is to provide a system of generalisations that can be used to make correct predictions about the consequences of any change in circumstances' (p. 4). This is to be done by 'the development of a 'theory' or 'hypothesis' that yields valid and meaningful (i.e. not truistic) predictions about phenomena not yet observed' (p. 7). The theory is to be a blend of two elements, a 'language' and 'a body of substantive hypotheses designed to abstract essential features of a complex reality' (p. 7). In its former role 'theory has no substantive content; it is a set of tautologies. Its function is to act as a filing system ...' (p. 7). In its latter role 'theory is to be judged by its predictive power for the class of phenomena which it is intended to "explain"' (p. 8).

The distinction between 'language', and 'substantive hypothesis' is the Positivist one between 'analytic' and 'synthetic'. So, when the Inductive problem arises, there can be no appeal to the filing system as grounds for preferring one hypothesis to another. Nor does Friedman wish to make one – 'the only relevant test of the *validity* of a hypothesis is comparison of its predictions with experience' (p. 8, his italics).

With admirable consistency, he then proceeds to saw off any other branch which he might be tempted to sit on. It would be an error, he says 'to suppose that hypotheses have not only 'implications' but also 'assumptions' and that the conformity of these 'assumptions' to 'reality' is a test of the validity of the hypothesis *different from* and *additional to* the test by implications' (p. 14, his italics). Hence he argues that it is no weakness of perfect competition models and no strength of imperfect ones, that the former have less 'realistic' assumptions than the latter. For, if the only question is which predict better, then that is the only question!

Nor should this move be underestimated. Imperfect competition models are often claimed to be superior because they are more realistic. But, once the realism of assumptions is admitted to matter, they too are open to heavy attack. Do supply curves really rise? How are marginal costs to be determined for joint production? Are outputs and costs really continuously variable? Do firms in fact know their marginal revenue curves? And the questions grow more awkward, when we go behind the cost curves to the true basis of supply, the production function. Can inputs really be much varied in the way supposed, without altering the characteristics of the product or the specification of jobs offered by the firm? Yet, if we cease to assume wide substitution in production, rising supply price, continuous variability, calculation of marginal revenue and so forth, we abandon traditional neo-Classical market behaviour theory. Admittedly there can be other behavioural theories,[14] even incorporating some neo-Classical insights.

---

[14] Cf. Cyert and March, *A Behavioral Theory of the Firm.*

But, so long as the aim is to preserve and defend the core of modern economic thinking, 'the grand neo-classical synthesis', as Samuelson calls it, the usual assumptions are needed. So Friedman's neo-Classical critics are well advised to agree with him that the realism of assumptions does not matter.

Without going into his own reasons, we can see why Friedman is bound to take this line on philosophical grounds. For a positivist, general synthetic statements can be known true only if they are reached inductively by comparison of their implications with experience. So there is simply no room for distinguishing between 'realistic assumptions' and 'predictive hypotheses'.[15] 'Realism' has to be a matter of confirmation through the testing of implications. Consequently recent critics who accept Friedman's Positivist tenets, while arguing for the greater realism of imperfect competition models, as distinct from their predictive power, are certainly wrong. The same applies to critics who argue that Friedman, in saying that success in prediction validates the hypothesis tested, has committed the fallacy of affirming the consequent. Friedman does not, in any case, say that, where H implies P and P is true, then H is true. He says that, where H implies P and P is true, then H is confirmed. And neither he nor they can possibly say anything else.

We now have a fine case of the inductive problem. Any particular statement is implied by many and mutually incompatible hypotheses. Which are we to prefer, when a prediction is confirmed? Friedman does not pose himself this question directly but his essay has the bones of what is perhaps his answer. Having earlier dismissed the analytic aspects of theory as a mere filing system, he now begins to claim that some filing systems are better than others. On further consideration of the notion of 'realism', he suggests that one hypothesis is to be preferred to another 'not because its "assumptions" are more "realistic" but rather because it is part of a more general theory that applies to a wider variety of phenomena ... has more implications capable of being contradicted, and has failed to be contradicted under a wider variety of circumstances' (p. 20). Generality, he explains, involves abstraction and analogy. Assumptions are best simplified to a point where it is 'as if' they were true (pp. 18, 40), even when interpreted literally, they are not true at all. For instance, à propos of the formula $S = \frac{1}{2} gt^2$, he writes, '... bodies that fall in the actual atmosphere behave as if they were falling in a vacuum. In the language so common in economics this would be rapidly translated into 'the formula assumes a vacuum'. Yet it clearly does

---

[15] This remark does not conflict with Nagel's distinctions of senses of 'realism', which we judge to be fair comment but addressed to parts of Friedman's case which do not concern us here. See E. Nagel, Assumptions in economic theory, *American Economic Review*, Vol. 1. 54, no. 2 (May 1963).

no such thing. The formula is accepted because it works, not because we live in an approximate vacuum — whatever that means' (p. 18).[16] The analytic part of theory contains ' "ideal types" ' (p. 35). 'The ideal types are not intended to be descriptive; they are designed to isolate the features that are crucial for a particular problem' (p. 36).

Now, we could see in this an answer to the Inductive problem, if Friedman were to claim that a hypothesis was strengthened by being expressed in a forceful 'ideal type'. But he cannot do so, while remaining loyal to Positivism. He does claim two merits for a forceful ideal type, its 'economy, clarity and precision in presenting the hypothesis' and, more ambitiously, that abstraction is a fruitful technique. 'A fundamental hypothesis of science is that appearances are deceptive and that there is a way of looking at or interpreting or organising the evidence that will reveal superficially disconnected and diverse phenomena to be manifestations of a more fundamental and relatively simple structure' (p. 33). But, since 'economy, clarity and precision' have no epistemological value and since his reason for appealing to this 'fundamental hypothesis of science' is that it has borne fruit in the past, he is still without any solution to the Inductive problem. The economist is to pick the most abstract, elegant and general theory, on the grounds that that technique has worked in the past. Our argument of earlier chapters that Positivism has no epistemological basis for induction is so far unshaken.

In any case, perfect competition models need more of a defence than this, since they do not predict better than a full cost 'classical' theory, in which prices are set by costs and normal profits in the standard range of operation, and output is regulated by demand. (That is, demand does not influence price nor do supply conditions influence output.) Having forsworn direct appeal to realism, Friedman tries to evade the consequences of relying exclusively on the criterion of predictive success — which would, as Schoeffler shows, undercut much conventional theory[17] — by stressing the importance of elegant and general basic theoretical structures. As already argued, such a move carries no epistemological weight within Positivism. But it does suggest that a well-entrenched and approved theory can be maintained against some vagaries of experience and so hints that Pragmatism has something to offer.

The hint soon becomes explicit. Since realism, when properly understood according to Friedman, is a matter of testing implications against experience, there is after all a requirement that assumptions be realistic. But

---

[16] He goes on to compare the assumption of Frictionless Motion with the assumption of perfect competition. Cf. our appendix to Chapter 1, where we rejected the comparison.

[17] Schoeffler, *The Failures of Economics*.

they 'cannot possibly be thoroughly "realistic" in the immediate descriptive sense so often assigned to this term' (p. 32). For that kind of realism would include such characteristics as 'the colour of each trader's hair and eyes, his antecedents and education, the number of members of his family, their characteristics, antecedents and education etc.' (p. 32). The right kind of realism is the abstract or 'as if' variety mentioned earlier. Since there is no difference between assumptions and general implications, the two can be interchanged (p. 27). It is an easy step from this to denying that theory and facts are independent. When the merits of abstraction are combined with the idea that diverse phenomena are 'manifestations of a more fundamental and relatively simple structure', then Pragmatism is imminent.

There may seem no need for Friedman to go so far, especially since it means dropping Positivism. Nevertheless he does so. 'If a class of "economic phenomena" appears varied and complex, it is, we must suppose, because we have no adequate theory to explain them. Known facts cannot be set on one side; a theory to apply "closely to reality" on the other. A theory is the way we perceive "facts" and we cannot perceive "facts" without a theory'. (p. 34). This strikingly conflicts with his Positivism but it is no mere careless flourish. 'There are many different ways of describing the model completely – many different "postulates" which both imply and are implied by the model as a whole. These are all logically equivalent: what are regarded as axioms or postulates of a model from one point of view can be regarded as theorems from another, and conversely' (p. 26). Since this line blurs the distinction between general statements and particular ones and also between analytic statements and synthetic ones, the seeds have already been sown. He is at once faced with the Deductive problem and with the snags of Pragmatism. The Deductive problem is lurking, in any case, but Friedman can no doubt avoid considering it by arguing that he is no worse off than any positivist. As soon as he makes this new and bold claim for theory, however, he must tackle it. If theory is only a filing system of tautologies and a body of hypotheses which confront the tribunal of experience, how can it be 'the way we perceive "facts"'?

Here, we suggest, Friedman must choose. If he sticks to Positivism, facts are given and concepts are optional. No sense can be given to the notion of more fundamental structures in reality and there is no room for interplay between pure model building, seen as logic and mathematics, and experience, seen as fact. Prediction remains the final criterion, with the consequences indicated by Schoeffler. If he prefers a pragmatist relation of theory to fact, he must withdraw his earlier account both of the filing system and of the substantive hypotheses. He can then defend theories which predict indifferently, on the pragmatist ground that any statement can be preserved in the face of experience and can defend 'unrealistic' assumptions, provided they are useful.

Friedman's Positivism runs him aground on the Inductive problem. He can edge himself off by claiming that theory plays an epistemological part in validating hypotheses. This beguiles him into Pragmatism. Yet, if our reflections in Chapter 6 are cogent, Pragmatism is simply another mud-bank and the only exit is by dropping Empiricism. With this cheering thought, we turn to Robbins.

Robbins' *Essay* is an attempt 'to make clear what it is that economists discuss and what may legitimately be expected as a result of their discussions' (1932, Preface). He wishes to distinguish between analytical or theoretical economics on the one hand and descriptive or historical economics on the other. In so doing, he is denying that economists should try to limit themselves to the projection of historical trends by induction from observed patterns. Indeed they could not, even if they wished. For economic generalisations have no claim in themselves to be regarded as laws. 'However accurately they describe the past, there is no presumption that they will describe the future' (1932, p. 101; 1935, p. 109 is almost identical). For 'there is no reason to suppose that their having been so in the past is the result of the operation of homogeneous causes, nor that their changes in the future will be due to the causes which have operated in the past' (1932, p. 101; 1935, p. 109).

He thus sets himself the Inductive problem in a fresh form. What is a 'homogeneous cause' and when have we reason to suppose we have found one? He gives two answers, both present in both editions but with different emphasis. The one emphasised in 1932 is in the spirit of von Mises' remark that 'in the concept of money all the theorems of monetary theory are already implied'[18] This is the solution which we ourselves proposed in the last chapter, neatly put by Robbins in these terms: 'In pure Mechanics we explore the implication of the existence of certain given properties of bodies. In pure Economics we examine the implication of the existence of scarce means with alternative uses' (p. 83 in both editions). 'Economic laws describe inevitable implications' (1932, p. 110; 1935, p. 121). It is definitions which have the 'inevitable implications' and that is why Robbins begins his *Essay* by discussing rival definitions. Any behaviour involving the allocation of scarce resources to competing ends is economic behaviour and all economic theory describes the inevitable implications of this.

That answer is absurd as soon as any concession is made to Positivism. If definitions are arbitrary, nothing of epistemological interest depends on them. Between 1932 and 1935 Logical Positivism gained its ascendancy. Robbins remained unrepentant but did give more weight to his other answer. Economic analysis, he says, 'consists of deductions from a series of

---

[18] L. von Mises, *Human Action* (William Hodge, 1949), p. 38. Robbins pays tribute to von Mises in his 1932 Preface.

postulates, the chief of which are almost universal facts of experience present whenever human activity has an economic aspect' (1935, p. 99). 'If the premisses relate to reality the deduction from them must have a similar point of reference' (1935, p. 104). 'In Economics, as we have seen, the ultimate constituents of our fundamental generalisations are known to us by immediate acquaintance. In the natural sciences they are known only inferentially' (1935, p. 105).

Here 'real definitions' are supplemented, and perhaps replaced, by 'postulates'. The key three postulates are that there is more than one factor of production, that we are not certain about future scarcities and that consumers have orders of preference. They 'do not need controlled experiments to establish their validity: they are so much the stuff of our everyday experience that they have only to be stated to be recognised as obvious... yet in fact it is on postulates of this sort that the complicated theorems of advanced analysis ultimately depend' (1935, p. 179). Economics thus comes to differ radically from mechanics, in that its postulates are qualitative and known by introspection. These postulates are synthetic and so economic theory can be conducted by the hypothetico-deductive method. Theory applies to reality because the postulates happen to be true, not because they are necessarily true. So, if a discreet silence is kept about the status of logic and mathematics, we can discern an empiricism in Robbins' second answer.

The second answer, we contend, concedes too much. We began from Robbins' objection to historical generalisations that 'however accurately they describe the past, there is no presumption that they will describe the future'. His postulates face the same charge. They are, he says, 'the stuff of our everyday experience', 'qualitative and known by introspection'. But there is nothing here to explain why this means more than 'very highly confirmed'. Introspection is a fallible way of arriving at generalities and exactly Robbins' claim has been made for now suspect postulates like 'We are all tainted with original sin' or 'Man is born free'.

Nor are his postulates evidently true.[19] There are few more contentious areas than the 'theory of value'. Socialists and Marxists have never bowed to marginalism; and modern growth theory reckons with prices, rates of return and capital values more reminiscent of Ricardo and Marx than of Menger and Marshall and determined without reference to preference scales. Engels Law is the best-confirmed empirical generalisation in household budget studies but does not necessarily follow from the usual theory of consumer behaviour. The Law of Demand itself is as riddled with exceptions as it is well-confirmed. Nor is there a shortage of rival approaches. American institutionalists from Veblen and Commons to Galbraith have steadily denied that individual scales of relative valuation are independent parameters of

[19] Cf. Koopmans, *Three Essays*, pp. 135–7, where another set of doubts is given.

the system, which in part determine the configuration of the other variables. On the contrary, they hold, such scales are determined, at least in part, by economic forces. They have denied, in other words, precisely what Robbins takes as a basic and self-evident postulate.

Nor, indeed, can we take it for granted that consumers order their preferences as traditionally supposed. Lexicographic orderings, for instance, have seemed to some thinkers to make better sense of household budget data, at the expense of certain theorems which then ceased to be derivable. Recently Lancaster has suggested that preferences range not over goods but over characteristics of goods,[20] a proposal supported by reflection on the famous diet problem in linear programming, as we showed in Chapter 5. Consequences for the theory of consumer behaviour are striking and, right or wrong, are enough to show Robbins' postulate less than self-evident.

Again, the past fifteen years have dealt unkindly with Robbins' belief that no one can 'really question' the existence of different factors of production. Joan Robinson, Sraffa, Pasinetti and others of the new Cambridge persuasion[21] have really questioned whether 'capital', construed as a quantity of resources measurable independently of the distribution of income, can have any empirical sense. Admittedly there is no questioning the existence of different inputs in the manufacturing process. But 'inputs' are not to be equated with 'factors'. An input is a commodity or service, a precisely defined product. A factor of production is the recipient of some category of income. Robbins says (and means) 'factors of production', inviting the objection that nothing can be both a produced input in the production process and, defined in the same way, a category of recipient of income. 'Capital' is a vector of material goods and services, from the first point of view, and a sum of value upon which income is computed, from the second. It is not self-evident that the two views can be combined; and, if Marx and the Cambridge critics are right, they demonstrably cannot be.[22]

The postulate about uncertainty is less open to question. But it is also indefinite. Depending on how it is made explicit, a battery of models can be constructed, each with different informational postulates. So it can hardly be true that any particular set of theorems can be derived from the postulate as Robbins states it.

We therefore object to Robbins' postulates, not because they are false

[20] Lancaster, *Consumer Demand*.

[21] See J. Robinson, The production function and the theory of capital, *Review of Economic Studies*, vol. 21(1953), pp. 81–106, and many other papers – cf. her *Collected Economic Papers*, vols. II and III (Basil Blackwell, 1965). See also Sraffa, *Production of Commodities* and the Pasinetti papers cited in the bibliography.

[22] G. C. Harcourt, Some Cambridge controversies in the theory of capital, *Journal of Economic Literature* vol. 7, no. 2 (June 1969).

but because they will not function as postulates. Since they are open to more than one interpretation, they do not entail a particular set of theorems. Since they are disputable, they are not self-evident. Since they can be reasoned about, they are not introspectible. We therefore maintain that 'real definitions' make a better basis than introspected postulates.

We should perhaps guard against a riposte to our claim that what is disputable is not self-evident. 'Self-evidence' can be defined psychologically, so that what is self-evident is written, so to speak, in capital letters on the surface of the mind. In this case it is a sufficient objection that children, savages and idiots do not perceive the allegedly self-evident feature of experience. But 'self-evident' can also have an epistemological sense, in which it means 'known without proof or evidence'. Here it matters not whether all mankind assents but whether it can be proved self-evident. This is less paradoxical than it sounds, if the argument we gave in Chapter 7 for the existence of real definitions and true axioms is sound. For instance, the law of non-contradiction is self-evident, in the sense that any proof can be proved to presuppose it. Similarly, if economic theory can be axiomatised, then its axioms will have to be self-evidently true. There will still be room for dispute about which the basic axioms are to be. But that does not cancel the search for those axioms which state the real definitions of the basic concepts of economics. Robbins' postulates are disputable, in that there is no pressing reason to accept them. This does not show them false but it does show that Robbins has no right to claim to know they are true.

That leaves us with Robbins' first answer, that economic theory consists of the logical consequences of conceptual definitions. There is an ambiguity in the claim that economic laws are 'necessities to which human action is subject' (1935, p. 135). What sort of necessity? In our own view not psychological nor physical necessity but *a priori* should be meant. Once again we return to real definitions and true axioms, repeating the *caveat* that real definitions are reached only after close observation and analysis. But here we finally part company with Robbins. Although committed to some kind of positivist analytic-synthetic distinction, he places little reliance on empirical and econometric studies. To concede the importance of statistical work would put his principal targets (Wesley, Mitchell, Kalecki, Frisch, and the early econometricians) out of range and rob his work of its main point. His notion of necessity is a psychological and subjective one. So, while agreeing that economic laws are 'necessities to which human action is subject', we finally disagree with Robbins. Without scope for real definitions and true axioms, economics as a scientific discipline is still somewhat hanging in the air.

8

THE ASSUMPTIONS OF NEO-CLASSICISM

We have been claiming that the variables of an economic theory are applicable in principle only to a social system which can produce and sustain appropriate bearers for them. Where the bearers are institutional agents, such as households and firms, whose activities and support use materials and energy, a production model has to be presented and solved, to demonstrate that there can be such bearers within the system; and so we sketched a simple production model of Classical-Marxian form. In this chapter and the next, we shall develop the point and shall elaborate our concept of a production model. We shall also present our fundamental arguments against neo-Classicism in a more detailed and systematic way than hitherto, starting from some matters raised at the end of the Introduction. Our contention will be that many significant differences between the neo-Classical and Classical-Marxian viewpoints spring from contrasting assumptions about the bearers of the respective variables. Because of its assumptions, neo-Classicism rules out important questions and propositions *a priori*. We would not object to this, since we ourselves have no inhibitions about theorising *a priori*, were it not that we believe these excluded propositions to be true, as we shall illustrate with an heretical example, a kind of Gresham's Law transplanted from the money to the product markets. The example may suggest that the issues are empirical. But we shall contend emphatically that they are, at the deepest level, conceptual, even though, in accord with our view of the relation of concepts to facts, we shall explore the assumptions about bearers of the relevant variables with reference to the way in which the system supports the bearers. In order to take the view we do of concepts and theoretical truths, we had first to reject Positivism. Consequently we could not raise the issues properly before and we regard the largely economic discussion of these final chapters as a development of our philosophical position.

We shall start by recalling our introductory contrast between neo-Classical and Classical-Marxian economics. This will prompt an indictment of neo-Classicism on five counts, directed against its major 'simplifying assumptions'. But, before reaching a verdict, we shall pick out two crucial theses, woven into these assumptions – that all market payments are exchanges in the same sense and that all market costs are costs paid for productive work in the same sense. We shall explain how the two theses complement each other and support the rest of the economic edifice and shall then present counter-examples, showing how a change in the assumptions involves a change in the sense of crucial theoretical terms, and, furthermore, a change in the political implications. This will amount to a strong *prima facie* case against neo-Classicism and a reconsideration will be called for. Yet it is too simple to say that neo-Classical theory is false and we shall next offer it a defence against charges of incoherence. The defence will begin with a distinction between 'impossible' theories (which contain contradictions) from 'impracticable' ones (which, although coherent, still cannot be applied because there are no bearers for the variables). Four current objections will be presented. These go to the heart of neo-Classicism but fail to prove impossibility. Nevertheless, they do show neo-Classical theory to be 'impracticable', as we argue by reflecting on the theory of production. And now, as the first item on this somewhat daunting agenda, let us take up some matters which we last discussed in the Introduction.

Neo-Classical contrasted with Classical-Marxian economics

By a neo-Classical theory we mean a model in which there are a large number of consumers, variously endowed with property, and a large number of producers of each kind of good or service. Each consumer's preferences are described by a utility function, with positive first and negative second derivatives. Each producer's technical possibilities are described by a production function, also normally assumed to have positive first and (after a point) negative second derivatives. Consumers purchase final goods, maximising their utility subject to the constraints of their incomes; they sell the services of factors, balancing disutility against expected return at the margin. Firms purchase factors, balancing expected productivity against cost, and sell final goods, setting quantities and prices so as to maximise their profits. Goods and services thus move in a circular flow: producers sell final goods to consumers, and with the proceeds from such sales they purchase factor services from consumers, which they combine into final products. With the proceeds from the sale of factor services consumers buy final products in accordance with their utilities. Competition ensures that demands and supplies will be equated in every market and that excessive profits will be eliminated. Briefly, marginal utility and marginal cost determine equilibrium in the final goods market; marginal disutility and marginal productivity do so in the factor market. This whole scheme is presented in Figure 2, p. 15.

By contrast, in a Classical-Marxian theory firms and consumers are not mentioned; only industries and social classes are shown. On the production side only the techniques of production appear, each industry being defined by the technique it employs. These are taken as given and are assumed to be costly to change. Given a set of techniques, including the amounts of labour needed for production at the unit level, the system will be termed 'productive' if and only if more of at least one good can be produced per period than is consumed in the aggregate in production, while at least as much is produced of every other good as is consumed. With given techniques productivity can be increased, for example, by working faster to cut down on the labour-time required per unit output. Prices are set (in the simplest case) so as to cover the technical costs of production, which are shown explicitly, and to return a uniform level of profit in all industries. Final demand depends on the spending propensities of the different social classes and will determine the level of employment and allocation of labour among the industries, but operating an industry at a higher or lower level of intensity will not affect long-run prices, which, in Keynesian fashion, are assumed to be less flexible than output and employment. Since the technical composition of each industry's input is shown explicitly, each industry's capital will be made up of different combinations of goods; hence, to set the level of normal or uniform profits, the prices of the inputs will have to be known. But since the outputs of some industries are the inputs of others, all prices and the rate of profit will have to be determined together. Yet the rate of profit cannot be determined until the share of profits is given. Once relative shares are fixed, however, prices, the real wage rate and the profit rate can all be determined. This means that there are two kinds of analysis of prices, wages and profits — movements of relative prices with real wages and movements of money prices with money wages. Consider the former. Given a wage rate, prices will be determined by the competitive condition that the rate of profit must be the same in every industry. To see the effect of changes in relative shares on prices, suppose the wage rate rises. At the given initial prices, labour-intensive industries will have to devote a greater than average share of their sales proceeds to paying their wage-bill leaving a less than average return on capital, while capital-intensive industries will find themselves in just the opposite position, with a greater than average return. To equalise the rate of profit, therefore, when the real wage rises, the relative prices of labour-intensive goods must rise, while those of capital-intensive goods must fall. Now consider profits, money prices and money wages. A general inflation of money prices, with money wages constant or rising more slowly, increases profits and so requires relative price adjustments; with money wages rising faster, decreases profits. Business therefore fights a war on two fronts, with its employees and with the general public. Profits are determined partly by the money-wage bargain struck between employers and employees and partly by the terms of the sale of goods and services to the consuming public.[1]

The contrast between neo-Classical and Classical-Marxian theories could hardly be sharper. The most obvious difference, and the one most frequently discussed, concerns substitution. In a Classical-Marxian system the coefficients of production are fixed; whereas in a neo-Classical system continuous possibilities of substitution are assumed. This is fundamental and we shall examine it in the next chapter. But it requires a careful statement, since switches in technique are possible in Classical-Marxian systems (due heed being paid to costs, discontinuities and other effects) and Walras, that pre-eminent neo-Classicist, in fact assumed fixed coefficients. For our present purposes the crucial differences emerge when we look at the way in which the flow of transactions is presented. In neo-Classical theory economic transactions are seen as a circular flow of goods and services, the stream in one direction in each market for goods or factors being matched by a corresponding traffic in the other. By contrast, modern Classical-Marxian theory emphasises the fact that payments to capital are *dispositions of a surplus and do not involve any kind of exchange.* There is simply no corresponding stream in the opposite direction. In neo-Classical theory both prices and quantities are determined by supply and demand acting in conjunction; in Classical-Marxian theory long-run prices are determined wholly by the conditions of supply; and demand (apart from some exceptional cases) is relevant only to the determination of quantities. In neo-Classical theory intermediate products are, as far as possible, eliminated; in Classical-Marxian theory they are given pride of place. In a neo-Classical system both supplies and demands are closely tied to individual decision-making units who are supposed to determine their behaviour patterns by maximising; in a Classical-Marxian system no such units are assumed, and what counts is the interlocking of possibilities and necessities rather than of motives plans and information. Maximising, although important, is not so central. In Marx, in particular, the widespread adoption of maximising behaviour is a consequence, rather than an assumption of the system.

We could go on, but we have already examined these contrasts in detail and the reader is invited to refer to the Introduction. It is, we trust, clear that the choice between the two systems of thought cannot be made on

---

[1] The amount of profit for a *given* level of real wages depends on labour's productivity, which means how much it accomplishes in a given time for which it receives pay. Labour may implicitly or explicitly threaten a slow-down to demand more pay (offer a speed-up in return for a bribe). Extortion and bribery are built-in strategies.

empirical grounds, since much of the dispute turns on criteria of evidence and rules for interpretating facts. Neo-Classical thinking does not, for instance, deny the existence of hierarchical social classes; nor does Classical-Marxian thinking deny that households and firms meet in the market. But each attaches a different importance to such features and advances a criterion of validity which supports its assessment. But we have already covered this ground and do not wish to repeat ourselves.

Simplifying assumptions in neo-Classical theory

Instead we shall move on to examine the 'simplifying' assumptions made in neo-Classical economics. We have already queried such assumptions but we did so previously in order to expose the more general Positivism needed to justify Positive economics. Having by now dismissed that Positivism we shall next query them again, this time in order to examine their role in supporting the neo-Classical vision. The indictment will be as promised, on five counts. In each case we will first contrast reality with the conventional assumption and then indicate the significance of the discrepancy for the neo-Classical world-view.

First, as there is now no justification for ignoring institutional forms, we can observe that neither firms nor households are the simple homogeneous entities of neo-Classical models. In reality the conduct of business varies between single proprietorships, partnerships, corporations, nationalised firms, public utilities, multi-national firms and conglomerates. There is an equal diversity among consuming units.[2] Moreover neither the goods produced nor the utilities they afford are in reality fixed. New products and new activities are facts of life, matched by changing tastes and patterns of consumption. Such changes are often economically rational, as linear programming studies show, and it is by no means 'as if' they were economically irrelevant. Nor, finally, are 'producing' and 'consuming' in reality the only occupations. Collecting and dispensing information, running and staffing organisations, planning innovations and, on the other side, educating oneself, adopting a new religion or acquiring a bank manager are examples of economically significant activities. The ways of 'meeting in the market' are therefore no less diverse and the terms on which parties meet are rarely 'equal'. Patterns of ownership and control, interlocking directorships and other relations between firms, collective bargaining, hire-purchase arrangements and consumer associations all have implications for the market. Nor should one overlook agencies which deal in information, under-

[2] Cf. R. M. Titmuss, *Income Distribution and Social Change* (George Allen and Unwin, 1962), Ch. 3.

write research and innovation, manage personnel or plan, forecast and organise the business of markets. Assumptions, in short, which reduce all economic activity to 'production' and 'consumption' are not even 'as if' true.

Admittedly neo-Classical thinkers know all this. It is only in the simplest heuristic models that we find the assumption that producing and consuming are the only relevant activities, and firms and households the only relevant units. That is fair comment but it remains worth asking how neo-Classicism pictures the market in its purest form, that is, what it regards as *essential* to understanding the market. Here neo-Classical and Classical-Marxian thought contrast most sharply. For neo-Classicism markets typically yield benefits to all parties participating, typically reach towards an equilibrium, and typically respond flexibly in the search for optima. The price mechanism is seen as one of the highlights of modern industrial civilisation, a flexible, sensitive method of reconciling competing claims on scarce resources, while preserving efficiency. For Classical-Marxian thinkers capitalist exchange is the means for accomplishing reproduction and exploitation in one stroke; the marketplace is the arena for the exercise of economic power, the battlefield in which the division of spoils between classes or subclasses is settled. For neo-Classicism then, exchange reduces to an allocation problem, and the only essential characteristic of a party to an exchange is what side of the market he is on – is he a supplier or a demander? By contrast for Classical-Marxian thinkers the first and most basic feature of exchange lies in its relation to the reproduction of the system, and the second in its contribution to the disposition of the surplus. Consequently, the essential characteristics of a party to an exchange are, first, the party's position in production, and second, his ability to command a share of the surplus. And that ability rests, in the end, upon power, and power derives largely from structural features of the system. So, from the Classical-Marxian perspective, all characteristics of agents which might have a bearing upon their ability to *gain at the expense of others* are relevant, whereas precisely these characteristics are pushed into the shadows by the neo-Classical presumption that market exchange typically tends towards an equilibrium in which all parties gain and, indeed, in the general case, gain proportionally to their productive contribution.

In short institutional forms confer power and advantage on some and deny them to others. It is not simply that neo-Classicism leaves out interesting features of the system; it is rather that by leaving out these features it is compelled to reinterpret power plays as 'tatonnements' and coercion as choice. (The Enclosure Acts produced a popular choice for urban living, as the people 'voted with their feet'.) The legal arrangements of capitalism provide employers with definite advantages in bargaining. Employers choose the place of business, the methods of production, determine the timing of production, the nature and design of the product, even the hours of work. The same legal arrangements also provide business with advantages with respect to consumers, local and even national governments, and so on. These can be neglected only if power is not fundamental in determining market exchanges.

The second assumption is that of 'perfect information'. The layman sees that information, like money, divides the world into 'haves' and 'have nots'. From a lay standpoint, the neo-Classical notion of information is perverse. Indeed 'perfect information', exhaustively either 'market' or 'technical' and passed anonymously along 'horizontal' channels, is an invention of neo-Classical economics. In reality information, more or less specific, is of many kinds, is usually 'addressed' and often passes 'vertically' through hierarchies. Policy, planning and forecasting (to say nothing of success in bargaining or in invading a market) may hinge on information or indeed on information about information. Information is not only about prices but, for instance, may concern competitors' intentions or government thinking and will normally be crucial in any competitive struggle. Moreover information costs money. The very notion of perfect information reduces economics to absurdity; but the apparently more reasonable idea of 'adequate market and technical information' is fully as pernicious. In the business world the correct term, with all its warlike connotations, should be not 'information' but 'intelligence'. Again the neo-Classical instinct for the antiseptic is misleading.

Thirdly, maximisation of profit or utility cannot be plausibly assumed to be the simple moving force of live economic behaviour. Whose motivation is in question? Middle managers and rising young executives have different ambitions. Whereas a production department will typically look for a steady flow of output at high capacity, a sales department may favour bursts and shutdowns for the sake of selling needs. Whereas productions and sales departments willingly carry large stocks of inputs and outputs respectively, a finance department is congenitally hostile to stocks. Such divergencies cannot show up in a model (even a maximising model) whose unit is the whole firm. Even within production, foremen and engineers are imperfect allies and each individual will be affected by what he judges his chance in the scramble for promotion to be. And what of the 'firm' as a whole? It may be out to expand, to capture the whole market, to retain an honourable reputation, to give security to its employees. Insofar as it is out to make profit, much depends on whose benefit is intended. Managers and shareholders may have a different judgement of profit. Similar discrepancies could readily be listed for the maximising of consumers' utilities. But there is no need to labour the point. To assume motivation without asking whose motivation, is like declaring oneself committed without knowing what one is committed to. Indeed it is debatable whether motivation should be assumed or whether it should be left to emerge from study of how it is produced, maintained and reinforced.

Fourthly, production cannot plausibly be assumed highly 'flexible' in the sense that the same goods can be produced in many ways and that factors can cooperate in many proportions; nor can technical change be plausibly taken to affect only methods of production and not products, consumption or work. Indeed, technical innovations are sometimes adopted not because they are more productive but because they permit better control of labour. Despite the protestations of advertisers, new techniques and combinations usually mean a new product. Technical change impinges on skills, conditions of work, properties of the product and household life and even the prospect of it can be significant, for instance for bargaining. A move along the production function is not readily distinguishable from a shift in the function. 'Inputs' and 'factors' are not in reality interchangeable.[3] Whereas a neo-Classical construction of cost curves depends on assuming increasing followed by diminishing returns, particularly with respect to capital per man, in reality there is no independent evidence for this nor can anything of the sort be found in engineering text books. Indeed, if it is supposed, in the name of 'flexibility', that there are ten genuinely different ways of making the same shoes, then, as modern theory has shown, it will rarely be possible to rank these methods unambiguously from most to least productive, independently of prices and the rate of interest. A method which is less productive than another at a high rate of interest may be more productive at a lower rate.[4] Moreover, as we explain and argue presently, whereas even under imperfect competition neo-Classical models assume all costs to be costs of production and assume the economy to be always on its efficiency frontier, in reality less efficient methods and worse products may prove more profitable. We shall return to this last point in a moment.

Fifthly, neo-Classical models tend to assume that all events happen at a logical instant (as argued in Chapter 5) or at least within some given period and that all expectations are formed with the same horizon. (Supply and

---

[3] S. Marglin, What do bosses do?, unpublished paper, Harvard University, 1971; cf. J. B. Clark, *The Distribution of Wealth* (Macmillan, 1899).

[4] Cf. Joan Robinson, *The Accumulation of Capital* (Macmillan, 1956), p. 109; Sraffa, *Production of Commodities*, Ch. XII, and Paradoxes in capital theory: a symposium, *Quarterly Journal of Economics*, Vol. LXXX, no. 4 (November 1966).

demand curves are assumed to hold for the same period.) In reality, however, different activities take different times, involving lending, borrowing, the holding of stocks and sometimes the hoarding of labour and goods. This is inescapable in any system which uses fixed capital. Different time horizons matter. Time has a cost, which cannot be less than that of supporting labour for the period and involves necessary materials. There are agencies, which make a living by coordinating time horizons and plans. An avowedly predictive model omits the impact of time at its peril. But of perhaps greater importance are the strategic features of time. In anticipation of a strike firms will stockpile. The best time to threaten a strike is when stocks are low and the firm has a large debt-servicing payment due. The time pattern of receipts and outgoings is crucial to liquidity and therefore to solvency. If we are to consider the strategies of competition, the relative strengths of large and small firms, of capital and labour, of business and government, we must take realistic account of the timing, as well as the interdependence, of the respective activities.

For at least those five reasons, then, neo-Classical models 'simplify' the contemporary scene by assuming the exact opposite of what is the case, thus eliminating from consideration some of the basic sources of economic power. Perhaps, however, the assumptions are warranted, if we take a longer span of time and try to discern historical trends towards a neo-Classical growth equilibrium? But, in fact, history is no comfort. Neo-Classical theory is essentially static and its growth models, which define a growth equilibrium in which all variables grow equiproportionally, portray nothing more dynamic than a 'dynamic stasis'. Historical trends, by contrast, can be argued to have been away from the neo-Classical assumption in each case. Large organisations, multiple information channels, more complex 'control' institutions for planning and regulation by governments and others, technology of growing complexity and greater product-differentiation are all commonplace now by comparison with, say, 1939. To save labouring the point, we shall offer Table 1 in summary (see p. 214).

It would be disingenuous to regard such discrepancies as damning in themselves and we are indeed perfectly willing to accept models based on 'unrealistic' or false assumptions, provided they do not concern essentials. But each of the five assumptions just discussed does concern an essential feature of the market system, namely bargaining power. Each describes part of the terrain of what is essentially a battlefield. The neo-Classical vision does not include battles and so takes the terrain to be irrelevant. Yet the outcome of a battle depends on the strategy and strength of the opposing armies, as partly determined by the terrain. So we have at least a *prima facie* objection to neo-Classical theory and one which Classical and Marxian models are less open to. In a simple paradigm modern model, for instance a

TABLE 1

	At present	Historical trend	Neo-classical assumption
1 Organisations and activities	Variety of type and level, influenced by new products and controls	Growing diversity of type, products and activities. Multi-level organisation. Increasing concentration of control	Firms and households produce and consume a virtually fixed list of products
2 Information	Various channels, vertical and horizontal	Growing diversity. Manipulation and strategic use of information	Market channels with horizontal flow
3 Motivation	Diverse, including non-market, role-oriented	Growingly role-oriented	Maximisation of profit and utility
4 Technology	Partially determines nature of product. Affects social organisation and life-style. Chosen to assist in control of labour force	Growing complex but becoming more flexible	Flexible connections but independent of social organisation
5 Time	Complex effect on planning and fore-casting. Cost always significant	Growing interest in calculating cost and effects	Either ignored or assumption of simultaneous behaviour patterns

two-sector, fixed coefficient growth model, we find:

(1) A multilevel organisation assumption which distinguishes between owners and workers, separates basics from non-basics and does not rule out other organisations. New products and activities are envisaged and the model is designed to analyse this. Crucially, it is made clear that owners and workers (and possibly other groups) divide the surplus and that what one gains the other loses. The power struggle is built in from the start.

(2) No assumptions about information, one way or the other.

(3) The motive of gain is normally assumed for all parties. But the assumption is tied to actual organisations, not to postulated or abstract entities. (In some Classical-Marxian models motivation for

capitalist firms is sometimes a theorem rather than an assumption. 'Expand or be destroyed' is a sort of Social Darwinist motif and one in tune with Marx.)

(4) Technology is assumed to be rigid and highly interdependent, therefore giving rise to dependencies among groups and firms.

(5) No assumptions about time.

Here, *prima facie* at least, (1), (3) and (4) are an improvement on the neo-Classical assumptions, while (2) and (5) are at least non-committal and do not rule out sources of advantage in the struggle for gain.

Two essential theses of neo-Classicism

If it is correct to see the market place as a battlefield, Classical-Marxian theories undeniably stand better. But neo-Classical defenders can at this stage retort that we have not shown it to be one nor have we shown the lack of bearers for neo-Classical variables. Indeed our argument earlier that theories tend to determine their own facts can cut both ways and what we have just presented as contemporary facts or historical trends may be merely the *obiter dicta* of Classical and Marxian theorists. So let us next enquire more kindly into the reasons for making neo-Classical assumptions.

We argued above that the assumptions are integral to the type of model, in that they underwrite a view of the nature of economic activity which is distinctively neo-Classical. Two theses in particular are essential and revealing. The first is that all market payments are exchanges in the same sense; the second that all market costs are costs paid for productive work in the same sense. The first says that factor markets and product markets are markets in exactly the same sense; potatoes have a price and so does capital, and both markets work in the same way. In equilibrium all parties gain, and if the equilibrium is competitive, and sometimes even if it is not, no one is exploited in any reasonable sense of the term. We have already made the contrast with the Classical-Marxian vision, in which the market figures as the arena in which the struggle over the division of the surplus takes place. The second thesis maintains that any work receiving a market remuneration is productive work, and, if the market is competitive, the remuneration will be proportional to the productivity at the margin. No economically significant distinction can be drawn between a machine operative and a salesman, between an engineer and an advertising employee. Both of these contentions underpin the neo-Classical contention that competitive equilibrium is 'Pareto optimal' – no one can be made better off without someone being made worse off. By contrast in the Classical-Marxian vision, productive work is sharply distinguished from unproductive work, thus making it possible to distinguish the expenses involved in production from those incurred in the competition for the surplus. Both are assumptions (or consequences of assumptions) which serve to determine the possible interpretations of the results of applying the model or as we put it before, assign characteristics to the bearers of the variables. They are not testable, since they are presupposed in testing, for instance, the postulate of diminishing marginal productivity (where firms have to be assumed to operate on their efficiency frontiers) or the claim of many development economists that capital scarcity is the crucial bottleneck (where there has to be a capital market in the relevant sense).

The relation between these two theses and the assumptions we objected to above is straightforward. If the theses are accepted, the assumptions seem reasonable enough, since, being to do with inessential matters, their admitted falsity would be unimportant. If all market transactions are exchanges and if all work is productive, there is no room for systematic exploitation. Although everyone struggles for the best price he can get, everyone nevertheless offers something useful in return. Big firms, which may be able to charge more than they 'should', can be counteracted by other big firms, since even giant corporations may 'behave competitively'. Even though imperfections may create a kind of systematic bias, the essential concept of the market is 'tit for tat' and 'you cannot get something for nothing'. So, the neo-Classicist can say, the market place is not a battlefield but an orderly shopping centre where, even if the odd customer is short changed or the odd item shop-lifted, people in the long run get what they pay for and pay for what they get. Let us next examine this apologia more closely.

The first thesis, that all market payments are exchanges in the same sense, is essential to the neo-Classical theory of the capital market. It contrasts with the Classical and Marxian notion that payment to capital is, although a market payment governed by competition, less an exchange than an appropriation or, even, a transfer payment. It contrasts also with the Classical and Marxian notion that payment to labour is less an exchange than an exploitation, where the 'surplus value' of labour is earmarked as a return to capital, before the exchange begins. In neo-Classical theory households save and firms invest, after selling bonds to households in return for their savings. A sort of social equipoise is presented, between households, who sell productive services to firms and firms who sell final products back to households. This view fails to distinguish between some of the households, who own all of the firms and the other households, who merely supply labour. The former group thus presumably find themselves facing themselves in the competitive market for services, selling to themselves what they own already. The latter are misleadingly credited with the positive power to decide their own strategy in the market, which belongs mainly to the former group. The power to withhold savings is more easily exercised than the power to withhold labour and, unless the working households are backed by strike funds, it is disingenuous to suggest an equipoise by speaking of the 'mutual dependence' of capital and labour. In general, neo-Classical thinkers have ignored property and have assumed motivation, without specifying in terms of institutional position, whose motivation. This results in an individualism and a uniform molecular view of society, which has only to be seen to be disbelieved.

The second thesis, that all market behaviour is productive work in the same sense, is a consequence of assuming that organisational details can be ignored, that technology is flexible and exhibits diminishing returns and that motivation can be postulated without specifying institutional forms. It is essential to the neo-Classical theory of cost curves, which are derived from the production functions of firms and are supposed to come from engineering data. Costs of selling, management, information and other functions are treated as overheads which can be varied in the long run. Long run cost curves are derived from long run production functions, which show the combinations of all inputs and outputs, including overhead input.[5] In consequence, cost curves yield supply curves also derived from the production function, implying that goods supplied are always produced by the most efficient engineering methods. This is true of models of imperfect as well as of perfect competition. After all, firms are being supposed to know all the techniques and to have no costs of acquiring information. They always operate on the frontier of the production function, without making technical mistakes. Long and short run functions, for instance, although they differ because some factors are fixed in the short run, are both equally well defined.[6] *Engineering* inefficiency is ruled out; when production is not at minimum average cost, there may be *economic* inefficiency and models of imperfect competition are designed to analyse this. The implicit assumption is, therefore, that engineering inefficiency can never be to the advantage of a firm or an industry. Being thus committed to denying that there is ever engineering inefficiency (in equilibrium), neo-Classicists are bound to dispute Veblen's contention that the demands of engineers conflict with those of the price system.[7] That, however, is a

---

[5] Some inputs are admittedly hard to measure and proxy variables will have to be found.

[6] A modern view, deriving from critics of neo-Classicism, distinguishes *ex ante* from *ex post* production functions. A point on the *ex ante* frontier may prove to have been a miserable mistake *ex post* and the firm be stuck with its results. This vintage approach, although retaining many other neo-Classical features, is a distinct advance.

[7] Cf. T. Veblen, *The Engineers and the Price System* (B. W. Huebsch, Inc., 1921).

logical requirement of neo-Classical theory and should be taken not as the refutation of Veblen but as a precondition for a neo-Classical analysis of cost curves.

On the other hand, if Veblen is upheld, then production models need to be separated from market models. Suppose, for instance, we discern a conflict in the production of light bulbs between engineers, whose task is to turn out cheap bulbs which will burn until doomsday, and sales managers, whose more profitable task is to keep the customers frantically replacing spent bulbs, then such a separation of models is called for. (The problem in national income accounting, of how money spent on research to reduce the life of light bulbs for commercial reasons is to appear in the national accounts, shows the ramifications of this conflict.) The easy reply is that neo-Classical theory does not consider the efficiency of products but only of factors. Light bulbs yield utility and it is up to the consumer to decide what kinds of bulbs he wants. But we can include factor inefficiency and contend that a firm may deliberately spend more than is needed to make an adequate product, precisely in order to reduce the lifetime of the product. The factor combination is inefficient and the product is worse. Neo-Classical theory does not envisage this sort of behaviour. The separation of production and marketing creates a distinction between value and price, for which neo-Classical theory has no place.

Elizabethan inefficiency and modern mousetraps

Already we can hear the cries of outrage from some of our readers. 'What? It is *impossible* for firms to make money by being inefficient!' And our critics can cite the well-known Mousetrap Law: the world will beat a path to the door of him who makes a better mousetrap. Very well, we will oppose this with our own home-grown version of Gresham's Law, adapted to the produce market: other things being equal, in the long term, under *realistically* competitive conditions, worse products will drive out better. In demonstrating this we shall show that firms can indeed make money by being inefficient (although, of course, they can also make money by being efficient).

Starting simply, consider an individual firm, producing a certain product in competition with a number of other firms. Suppose the product is shoes, and the firm, like the rest, produces sound high-quality, durable footwear. By reducing the quality of its product it will, as word gets round, lose sales to its competitors, although it should be possible for it to produce shoes that *look* tough and solid. But on the other hand, by cheapening its product it will release funds with which to engage in an advertising and sales campaign, while leaving its total variable costs (production plus marketing) the same. If a sales campaign will bring in more sales than are lost by the qua'ity reduction, the firm should reduce quality and begin intensive marketing; quality should be reduced, in theory, up to the point where the loss in sales from an additional drop in quality just equals the gain in sales from the extra marketing effort made possible with the funds transferred from production to marketing. (Figure 31, though labelled for the case of planned obsolescence, also illustrates this case.)

What should the firm's competitors do? Let us suppose that the aggregate demand for shoes depends largely on the number of feet, and the size and distribution of national income, and that none of these will change in the short term. In the short term there are no aggregate gains to be made. Further let us suppose that, if everyone cheapened the product, the net effects would cancel out and nobody would be any better off. Now consider the position of any one of the competing firms *vis-à-vis* any other, or the rest taken together. If both maintain quality nobody gains, if both cheapen nobody gains, and the customers, society as a whole, lose. Nevertheless under the circumstances we are considering both will cheapen, for each will observe that if *he* cheapens, and his competitor does not, he will gain, through his marketing campaign, a fraction of his competitors's market. Similarly he will observe that if his competitor cheapens and advertises, and he does not, he will lose a fraction of his market. The only safe course is therefore to reduce quality and shift resources into marketing. A very simple diagram (Figure 30) illustrates the dilemma quite clearly. The optimal strategy for both is to cheapen the products. This would be true if both cheapening meant an actual loss, as consumers turned to imported shoes, so long as that loss was *less* than the loss, L, of a firm to its competitors when they cheapen and it does not.[8]

This shows that, under simple and realistic assumptions, bad products can drive out good. The conclusion is conditional; if the gain from the marketing drive would not compensate for the loss in sales due to cheapening, product quality will be maintained. But there can be no general presumption of this, particularly as advertising and marketing techniques grow more sophisticated, unless, of course, we rule the whole matter out

---

[8] The turn towards imports will not rescue the competitive model for two reasons. Once established in the market, foreign manufacturers will face the same pressure to reduce quality. Also, and perhaps more interestingly, they may never get established, since the threat they pose may cause domestic producers to band together and lobby for a protective tariff.

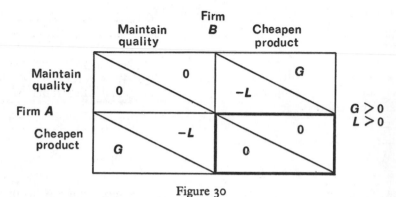

Figure 30

of court by assuming that consumers always have 'adequate market and technical information'.[9]

Yet this is only the beginning. Let us now look at the problem in long run terms. But this time let us consider, not shoes, but consumer durable goods, say, refrigerators. Upon the development of the product, commercial opportunities will be seized and firms will enter, building plant and install-ing equipment. Each firm will install the largest and most modern plant it can afford, for if it does not, its competitors will be able to grow faster and undersell it. (This may well result in over-building capacity. For, as in the case illustrated in Figure 30, it might be better for everyone to install a relatively small and modest plant, but, so long as a firm can gain more at the expense of its competition by building large than it would gain if everyone stayed small, competitive pressures will force everyone into extensive invest-ment.) The number of possible sales of refrigerators, however, is limited by the number of families; the growth in sales by the growth in population. The competitive scramble leads to investment appropriate for the opening of the market. What happens when every family has a fridge? One answer might be to shut down the plant and put it in mothballs until replacements

---

[9] Out on the Illinois prairie they will say that the cheaper product is what the market prefers. A decision about how much to put into quality and durability must be made; and the Chicago criterion is Do what the market will accept. This misses our point, which is that the product but not the price is cheapened. Total variable costs are the same but the composition has changed, with selling costs rising at the expense of production costs. Moreover, we reject the postulate of 'adequate information' on the grounds that manipula-tion of information, including deception, is a useful market strategy, dictated by the profit motive. A firm, like a government, should practise deception to the point where the additional gains from further lying are just balanced by the additional costs due to discovery and exposure.

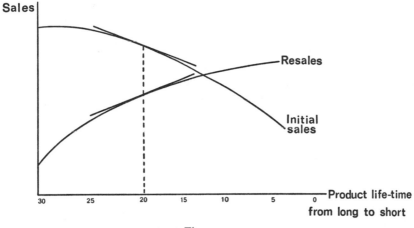

Figure 31

are needed. A good refrigerator might last forty years.[10] Capitalism has a simpler and better answer – reduce the life-time of the product and introduce frequent superficial model changes to encourage turnover. For any individual firm, reducing the life-time of the product (building in obsolescence) will reduce initial sales, but by the same token, will increase resales, particularly if customers can be tied to the firm by such devices as trade-in reductions or special attachments, which can be kept on from one model to another but will not work with the products of competitors. We can readily determine how far, in theory, the product life-time should be reduced. So long as resales are rising faster than initial sales are falling, as product life is reduced, the reduction should continue. At the point where the loss in initial sales from a further reduction just matches the gain in resales, total product sales will be at a maximum. In Figure 31, this will be the point where the absolute value of the slopes of the two curves are equal. The situation for the market on a whole will be that laid out in Figure 30. We have kept the argument as simple as possible by talking about sales, but it should be remembered that it is earnings that firms are interested in. It will therefore be worth their while under these conditions to incur expenses, either current or capital, over and above those required for normal production, to shorten the life-time of the product, so long as

---

[10] Nell bought a 1928 General Electric silent refrigerator in 1959 for £5, reselling after two years of trouble-free use for £4. In 1971 the person to whom he sold it, having used it for 10 years, installed it in his tenant's flat, after a more modern refrigerator broke down.

earnings from additional resales, minus such expenses, outweigh the corresponding loss in initial sales. Hence it may well pay a firm to be 'inefficient'.

This, we believe, is enough to establish our point, though it hardly disposes of the problem. For that we should have to present a more sophisticated model, in which firms begin with a technically sound product and then gradually cheapen it, the problem being to determine the optimal rate of cheapening, so as to maximise the firm's prospective rate of growth. There are also many refinements that could be made to deal with collusion, with new entrants after market shares and product life-time have been established and so on. But our concern here is methodological. So let us look back at the assumptions and basic neo-Classical theses from which we began.

According to basic neo-Classical doctrine, all costs are production costs (cost curves are derived from production functions) and the economy always operates on its efficiency frontier in equilibrium, though it need not be at the optimal point on that frontier (economic inefficiency).

According to our own reckoning, if durable capital goods are used to produce durable consumer goods, or if advertising and marketing techniques are sophisticated and consumer goods complex, the economy will generally operate inside its efficiency frontier in equilibrium, and will be incurring substantial non-production costs.

In order to argue our case we had to reject the neo-Classical assumptions about information, mobility and the time structure of production and consumption. We also found it necessary to distinguish between the production and sales operations in the firm, and we demonstrated that, in the absence of these assumptions, the basic thesis, that all economic activity is productive in the same sense, could not be maintained. Our object was to show the significance of neo-Classical assumptions in determining the neo-Classical viewpoint and this example has surely shown that. Moreover, while a detailed analysis and defence of our neo-Greshamite law is beyond the scope of this work, there is plenty of causal empirical support for it.[11] Whereas the corresponding neo-Classical proposition taken at face value, is either false or empty, depending on the sense given to 'in equilibrium'. We suspect that a case of sorts could be made against neo-Classicism here on empirical grounds. But that is not our intention. Instead we want to emphasise the fact that our questions cannot be raised, nor our propositions presented in the neo-Classical framework. We had to change the meanings of terms like 'cost', 'production' and 'efficiency' to present our position. This means

[11] Cf. V. D. Packard, *The Waste Makers* (D. McKay Company, 1960); D. Masters, *The Intelligent Buyer and the Tell-Tale Seller* (Alfred Knopf, 1966).

that any empirical case would necessarily miss its mark. We shall have to dig deeper, and for that we must look again at the way neo-Classicism hangs together.

Neo-Classical theory is inapplicable, not false, and impracticable, not impossible

The two neo-Classical theses complement one another. By the first, the services of capital and labour are the wares in the factor market; by the second, suppliers always choose technically optimal combinations of factors. Together the theses imply that economic theories of capital and production can ignore technical or engineering detail. The services of capital are sold in return for interest and it does not matter what the capital is embodied in. The rate of return received is supposed to determine the point on the production function at which firms are operating. Details of technique supposedly need not concern economists.

The upshot is that neo-Classicism has led us into political economy by, so to speak, the back door. A capitalist society is one where owners of capital receive income as a result of their ownership, as distinct from their work. In the neo-Classical view this is an institutional detail to be ignored for economic purposes (any political ill effects can be corrected, for instance, by some combination of taxes and subsidies). The economist's purpose is to find the economically most efficient combinations of capital and labour and to identify the patterns of incentive which encourage it. The meaning of 'efficiency' depends on assumptions, which are chosen for the sake of the resulting model's predictive power. There, it is said, his job ends. This looks at first like a modern scientist's refusal to pass value judgements. But in fact it is an old fashioned liberalism. For the separation of economics and institutions, implicit in the idea that there are optimal combinations to which institutions either are irrelevant or ought to conform, depends, unexpectedly, on there still being an Unseen Hand. Or, to put it more plainly, it depends on assumptions which remove all the sources and opportunities for the exercise of economic power. Otherwise it will not be true that economic behaviour tends to exhibit regular patterns conditioned only by the state of technology and individual preferences and still less true that these natural patterns are the best ones. The economist who says 'I cannot tell you how you ought to arrange your institutions; I can only give you the scientific answer to the problem of how resources are best allocated' is to be reckoned a rejuvenated liberal with his scientific tongue in his check.

There is no doubt, then, that neo-Classical theory depends on making just those assumptions which critics find so implausible. Neo-Classicists are often quite cheerful about their lack of realism, since they believe they can parry objections with the philosophical doctrines discussed in earlier chapters. Neo-Classical theory needs Positivism as much as it needs its own assumptions. But Positivism is indefensible, the assumptions are mistaken and the former cannot be allowed to buttress the latter.

The moral we draw is not that neo-Classical theory is false. It is rather that, since its assumptions serve to define the conditions of application of its models and since those assumptions are false, neo-Classical theory is inapplicable. To put it baldly, there are no bearers for neo-Classical variables. But we are not yet ready to cash our winnings and shall next discuss the notion of inapplicability with more circumspection.

A model will be theoretically unsound if, in principle, it cannot be applied. There are two conditions to be met: the model must be both possible and practicable. In calling it possible, we have in mind the familiar requirement of consistency, which we choose to put in the less familiar form that no sound model can ascribe contradictory properties to the same bearer of its variables. For example, Harrod argues that the theory of imperfect competition attributes a kind of schizophrenia to firms, whom it supposes to think in short-period terms when defining marginal costs, in long-period terms when assessing marginal revenues and in both when determining output by equating marginal cost to marginal revenue.[12] If he is right, then, since there is no possible way of equating what is defined in incompatible terms, the model, taken strictly, is inapplicable because impossible. The other condition, that the model be practicable, will eventually need a more careful explanation but, to put it loosely, if a variable is so defined that an economic agent, to whom it applied, could not last long in the market (given the assumed social order) or support himself materially (given the laws of nature), then the model in question is impracticable.

The conflict between the Mousetrap Law and our own home-grown Law of Products looks empirical at first sight. On reflection, however, it is evident that it cannot be resolved by evidence, for the two sides attach different meanings to 'efficiency', 'cost', 'production' and even 'competition'. These meanings depend on assumptions about the bearers of the behavioural variables, and we rejected the neo-Classical assumptions. We think it plain that neo-Classical assumptions are never fulfilled and rarely, if ever, even approximated. Moreover, we think our examples have shown that those assumptions underlie an optimistic and politically naive vision of the economic system. Our rather harsh metaphor of the market as a battlefield was deliberately chosen to heighten the contrast and we do not necessarily want to saddle Classical-Marxian economics with the full burden

[12] R. F. Harrod, Theory of imperfect competition revisited, in *Economic Essays* (St Martin's Press, 1972), esp. pp. 146–51.

of this, although we think it much nearer the truth than the vapid prattle of optima so common in neo-Classical texts.

But interesting as this may be, it falls considerably short of our mark. We are not content to say that, *in fact*, there *are no* bearers for neo-Classical variables. Nor, however, do we wish to claim that there *could not be* such bearers under any conditions. We are staking out a kind of middle ground, contending that, given the laws of physics and engineering and given the legal foundation of capitalism, there cannot exist neo-Classical bearers, since neo-Classical assumptions cannot then be fulfilled. We are thus claiming that neo-Classicism is more than empirically false and less than impossible and our next task is to introduce the concept of 'impracticability' in a persuasive way.

The impracticability of neo-Classicism

To sharpen this distinction between 'impossible' and 'impracticable', we shall next deploy an example. Then we shall consider some recent objections to neo-Classical models and argue that they show not that the models are impossible but rather that they are impracticable. Even granting that some objections can be met by reworking the framework of neo-Classical theory, we shall find others which require an elementary Classical or Marxian model. Our own case, presented in the next chapter, will be that neo-Classical theories, being exclusively concerned with action variables,[13] presuppose a structural model of economic agency, with which they are incompatible. In other words a structural model (or the structural features of a model) embodies the conditions for the model's practicability and so defines the sort of bearers needed for its variables. Neo-Classical theories, we shall claim, call for bearers who would fail to support themselves or go out of business. The ground will then be clear for a Classical or Marxian approach.

An example of impracticability is raised by the concept of short-run 'supply price'. Suppose the demand for the product of a firm in imperfect competition falls, with the result that price and quantity are lowered (as under perfect competition) to minimise the loss. Diagrammatically, demand falls from AR_1 to AR_2, so MR_1 falls to MR_2, and short-run equilibrium price and quantity are both reduced (Figure 32). Now consider the firm's capital situation. At any time part of their working capital is tied up in stocks. (At one time, indeed, all of it has to be.) So, when price is cut, there is a permanent loss of working capital. Since fixed costs do not fall, the

---

[13] There is some doubt about the interpretation of the supply curve. Cf. Kornai, *Anti-Equilibrium*.

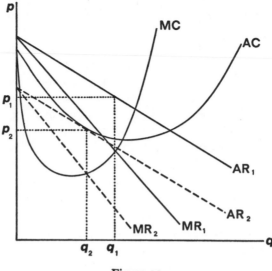

Figure 32

firm's debt-equity ratio rises. Yet a certain debt-equity ratio is needed to keep the firm out of receivership.[14] There is thus a conflict between the theorem derived from the concept of 'supply price' and the need for an upper limit on the debt-equity ratio.

The conflict can be resolved by taking time into account, which also helps to explain why prices are sticky downwards. When demand falls, it takes longer to sell off stocks and so to recover working capital. But time has a cost, in this case in interest. The loss to the firm at a given price will be due to the extra time required to recover working capital and will appear as additional interest payments on the firm's debt, while stocks are sold off. Suppose, instead, that prices are cut so that stocks are sold off in the normal period; then the fraction of working capital lost will equal the percentage of the original price by which price has been cut. Business will wish to minimise its loss of working capital. Prices will be sticky or flexible according as the original debt-equity ratio, the rate of interest and the elasticity of demand are low or high. The debt-equity ratio is thus a relevant variable, whose effect may even make it worth raising price, when demand falls, and whose impact can be allowed for by taking account of time.

Three points emerge from the example. First, 'supply price' is usually defined without regard to the continued existence of what we call 'the

---

[14] The limit is set by the amount that can be shifted from paying dividends and applied to interest charges.

bearer of the variable', in this case the firm. It is simply assumed that the bearer can maintain its physical and legal being. Secondly the postulated motivation, in this case the maximising of profit, is assumed not to conflict with motivation to continue to exist. But, as in the example, motivation to keep capital intact or to minimise losses of working capital can conflict with the profit motive. Exclusive pursuit of the most profitable final position, in other words, could have the odd result of driving a firm into receivership along the way, Yet, thirdly, perhaps the most important point is one often stressed by Joan Robinson.[15] A firm faced with a shift in its demand must *change* its behaviour pattern. Change takes time, which has a fixed cost in interest. But neo-Classical time is a sort of logical abstraction, where each position on a supply or demand curve has its own infinite past and future and represents a hypothetical fully adjusted equilibrium situation. There is no *movement* from point to point on a neo-Classical curve. There is only a hypothetical *comparison* of what might have been. The conditions for the continued existence and operation of the bearers are assumed to be met at every point, without ever being shown explicitly or their resulting constraints being set forth. But actual events occur in historical, not in logical, time and actual bearers need actual support, creating real constraints.

Neo-Classicists may not grant this, since they are wont to 'ignore working capital', by assuming that firms either operate without it or can raise it without limit at going rates. In our view, this is just the sort of 'simplifying' assumption which renders a model impracticable. It is not merely that actual firms do need to pay for working capital and that this fact does actually influence their behaviour. It is, rather, that if the model is to be a model of a *firm*, then the conditions for the firm's continued operation are presupposed. Production is essentially a time-consuming process of using up material goods to produce material goods. Capitalist production is the assigning of the net proceeds of this operation to owners, who are at liberty to reinvest, lend or spend them. A model must show how this assignment can be carried out as production carries on. Price-cutting endangers this and a model which predicts price-cutting, without demonstrating how the institution can successfully maintain its existence, is not an applicable model.

In a preliminary way, then, we suggest that economic concepts referring to bearers of economic variables must not be so defined that the bearers referred to could not sustain their role in the economic process. A model using such concepts will be inapplicable, because impracticable.

Neo-Classicists, accepting that models need to be applicable, might be

---

[15] Cf. for instance, *Essays in the Theory of Economic Growth* (Macmillan, 1962), Ch. I.

tempted to say that applicability is simply a matter of making allowance for relevant facts. If, for instance, considerations of working capital affect a firm's behaviour, thus upsetting the economist's predictions, then suitable values should simply be assigned in the model. In our view, however, this conflicts with what we said earlier about the kind of assumptions to which neo-Classical economics is committed. A Classical or Marxian notion of what is relevantly part of the productive process calls not for adjustments to neo-Classical assumptions but, as we saw at the end of the last chapter, for a different sort of model. Moreover this other sort, which we will call 'structural', is theoretically prior to an equilibrium analysis since no bearer of economic variables can achieve equilibrium, if he has already failed to sustain himself adequately or gone out of business.

Four objections to neo-Classicism

Economic models (including neo-Classical models) typically have variables, whose values are the actions of economic agents. Consequently they apply only to agents capable of performing the actions required. Included in the model are definitions of which agents can perform which actions. A 'household', for instance, is a consuming unit. The bearer of a supply variable has to be a supplier. Firms necessarily do not supply factors of production. Such definitional statements of what various sorts of agent do or do not do are, when true, necessarily true. If our account of necessity is right, they state what must be in fact true of an economic agent who is a possible bearer of a given sort of variable.

With this in mind, we turn to four objections to conventional theory, common in recent debates. All seem to allege incoherence in the theory and might be taken to show the theory impossible. We shall defend orthodoxy against charges of impossibility but shall then press for a conviction on charges of impracticability. (This will leave some arguments which we think yet more powerful for the final chapter.)

The first objection is to the neo-Classical model of perfect competition and alleges that no bearer could possibly both be rational and be possessed of perfect or complete market and technical information. The proof is apparently simple. To say that a bearer has perfect information is to say that no further information could improve his profits or productivity, and so to say that the marginal product of information is zero. Information will normally have a positive marginal cost; extra time and effort, which could be profitably used on other projects, must be expended in order to acquire extra information. But if the marginal cost of information is positive, the expected marginal product will be equated to it, and so will never fall to zero. Information will always be incomplete in equilibrium.

An apparent escape for the neo-Classicist lies in arguing that information has zero marginal costs, since all its costs are overhead costs. But that reply is both implausible and disastrous. It is implausible, because, as already argued, it takes time to absorb information and time has an opportunity cost. It is disastrous, because overhead costs still need a marginal analysis. Capital will be invested in information producing activities to the point where long-run expected marginal return equals the going rate of interest. Since this is always positive, investment in information has no chance whatever of generating a perfect supply of information.

Before judging the objection, we shall deploy the others which we wish to discuss. The second alleges a contradiction in the notion that investment is governed by considerations of marginal productivity, on the ground that, whereas the actual capital stock reflects the technical possibilities of the past, the production function reflects those present or expected in the future. Since knowledge accumulates, the two influences have different effects. Meanwhile capital goods are durable and, once installed, can be changed only as fast as they wear out. Since there are complementarities in capital goods, techniques chosen in current investment will be constrained by past decisions. They cannot, therefore, be correctly described by a theory which makes the capital-intensity chosen a function solely of the rate of interest in the usual way. The rate of interest matters precisely because the equipment is durable and generates returns, which must be discounted to obtain present value. Yet, precisely because the equipment is durable, the rate of interest cannot govern a marginal choice, since durable equipment chosen in the past still exists and will influence the choice. To put it summarily, a society cannot both use and not use durable equipment. The very feature that might make marginal productivity relevant also ensures that it cannot be the governing factor.

The third objection alleges a contradiction between assumptions of perfect mobility and perfect information. In deciding whether to enter a market, a firm needs to know what supplies other firms in or about to enter the market can give. Otherwise, perfect mobility being assumed, the prospect of profit in any market would lead all those in all other markets to enter at once. Conversely the moment profits dip below normal, all firms would abandon the market like startled rabbits. Perfect mobility, in other words, coupled with lack of information about other suppliers means perfect instability. In practice firms do know what others are going to do and, when some enter, others hold back. But such knowledge is possible only because there are known constraints on the actions of the other firms, arising partly because all firms cannot in practice act at once, and partly because of indivisibilities and inflexibilities. Durable capital goods, for instance, are not fully adaptable to producing for all markets. Perfect information thus necessarily includes information about constraints, which imply that there cannot also be perfect mobility.

The fourth objection is that assumptions of perfect mobility and rationality conflict. The reasoning is again that given for the impossibility of combining perfect information with rationality. Mobility has a positive marginal cost, which, arguably, rises as the volume of resources shifted from one line of industry to another increases. While marginal cost is positive, mobility must be imperfect. If, in reply, the costs of mobility are argued to be overhead costs, then the retort is again that such a move is implausible and, in any case, simply shifts the difficulty to the long run.

The four objections are powerful. But, presented as claims that neo-Classical models are impossible, because contradictory, they can be easily evaded. The evasions are, to be sure, disingenuous and take the form of adding epicycles to the original theory. The line taken is to grant the arguments and then to incorporate them by adding 'corrections'. Information is admitted not to be perfect, with the result that some technical opportunities are missed, some prices fail to be uniform, some chances of entry or exit are overlooked. These imperfections can be seen as either systematic or random. If they are systematic, then a function can be postulated, showing the deviation from perfect competition equilibrium. If they are random, a random shift variable can be introduced into all affected functions. This sort of device can be used to deal with all four objections, after which the neo-Classicist continues as before, now regarding his competitive theory as an 'idealised case' or 'ideal type', against which actual departures from the model can be measured.

We do not intend to try to decide finally whether this sort of reply suffices, since we are only clearing the ground for what we want to say on our own account. Nevertheless, we wish to air some suspicions, before passing on. We recall again our earlier distinction between two kinds of assumption. Information and mobility occur in the neo-Classical world not as variables in their own right but as consequences of the definitions of other variables. To assume that information or mobility is perfect is not to assign to a variable with a value range of 0 to 1 the value 1. For no such variable with such a range has been defined. When information or mobility are imperfect, other variables do not so much shift as become inapplicable. For instance the theory requires enough information to ensure that prices and rate of profit are uniform. Lack of uniformity would mean not a shift in the value of the variables 'price' and 'rate of profit' but the end of talk about *'the* price of good x' or *'the* rate of profit on capital'. There would be various prices and various rates and no reason to suppose that the extent of deviation from uniformity would remain constant, as other indices changed. To restore order, we would have to know the exact patterns of information flow, its speed of travel compared to speeds of market adjustment, its cost and usefulness, as functions of the date and amount of different kinds of information; and so forth. With all these additions, the basic model would by now have changed beyond recognition.[16] Much more important, when information and mobility are less than perfect, control over information and timing of mobility become strategic variables in competition, which require us to conceive of the market place in a different way.

There remains also our repeated argument that the equilibrium model is untestable. Yet the function relating deviations from perfect information and mobility to deviations from equilibrium cannot be constructed, until the model has been tested and found true. To treat observed correlations of degrees of information and mobility with variations in price-quantity patterns as significant for equilibrium theory is to beg a huge question. The circularity detected in earlier chapters is not waved away by construing the theory as an 'ideal type'.

Similarly a conflict between assumptions of perfect mobility and of perfect rationality also prevents the formation of uniform prices and uniform rates of return. To restore order, we would need to know the exact costs and benefits of mobility in various industries. This can be done, but only by changing the model so that it conflicts with most textbook ones. Again, however, the central neo-Classical vision can surely survive a change in its textbooks.

The other two objections have more teeth. At the simplest level, both cast doubt on the responsiveness of technical processes to market incentives. The one alleging conflict between assumptions of perfect mobility and of perfect information reminds us that knowing what other people are likely to do depends on knowing the immobilities constraining them. Since there could be no stable market adjustment pattern without such constraints, the argument threatens to reduce to absurdity the view that social atoms can be combined to form any number of different social and economic systems. The other objection, to do with investment criteria and marginal productivity, reminds us that a modern capitalistic productive process produces not only a commodity output but also partly-worn out equipment. Anyone who once thinks of gross output in this way will find it hard to suppose that factors can be substituted for one another in producing the *same* output. An isoquant will become harder to comprehend. The amount of output, being composed of incommensurables, must be expressed in value and, to know the value of partly worn-out equipment, we must know prices

---

[16] This point is, we confess, more polemical than profound and we aim it only at those minor objects of pedagogic veneration, the models in basic and intermediate level textbooks.

and the rate of interest. These objections go to the heart of neo-Classical thought about capital and supply and we shall press them further in a moment. But, when we do, we shall change the context. So long as we continue to treat the assumptions as concerned with the *behaviour* of given agents, we remain within the confines of the neo-Classical vision. And all four of these problems can then be dealt with by adding suitable epicycles, even if at some cost to the authors of textbooks. Instead we shall shift our ground and set the question in a Classical-Marxian context, making the issue whether agents so defined can continue to reproduce themselves and their economic setting consistently with the behaviour postulated of them.

The continuing argument among economists about neo-Classical theory is hard to adjudicate but, if the charge is that neo-Classical models are impossible, because inconsistent, we judge it so far unproven. Whether they are impracticable, however, is another matter. We shall next argue that they are and that they presuppose a structural model which turns out to be Classical or Marxian.

9
RATIONALIST FOUNDATIONS FOR ECONOMIC THEORY

We have just seen how neo-Classical assumptions underwrite the neo-Classical picture of the price mechanism as a sensitive flexible instrument for allocating resources optimally while resolving questions of exchange and payment to the benefit of all parties and in the process preserving and even enhancing efficiency. We have argued not only that these assumptions are not fulfilled, but also that they cannot be, given the world we live in. Given modern technology and the role of durable goods in it, the assumption of easy, costless transfer of resources is nonsensical. However, when we try to make it look plausible, by admitting that there is at least some cost to transferring resources, the model is weakened, as the assumption of mobility comes into conflict with the assumption of rationality. Exactly the same happens to the assumption of market information; when we take account of the reality of communications and information technology and allow for the cost of information, the same conflict emerges. In addition and perhaps even more interestingly, some crucial information, strategic information about competitors' intentions, actually presupposes immobilities and inflexibilities. The neo-Classical world ignores power and power thrives on rigidity. Once we allow that there must be immobilities, information gaps, and imperfectly adjusted durable capital structures, we can expect a world where, for instance, bad products drive out good.

Two properties of bearers

Let us examine this further. The four objections can be met with epicycles, while we remain within the neo-Classical system. But they cannot be evaded, once we turn to considering the necessary conditions for reproduction. The objections then show, we maintain, that neo-Classicism is not so impossible but nonetheless impracticable; that, given our world, a social order must, in reproducing itself materially, endow its institutions with certain properties in conflict with the neo-Classical assumptions. If the assumptions are made at all realistically, then they generate the four objections, which suffice to show that neo-Classical optimality cannot be guaranteed, indeed, could be achieved at best by accident. If the assumptions are not realistic they conflict with necessary properties of the bearers; and so the model will not apply at all.

Two such properties stand out. (It should be remembered that we are talking about repeatable and repeated patterns of action.) First, actions which are either involved in material reproduction or underwritten by its results use up material goods and services or the time of persons supported by material goods and services. Such actions take time, can be well or badly done, are completed or fall short and can succeed or fail. They are *productions*, not performances, as we pointed out at the end of Chapter 5. This point is central to all four of these objections. Acquiring information takes time, and can succeed or fail, be well or badly done, as all students know. Moving resources from one line of business to another uses up time and resources and can be well or badly executed; and similarly for installing durable equipment. Once one treats these activities *as what they are*, namely as productions, the four difficulties just canvassed arise, showing that the assumptions no longer support the neo-Classical vision of the price mechanism. Actions are not what neo-Classicists would like them to be, and this is devastating to their scheme of things.

Secondly, technology is not what the neo-Classicists take it to be; and this is equally devastating. All four objections arise because technical processes including communication and the processing of information take time and require inflexible, because specialised, resources. Technical processes, not surprisingly, are productions. They are therefore, to neo-Classical eyes, 'inflexible and rigid', giving rise to 'discontinuities and externalities'. We put these phrases in quotation marks, because no one who was not steeped in neo-Classical lore would ever think of describing modern technology in this way. What to most everyday observers would seem the most flexible and adaptable equipment ever made, say, for example, a modern automated steel rolling mill, must be described as the very opposite and be blamed for discontinuities and rigidities marring the neo-Classical picture of production simply because it is efficient, well-adapted to its purposes and long-lasting. Our argument has repeatedly indicated the importance of 'flexibility', and easy costless substitution to the neo-Classical picture. Where equipment is specialised, durable, and costly, and information is imperfect, the conditions for our home-grown law are present. And we see now that, if technical processes are conceived as productions, as they must be if the model is to apply, then they will generate the four problems considered at the end of the last chapter. This shows that neo-Classical assumptions cannot be made strong enough to guarantee sufficient 'flexibility' to ensure that only neo-Classical conclusions will follow.

The production function and the Law of Substitution: a critique

We now propose to take this argument a major stage further. We shall contend that the basic neo-Classical picture of an economy in which the production system is governed by the Law of Substitution, as understood in the neo-Classical framework of thought, is inconsistent with the regular reproduction of the social order, given the laws of physics as we know them, and the very simplest notion of property. So far we have drawn out the implications of technical processes being productions rather than performances; now we must examine productions more closely. At the end of Chapter 4 we found that the more precisely we described a particular economic activity the more we uncovered its *logical* interdependence with other economic activities. For this reason we were unable to isolate a set of economic activities capable of serving as atomic facts. Now we set out the regular reproductive system, as a set of ongoing social activities, and examine the patterns of logical interdependences. We remember that the ability to refer to social entities, ongoing institutions or repeatable patterns of activity, depends on the ability of the system to reproduce and maintain such entities. Our question will therefore be whether the regular reproduction of the neo-Classical entities is consistent with the picture of production as governed by the Law of Substitution? And our method will be to set forth a simple production model and to examine the logical connections implied in the productions contained in it.

Let us advance by considering two interpretations of the production function. The first, and more conventional would write it:

$$q = q(f_1, f_2, \ldots, f_n)$$

where q is the firm's output and $f_1, \ldots, f_n$ are the inputs of factors acquired by the firm and applied to producing q. Here the firm is the bearer of two variables, output and acquired inputs, and different firms can produce the same good, while having differing production functions. The second interpretation leaves the firm out altogether and regards the production function as a summary of what is needed to make a given product with the going technology. It is an economic report of engineering possibilities and shows the design of a good. So, whereas the first interpretation shows the results of action, the second shows possibilities for action. Whereas the first requires that there be already a bearer for the variables, the second does not: or, to put it another way, whereas the first shows the production function of a firm, the second shows the production function of a good. We contend that the production function in the first sense depends on the production function in the second sense. Let us see what this means.

Suppose that what is produced is an economic agency, a household, and consider the minimum amounts needed to support an average family of wife at home, man at work and two children being reared to replace them. For each period of time an input of commodities and services will be needed. Each input is itself the product of inputs, themselves the product of inputs. If we list the inputs, the inputs of those inputs and so on, until the list repeats itself, we shall have recorded the complete structure needed to support a family. For instance:

$$a_1 \,\&\, b_1 \,\&\, c_1 \to a$$
$$a_2 \,\&\, b_2 \,\&\, c_2 \to b$$
$$a_3 \,\&\, b_3 \,\&\, c_3 \to c$$

where a might be a bundle of goods able fully to support labour, b might be tools and c might be raw materials. Since a, b, and c are used in each other's production, the output of each has to be divided among all three activities. Each input takes time to produce; the aggregate output is the minimum set of goods, given the available technical knowledge, that will support work time at the end of the stated time. The system will not be practicable, unless in each case aggregate input is less than or equal to aggregate output:

$$a_1 + a_2 + a_3 \leqq a$$
$$b_1 + b_2 + b_3 \leqq b$$
$$c_1 + c_2 + c_3 \leqq c$$

And now we have a highly simplified design or structural model, showing not what happens nor what anyone will do but what conditions have to hold for any bearer of the variables to continue to exist.

Some important economic results follow almost at once. Suppose first that aggregate output is just sufficient for replacement. Then, writing p_a, p_b, p_c for the barter exchange ratios, we determine these:

$$a_1 p_a + b_1 p_b + c_1 p_c = a p_a$$
$$a_2 p_a + b_2 p_b + c_2 p_c = b p_b$$
$$a_3 p_a + b_3 p_b + c_3 p_c = c p_c$$

Any one of the prices can be taken as a standard and the others expressed in terms of it. If more is produced than is required for productive consumption, we can speak of a surplus. The exchange ratios will not be determinate until the disposition of the surplus is settled. We will discuss this further shortly.[1]

---

[1] For a fuller discussion, cf. Sraffa, *Production of Commodities*, Ch. 1 and 2.

We are now ready to press home the two sharper objections above, in order to show that the conditions for the continued existence of households and firms (the bearers of neo-Classical economic variables) conflict with an essential presumption of neo-Classical economics. Let us look more closely at our simplified structural model. Subject to the feasibility condition that aggregate output in each case at least equals aggregate input, as have:

$$a_1 \& b_1 \& c_1 \to a \text{ (worker support)}$$
$$a_2 \& b_2 \& c_2 \to b \text{ (tools)}$$
$$a_3 \& b_3 \& c_3 \to c \text{ (raw materials)}$$

The rows, read across, show production-supply; the columns, read down, show productive consumption—demand. Now suppose that some other way of producing the same amount of b is proposed. In neo-Classical theory this is a simple and common case, since b can normally be produced in infinitely many ways, involving relatively more or relatively less labour. Moreover, in neo-Classical theory, the household's utility functions are unaffected by the way chosen to produce b and the only repercussions on other industries are through influence on factor and product prices. After all, in the words of Samuelson, 'Substitution is the law of life in a full employment economy'[2].

But this is an implausible picture.[3] A change in a productive process has far more effects than are dreamt of in neo-Classical theory and, we contend, necessarily so. A change in the material input-labour ratio must affect job definitions or product specifications or both.[4] New job definitions call for new skills, thus affecting the training of workers, the pattern of consumption and perhaps even styles of family living. Hence utility functions are almost sure to shift, following a move along a production function. New product specifications change the potential usefulness of the product, causing users to adapt to its new qualities and to modify their processes of production. If such changes are economically significant, neo-Classicists will be embarrassed. For a change in the value of a variable will have caused some parameters of their model to shift.

Let us consider what happens when b is produced in a new way. If we suppose, for the moment, that the product specification is unaltered, then it follows logically that design and raw materials are also unaltered. Hence the change shows itself in the organisation of work, in the tools for

---

[2] P. A. Samuelson, *Economics*, 6th ed. (McGraw-Hill, 1964), p. 19.

[3] John Hobson pointed this out long ago in *The Industrial System* (1910; new and revised ed., A. M. Kelley, 1969).

[4] This is argued by Hobson, *ibid*. Whether these effects are economically significant in any given case is an empirical matter.

shaping the material or in the source of energy. If it happens, for instance, that machines are brought in to guide or replace human labour, job specifications are bound to change. The change may well be economically significant. If we suppose, alternatively, that a new raw material is used to produce b, then the product specification is bound to alter. Here is a case where what the product is, what goes into it, who makes it and how it is made are logically connected. There are logical limits on possible substitutions.

The Law of Substitution, therefore, cannot be reckoned a universal law. Where rational or optimal changes are made, previous patterns of training and consumption will rarely serve. Where equilibrium requires that, for any given pattern of aggregate job specifications, job training and worker consumption be optimal, any change in the skills demanded will call for some change in worker training. Similarly, where product use is to be optimal, changes in the product will call for adjustments, even though the users could make do at less than optimum.

Technical change

Conventional use of the Law of Substitution thus involves abstraction which ignores essential features of production. This is not to say that in given cases these neglected features will always be practically significant. The actual relevance of changes in product or job specification is a matter for practical observation but their potential relevance is a conceptual consequence of defining 'production' in terms of the using up of resources. The neo-Classicist may defend his abstraction on the ground that these conceptually necessary changes in parameters do not always matter and can, in any case, be dealt with by 'adjusting' the data. But, we reply, the defence falls, since he has deprived himself of all criteria for deciding when the changes, which are crucial aspects of the impact of technology on society, are economically significant. For an effect will be judged economically significant only if it affects the equilibrium values of rates of return or quantities of factors employed; but equilibrium in turn depends on supply and demand functions, which are constructed on the basis of the Law of Substitution. Consider, as a case, the neo-Classical analysis of technical change during growth.

Here the issue is usually conceived in terms of the effects on the returns to factors, which are taken to depend in turn on the role of various factors in sustaining a given level of production. Technical progress is said to be 'neutral' when some definitive index of returns is unaffected. Three definitive indices have been proposed by eminent authorities. Technical progress is Harrod-neutral when, for a given capital–output ratio, the production function shifts upwards, leaving the rate of return to capital unchanged. It is Hicks-neutral, when, for a given capital-labour ratio, the function shifts upwards, leaving the relative shares of labour and capital unchanged. It is Solow-neutral, when, for a given productivity of labour, the upward shift leaves the wage rate unaffected. These indices are put to various uses. Is there, for instance, any systematic aggregate bias in technical change over the years? Is there any theoretical reason to prefer one index (usually Harrod's one) to the others? What influences the rate of technical advance? How does the date of manufacture of equipment (as opposed to the date of its first use) affect change? Questions like these indeed merit investigation but our concern is not with them but with a premiss of the approach.

The neo-Classicist is concerned with the effects of technical advance on returns to factors and his premiss is that returns to factors reflect and are ultimately determined by uses of technically defined inputs. He does not actually distinguish between 'factors' and 'inputs' – or, rather, he supposes that the latter can be combined into the former; witness the books and articles supposedly about technical change, which neither mention nor analyse any actual invention or improvement. When the distinction is drawn,[5] he has to hope that factor variables, such as 'capital', constructed by aggregating inputs will behave in accordance with neo-Classical production function theory; that it is at least 'as if' there were a suitable production function.[6] Yet the hope has been conclusively dispelled in recent controversy. Our argument complements this conclusion. For, on examining the connections between inputs as they appear in a 'production', we find that there are logical connections between different kinds of inputs, which sharply limit the possibilities for things being 'as if' neo-Classical substitution took place. But if the Law of Substitution is not generally valid, we can no longer suppose that the Principle of Scarcity operates here. The price mechanism, in short, as understood in neo-Classical thinking, will not have a home here. Inputs will not aggregate into well-behaved 'factors' and the returns to factors will not depend on the productive use made of inputs.

Once the premiss is rejected, the way is open for a fresh treatment of technical change. Looking instead for effects on the use of *inputs*, as opposed to 'factors', one can ask, for example, how change will affect the skill-composition of the demand for labour. How will vocational education be affected? In what conditions and to what extent will mechanical,

---

[5] We drew it earlier and shall press the point later.
[6] E.g. P. A. Samuelson, Parable and realism in capital theory; the surrogate production function, *Review of Economic Studies*, Vol. 29, no. 3 (June 1962).

electrical or other energy replace human effort? Does technical progress require ever more bureaucratic organisation of labour? What happens to the aggregate of kinds of job offered? Must jobs be organised hierarchically? Does unskilled labour systematically yield to white-collar jobs? How do the qualities, for instance the durability, of the product respond? Is there sometimes, as we, following Veblen, have maintained, resulting market pressure to lower the technical quality of goods and perhaps of labour services, in the spirit of Gresham's Law? The task of theory will typically be to determine the conditions in which an innovation occurs (for instance a machine which replaces labour but needs much labour to introduce) and the consequences it brings. There is nothing in textbook neo-Classical theory capable of tackling such questions and neo-Classical theorists have in fact left them alone.

Indeed one striking characteristic of neo-Classical thinking about technology is the small scale of the questions asked. Historians and archaeologists have christened whole eras by the technology used. After the Bronze Age, the Age of Steam, the Atomic Age, what about the Harrod-neutral Age? Marx even claimed that 'The hand-mill gives you society with the feudal lord; the steam-mill society with the industrial capitalist.' We cannot assess such contentions in this book but they do indicate a neo-Classical blind spot. To raise such questions the economist needs a framework of careful conceptual connections among the elements entering into the material reproduction of the social system.

Provisional summary of the critical case

Let us take stock now. We contend that this broadside, taken in conjunction with our earlier cannonades, is enough to sink the neo-Classical ship, although we hardly dare hope that many of its passengers or crew will join us in the Classical and Marxian lifeboats. Nevertheless, let us state our claim as baldly as we can in the form of a dilemma: *either* economic agents and activities are conceived in such a way that the neo-Classical assumptions are sufficient to entail the vision of optimality resting on the two critical theses, in which case the model cannot, in principle, apply to a world in which our present laws of physics and engineering hold: *or* economic agents and activities are conceived in a manner consistent with regular reproducibility, in which case the model can apply, but adulteration in the product and exploitation in the factor market are both conceivable, even likely, in equilibrium, optimality is a farce, and the door is open wide in welcome to both Veblen and Marx.

Positivism provided neo-Classicism with defences, which we had first to break down. But our critique of neo-Classicism finally rests not on our critique of Positivism, but on our alternative to it, Rationalism. For the basic contention that neo-Classical models are either inapplicable or incapable of generating neo-Classical conclusions arises from the conflict between standard neo-Classical assumptions and the real definitions of economic activity. Neo-Classicism finally falls foul of necessary but not purely logical truths. And it is such truths which make it possible for the economist both to provide explanations, even where his predictions have failed, and to act as a critic and judge of the economic aspects of society, the role we proffer in place of the positivists' passive and neutral observer. We hope our arguments will lead the reader to agree with Joan Robinson:

The success of modern capitalism for the last twenty five years has been clearly bound up with the armaments race and the trade in arms (not to mention wars when they are used); it has not succeeded in overcoming poverty in its own countries and has not succeeded in helping (to say the least) to promote development in the Third World. Now we are told that it is in the course of making the planet un-inhabitable even in peacetime.

It should be the duty of economists to do their best to enlighten the public about the economic aspects of these menacing problems. They are impeded by a theoretical schema which (with whatever reservations and exceptions) represents the capitalist world as a kibbutz operated in a perfectly enlightened manner to maximise the welfare of all its members.[7]

Our critique of Positivism, however, has led us to develop Classical and Marxian models. For Positivism could not account for the relation of theory either to fact or to hypotheses. Economic facts are not independent of economic theories, as they would have to be under Positivism, and theories do support hypotheses, as they could not according to Positivism. In providing an alternative account, we were obliged to look more closely at the basic concept, production, whose real definition, we held, provided the only safe foundation for the subject of economics. In trying to find a level of economic atomic facts, for instance, we found instead that the more closely we looked at particular economic activities the more precisely we came to see their interdependence. Such interdependence, however, we found grounded in the material relations of production. For economic activities are performed by agents, who require support both for themselves and for their regular patterns of activity. The interdependence of activities led us to the material dependence of agents upon each other and upon basic production activities and this in turn led us to develop a rudimentary production model or basic theory of material support, which then provided us with a rudimentary theory of exchange and even of distribution. Thus, in attempting to answer

[7] *Economic Heresies*, pp. 143–144.

the questions with which we floored Positivism, we developed an alternative philosophy, which has led us into an alternative economic theory, admittedly still elementary, yet capable of attempting the root questions. We now propose to spend the rest of our final chapter showing that this theory does indeed answer the questions and is, in fact, Classical-Marxian in form.

An objection: production 'need' not be basic

First we must dispose of a possible crucial objection. To see where it arises we must review our position again. In Chapter 6 we argued that different subjects are and must be formally distinguishable from one another by 'non-logical constants'. The definitions and axioms introducing the non-logical constants, and so demarcating the subject, are, we maintained, necessary but non-analytic truths. In the traditional rationalist term, the subject must rest upon *real definitions* of its fundamental concepts. In Chapter 7, developing the ideas of Chapter 5, we contended that the fundamental concept was *production*, taken in an extended sense. For economic variables apply only if they are predicated of appropriate bearers. Bearers in turn are characterised by the assumptions of the model, and a necessary condition of a model's applicability, we argued, is that a social system of the kind the model seeks to describe should be capable of regularly reproducing and supplying bearers who have the specified characteristics. This then required developing a simple model of production, which led on to a basic notion of exchange.

A critic might accept our contention that the subject must rest on real definitions and yet object to taking production as the basic concept. For instance, he might contend that, since production methods are chosen, 'choice' in the sense of allocating scarce resources among competing ends, should figure as the basic concept. This, indeed, is how we interpret Robbins' position, at least his earlier position. Nor is choice the only possible alternative: exchange, the market, money, labour and capital, all spring to mind as possible candidates. Why should we claim a necessarily privileged status for 'production', or, more exactly, for 'reproduction of the economic system'?

The question is as dangerous as it is apparently difficult. For if we cannot provide a satisfactory answer, our whole argument is in jeopardy. Our account of explanation and of the role of the economist as social critic rests on necessary truth of conclusions validly derived from sound and applicable economic theories. Counting equivalent sets as the same, there can therefore be only one set of fundamental economic definitions and axioms. There can be only one economic science. Of course there can be many different aspects to it and many different branches, just as there can be many different kinds of explanation for the same event, so long as each different kind explains a different aspect. But necessary truths cannot conflict; alternative theories, that is, theories with incompatible implications, are not allowable, and even complementary theories must be fitted together and made to cohere. We cannot allow the possibility of different fundamental concepts, for different concepts will give rise to different theories, as different as Robbins and Marx. Pragmatists might simply shrug agreeably and wait to see which worked out the best. No such cheerfully casual course is open to us.

Nor, however, is one necessary. For, we believe, we have already given sufficient reasons to rule out every one of the above suggestions. The general point is simple. Choice depends upon choosers, exchange upon traders, labour upon workers, and so on. Choosers need reasons and abilities, traders must have goods and skills, workers jobs and skills. Hence the agents in question, and their replacements when they grow old or ill, when they die or retire, must be trained and supported, as must the context in which the agents characteristically operate. The reproduction of the system, in short, is primary. Nevertheless, let us take each suggestion in turn.

First, choice, since it is the most obvious and widely canvassed alternative. Our answer is simple: choice depends on the context and activities of the choosers. We do not want things in a vacuum, we want something 'under some aspect' as philosophers would put it. If we want a good or service, that is, if we want it *regularly* on a continuing repeatable basis, not as a once for all whim, then we want it *for* something, *in order to* do something with it, because it fits into a project or activity of ours. So some aspect or other of the thing must relate to the reason for wanting it. Some very important conclusions follow, which we have already met in Chapter 5. First, the formation of relative preferences among goods and services, if *it is to be rational, must* involve solving typical *production* problems. Preferences for goods and services, what economists normally call 'tastes', cannot be among the fundamental raw data of economics. Preferences for commodities must be calculated and the calculation will be based, as in the linear programming example, on the way the characteristics of different goods contribute to the objectives of the choosing agent. Secondly, what one wants and what is good for one can, and frequently do, conflict. One may like cigarettes but one's doctor may know better. To function properly and effectively in his appointed roles, a person must maintain both his health and his levels of training and competence: and in either or both of these areas personal preference may be at variance with rational choice. Both points imply that choosing is a concrete activity taking place in specific circumstances. We choose what we do because the context we are in provides us with certain options, certain resources and certain goals. Apart from the context neither 'choice', nor any of its synonyms amongst economists, (preference, wants, etc.) have significance. But once we allow that the chooser *must* exist in a specific social context, then the characteristics of the chooser we can assume are limited by the requirements for the maintenance of the context. The conditions of reproduction are prior to because determining, those of choice.

But what of the argument that we choose the methods of production, that choice determines the system of production, and so the basic context itself? We have already answered the argument, if it is to mean that such choices take place in accordance with the neo-Classical scheme, by pointing out that durable capital goods are among the determinants of choice. Nevertheless there is a point here. Our contention is based on the belief that society as a whole is responsible for what exists in it. A social system is a process which regularly uses itself up and recreates itself. In the course of this, and by rules which the system itself establishes, new products, new skills or new methods of production may be introduced, and new social positions may be created. In this sense, whatever is may be so because it has been deliberately chosen. But it also may *not* have been chosen, nor may it have come about *as if* it has been chosen. It is entirely possible to conceive (and anthropologists have written) of self-sufficient, self-reproducing economic systems, with specialisation of function and exchange, producing a surplus which is distributed according to definite rules, in which there is no mechanism by which a new method of production or new products could be introduced. It is true that in our time the area of conscious control over economic activity has widened and that we are moving towards a time when perhaps we may be able to control and determine the shape and form of what exists in society. But we certainly do not at present, and to pretend that we do is cruel mockery.

Secondly, 'exchange' is a less plausible candidate for the basic concept than 'choice'. Not only must traders be supported, and have reasons for wishing to trade, which implies that they must be functioning in a definite context, requiring maintenance, but they must also have something to trade. The regular supplying of traders with their wares must be explained before we can explain a regular pattern of trade. Exchange depends on having something to exchange, so must be placed in a context of production. Thirdly, exactly the same arguments can be applied against a claim of priority for the concept of 'the Market'; we must first account for the existence of what is to be marketed, and for the maintenance of the institutions of the market itself. (No doubt the *development* of the market will *encourage* production. That is quite another matter.) Fourthly, 'Money' is simply a means to exchange and assist accounting; also a store of value. It therefore depends upon the prior development of exchange and the market. Fifthly, 'Labour' is either a *part* of the production process, and therefore an inadequate, because incomplete, candidate for the role of fundamental concept (how is it supported, where does it get tools, what happens to products?), or it may be thought of as wage-labour, in which case it is peculiar to capitalism. In the theory of capitalism, wage-labour is indeed fundamental, as Figure 3 in the Introduction shows, but for that very reason it cannot be fundamental to economics as a whole. Sixthly, the same applies, *pari passu*, to capital. Either it means 'means of production', in which case the concept is *part* of what we want, or it means 'self-expanding, circulating fund of value', in which case it is peculiar to capitalism, where it is indeed a fundamental concept. Therefore none of these alternatives will do, and interestingly, the more carefully we examine them, the more we are brought back to the conditions for the reproduction of the system, the very concept we want.

Perhaps there is some kindly critic, who applauds our conclusion as a description of some general facts of social experience but adds, like Porgy, that it ain't *necessarily* so. In other words, does the 'priority' we have been claiming for the concept of production rest on more than physical constraints of the world we happen to live in? If not, what we have paraded as conceptual necessities will turn out to be at best physical necessities, whose epistemological status is notoriously doubtful. An ambitious reply would be to carry the argument a stage further by connecting some 'laws of nature', for instance the elementary laws of mechanics and the conservation laws, with the concept of a 'material object', arguing that this concept was itself a conceptual primitive for any understanding of an objective, experienced world. But this, although tempting, would be far beyond our scope. So, more modestly, we reply by pointing out that production necessarily involves the using and using up of materials. The necessity is conceptual, even though physical necessity is involved too. Action equals reaction, if we cut wood we dull the blade, if we sharpen the blade we wear down the grindstone. When we apply force we consume energy. If we are to continue a pattern of activity, we must replace what is used up and support a continuous flow of energy. It is not contingent that outputs require inputs. Physical necessities aside, production necessarily involves more than an act of will and necessarily depletes some of what existed before. By appealing to the idea of change subject to constraint, we can claim to satisfy the critic.

A grammatical matrix of production

It is odd that the necessities involved in production and reproduction are not more widely recognised, since they are deeply embedded in our language. Indeed, they are entrenched in our grammar itself. To show this we will now present what we believe to be a correct, although simplified, form of the conceptual basis of the reproduction system of an economy, *as a grammatical matrix.* For the formalities of grammar distinguish different relationships between man's activities and the world. Following Jesperson we distinguish between verbs of activity, denoting a continuing, on-going process, and verbs of accomplishment, and between various kinds of objects: direct, instrumental, material, and, finally, objects of result. These categories embody a number of distinctions we have been making. For example, verbs of accomplishment are what we have called productions, verbs denoting the moment of point of accomplishment, are what we have called performances, whereas activities are verbs indicating the various operations that go to make up the whole production. (Activities of course, can also stand on their own.) The distinctions between the grammatical categories of instrumental objects (with which or by means of which something is done), material objects (on or to which things are done), and objects of result (the end-product aimed at by a verb of accomplishment) are precisely those traditionally drawn between instruments of production, raw materials and products. The relations between the categories are evident, too. The skills of the subject must be such that he can apply the instruments to the materials, in such a way as to bring about the result. The materials must be such that the intended design can be imprinted on them; the tools must be such that they can be used to bring about the intended result. These are all conceptual relationships, and their implication is that an economic system must meet certain minimal requirements if it is to form a coherent whole. For the categories must be filled; instruments must be designed and produced, materials supplied. Thus each of these will also appear as objects of result. Supply must be adapted to demand not only in quantity, but also in nature. This is the basis of our critique of the Law of Substitution – a change, say, in the design of instruments entails changes in the jobs performed with those instruments.

Now let us look at the matrix (Table 2). Parents teach the skills of II, and supply the socialised people who are then endowed by the educational system with skills and divided up among the roles of I. Farmers supply III, teachers V, workers VI and VII. VIII, however, contains a miscellany. Miners produce materials, but land is given. It enters into the system, but is not itself produced.

We are proposing as an example of the real definition of a reproduction system a matrix with six different outputs which in turn also serve as inputs. The most obvious question is, why six? The answer is simple; it seems enough variety to illustrate our points without becoming unbearably complicated. The actual number of different products is, in our view, an empirical matter, as is the degree and pattern of interdependency in the matrix. That interdependence exists, we hold to be necessary; how much at any time or place, contingent.

TABLE 2. *A Grammatical Matrix of Reproduction*

| | Maintenance demand | | | Replacement demand | | | | | |
| | Activity verb II | Direct object III | Activity verb IV | Instrumental objects V | VI | VII | Material object VIII | Verb of accomplishment 'to produce' | Object of result |
Subject I									
Farmers	Eat etc.	Food etc.	Farm using	Skills	Energy	Tools	Land	→	Food etc.
Workers	Eat etc.	Food etc.	Work using	Skills	Energy	Tools	Materials	→	Tools etc.
Workers	Eat etc.	Food etc.	Work using	Skills	Energy	Tools	Materials	→	Energy etc.
Miners	Eat etc.	Food etc.	Mine using	Skills	Energy	Tools	Land	→	Materials etc.
Teachers	Eat etc.	Food etc.	Teach using	Skills	Energy	Tools	People	→	Skills
Parents	Eat etc.	Food etc.	Supervise using	Skills	Energy	Tools	Their children	→	People

Note. Parents, that is, families reproduce the *population*; the educational system endow them with *skills*, thus dividing the population into *farmers*, various kinds of *workers*, *miners*, etc. Everyone requires maintenance, *food*, etc. Every production process requires (or may require) *energy* and *tools*. *Workers* require raw *materials*; *farmers* and *miners*, however, apply their *skills* to the *land*. All the objects of result re-appear as productive consumption in the column; only *land* is not produced.

The necessity of multiple interdependent activities and the consequences

Our position will be established if we can show that there must always be at least two interdependent activities. Our argument proceeds from the premiss that the world is the way it is: energy consumed must be replaced, and man is mortal. Hence if a society is to continue, not only must new generations succeed old, the existing members must be supported. So supporting life and producing and training new members of society – in short, family life – is one activity. For this activity to be carried on there will have to be food, providing energy. The production of food will require work, whether of hunting and gathering or settled agriculture, and this work will depend on the training and support of family life. So we have as the minimal realistic model the one we met at the end of Chapter 7. There are two activities, supporting and replacing a working population, or family life, and producing food, each of which depends on the other. An exchange rate is defined between them, and if more is produced of either than is consumed in the aggregate, and no less of the other, a surplus will exist. By re-allocating effort, this surplus may be made to consist either of food or of work-time. This is important, as is the existence of the ex- change ratio or real wage. For it means that this two-sector model differs fundamentally from the conventional one-commodity growth models which permeate the textbooks. If we are correct, such models are inapplicable in principle.

So large a claim needs further explanation. We contend that there *cannot* be one-commodity worlds. It is open to defenders of the faith to agree, provided they continue to hold that it is 'as if' there were.[8] Neo- Classical one-commodity growth models depend heavily on bringing capital and its price, the rate of profit, under the scarcity principle: when capital increases in relation to labour, when it becomes less scarce, the rate of profit falls; when it becomes less plentiful, the rate of profit rises.[9] Now

[8] Cf. Samuelson, Parable and realism in capital theory, pp. 193–206.
[9] This is easily illustrated by a widely-used diagram. When a production function, whose arguments represent the combinations of the whole society's capital stock and labour force needed to produce various levels of G.N.P., is 'well behaved' (cf. R.G.D. Allen, *Macro-Economic Theory: A Mathematical Treatment* (Macmillan, 1967), Ch. 3, esp. pp. 41–4) it can be drawn as in Figure 33. y represents output per head, k capital per head. A point k^* is thus a level of capital per man. The tangent to the function is thus the marginal product of capital, equal in competitive conditions to the rate of profit; and from simple geometry the line segment from y^* to Q must equal rk or total profits per head, so that QO will be the wage rate*. Hence, given the production function and competitive conditions, the division of income between wages and profits depends only upon the amount of capital per man.

248

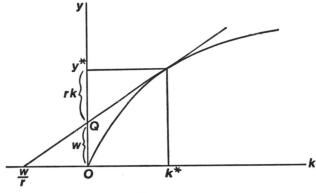

Figure 33

let us look at our two-sector model and let us assume everything the neo-Classicals normally assume – competition, easy, flexible factor mobility, perfect information and the like. Let profits be earned upon food and suppose the whole of net output consists of handiwork goods made in the extra work time. Then the following identity holds:

$$\frac{Y}{N} = r\frac{K}{N} + w$$

(where Y is net output and N the number of workers) so that:

$$\frac{K}{N} = \frac{(Y/N) - w}{r}$$

which can be drawn as a straight line on the graph which we introduced earlier as Figure 29. It is clear from Figure 34 that, as the rate of profit

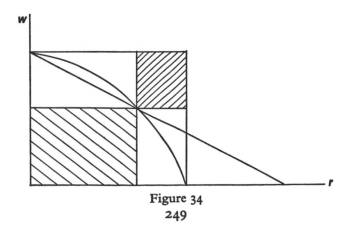

Figure 34

249

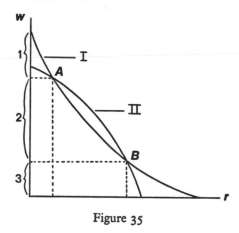

Figure 35

increases, so does the value of capital per man, just the opposite of what the neo-Classical scarcity principle states. Suppose next that we consider two technical systems and ask ourselves which, under ideal conditions, would be the desired system for profit-makers, as we allow the wage to vary in our imaginations (Figure 35). When the wage is high, in range 1, system I would be most profitable. In range 2, system II would yield the highest rate of profit. But in range 3, I would again be best. Now look at the 'switch points' A and B. At point A a small rise in r is associated with an imaginary change over from a high capital per man to one with a low capital per man. But at switch point B just the reverse is true. Switch point A is compatible with the neo-Classical way of thinking but the 'reswitching' point B cannot be accommodated.

We submit then, that, the real definition or basic concept upon which economics must rest is that of a system's ability to reproduce itself. Table 2 (p. 247) expresses a nexus of conceptual relations, intended to articulate the basic notion while leaving it open or contingent how these necessary interdependencies are actually instanced in different societies. The actual details of different social structures are facts independent of economic theory and this means that pure economics can provide only part of a picture, which requires political economy in the first instance and finally a general sociology to complete. Nevertheless the *a priori* ramifications of the concept of ability to reproduce are, we believe, the root of production theory and so of any sound general economic theory. This is our final answer to the regress confronting Positivism in Chapter 4, which a vain hunt for independent atomic facts failed to stop and which, when nourished with pragmatist rejection of the traditional senses of necessity, reduced all enquiry to chaos. In other words, we have argued philosophically that economic theory must be treated axiomatically, and, that its axioms must be true and that some of them must introduce the basic and definitive concepts of economics; and we have then argued that the concept in question is that of Reproduction, whose nature and significance we have now outlined.

Finally, we observe that our real definition of reproduction also supplies an explanation of the necessity of the equilibrium conditions. The condition that supply equal demand is the condition for the solvability of the models, and this, in turn, is the condition for reproduction. When there is a surplus, it will be disposed of in some fashion and the ability of the society to continue operating as it has depends on the surplus being disposed of in the same manner as before. Hence the supply must be distributed according to the pattern of demand.

Reproduction and distribution

It may still strike the reader that we are being somewhat furtive about the transition between philosophy and economics. Our espousal of rationalism certainly commits us to belief in the explanatory power of axiomatic theories and to insisting that economic theory must rest on real definitions. But does it commit us to reproduction as the basic concept or has the discussion just passed wholly into economics? Our reply is that we are committed to a method of enquiry and that we regard the ramifications of the basic economic concept as philosophically significant.[10] But this is enigmatic and, in illustration, we shall now offer the reader a summary account of what we are calling 'production models' in relation to rationalist philosophy. We have already noted that neo-Classical variables are mostly, if not wholly, action-variables, whose values result from intentional acts. (Buying and selling, prices and quantities, costs and outputs, borrowing and lending, saving and investing, rates of return are typical examples.) Yet neo-Classical agents — households and firms — lack many characteristics which we have given reasons for thinking relevant. A 'production model' is an attempt to restore a range of these characteristics. Production can occur only where there is continuity – social organisation and its analysis must therefore allow for reproduction of what is used up.

---

[10] As already hinted, the authors are not wholly unanimous. Hollis, as philosopher, does not feel obliged to offer a particular basis for economic theory, whereas Nell takes basic economic theorising to be fully an exercise in philosophical reasoning. This is not a disagreement of principle, since we share the view advanced here that economic theory is a branch of a more general tree of knowledge but it does mean that the substance of these final two chapters is Nell's, with Hollis being content on grounds of economic ignorance to observe that the earlier criteria of sound theory do indeed matter for judging between economic theories.

Production models as we present them, show what has to be, if the system is to reproduce itself.

The very simple model of household support given earlier shows what we have in mind. Activities are arranged in rows with material components to the left of the arrows and proposed results on the right:

$$a_1 \ \& \ b_1 \ \& \ c_1 \rightarrow a$$
$$a_2 \ \& \ b_2 \ \& \ c_2 \rightarrow b$$
$$a_3 \ \& \ b_3 \ \& \ c_3 \rightarrow c$$

We have already discussed this model and shall analyse it further in a moment, defining the region of 'feasible' outputs and connecting input-output relations with exchange values. But first we must enter some *caveats* about what the model does not show. Compare it with the grammatical model in Table 2. There we distinguished direct, instrumental and material objects and described the subjects and their activities. Here we indicate the subjects and their activities by the amount of their labour time and the various inputs only by their respective quantities. All qualitative distinction is reduced to quantitative uniformity and all the relations between the elements to '&', which, when we solve for barter exchange ratios, will become '+'. There is a good reason for mentioning this. The production formulae represent technology and, as we shall see, can be combined with any of several distributional schemes, so that, apparently, the same production system might be organised on a feudal, a capitalist or a socialist basis. This is profoundly misleading. From a set of production coefficients, taken alone, we can tell nothing about the social system precisely because the degree of abstraction is so high. Hence, in order to represent a social system, an input-output system must be supplemented by what we shall call a Rule of Distribution. But it does not follow that the production system is independent of the relations of distribution. Indeed the connection is too intimate to allow any point of demarcation – the serf's relation to the overseer or the worker's to the foreman falls on neither side of a divide between production and distribution. The relations of dominance and subordination which develop in the management of production will normally be among the central determinants not only of distribution but also of most other social relationships.

Bearing in mind, therefore, that the representation of production shows much less than there is in the system and that production and distribution relations are not independent, let us see what a mathematical model can tell us. The columns in the example given above show automatically the disposition of outputs *as input*. It can be seen immediately whether a given set of activities is viable on its own or whether it requires support from outside. Indeed the amount of support can in principle be calculated, as follows. First check for columns (representing inputs needed) which have no corresponding row (representing productive activity). If there are any, then the inputs must come from outside or the set of activities be augmented. Next add up each column to find the total input needed and compare the total with the output of the corresponding activity. If each corresponding output at least equals its input, the system is viable. If outputs are less than their inputs and there are no compensating excesses, the system is not viable without outside support. If there are some deficits and some excesses, viability depends on the scope for selective retailoring and switching.

Each activity leaves the agents temporarily in possession of their own output but in need of the outputs of other agents. For the system to continue there will have to be exchange. This now becomes a conceptual point and shows that, in linking the notion of production to that of viability, we have to relate it also to the notion of exchange. In introducing exchange we shall want to be able to calculate exchange values for a viable system. But the calculation will follow determinately from the activity table only where each output exactly equals what is needed as input. Where output is in excess – or, to use the famous term, surplus – more information is needed. In particular, who gets the surplus and how? (For Marx and, differently formulated, for Ricardo this was the central question of political economy.) So we shall need to define a new variable, or set of variables, and to postulate a rule of distribution, specifying how the surplus will be spread among the bearers of those variables. For instance, at its most simplistic, the rule might assign the surplus in material form to a ruler or chief, to be distributed as he or the elders see fit. In this case the existence of a surplus would not affect exchange ratios, which continue to be determined only by needs of production, and distribution would not take place through the market mechanism. But again we must caution against thinking that, having defined the production system, we add, contingently, a distribution system to complete the picture. The temptation results from the abstraction needed to set up mathematical formulae for production; but, as our grammatical matrix shows, the relations of production are truly much richer. In particular they involve relations of dominance and subordination, as with teachers and pupils or with supervisors and workers, which cannot easily be separated from distributional relationships. The rule of distribution is therefore best thought of as a further specification of the production system itself.

In general, to demonstrate that an economic system is viable, we must be able to specify the inputs and outputs of its activities and show how exchange satisfies the input requirements. The Rule of Distribution for that system defines the kind of economic system it is. Thus a *market* economy is essentially one where the surplus is distributed through the exchange mechanism, whereas in a *'natural'* economy the surplus is appropriated directly, as in primitive forms of feudalism. Among market economies there are at least three familar types, one where the surplus is distributed in proportion to the labour time needed for each activity (as a function of the subsistence requirements of the workers for the period), another where the distribution depends on the value of the inputs advanced and the third a mixture. These differences are not captured merely by the introduction of a new variable into the table, in order to make up the difference between input and output and so to represent the surplus. For, although this would allow the calculation of exchange values together with the 'rate of surplus value' (the ratio of the value of the surplus to the value of the subsistence inputs), it would not serve to determine whether the system was, for instance, Feudal or Socialist. That would require a further precise interpretation of the 'rate of surplus value' or, in others words the exact rule of distribution.[11] Hence it is the rule of distribution which gives the essential character of the system.[12]

In terms of rationalist philosophy, we have just illustrated the point of applying the notion of 'real definition'. The concept of 'production' is to occur essentially in any analysis of an economic system, in that no theory is an economic theory unless it involves 'production'. Moreover no system is viable without exchange and the concept of 'exchange' needs to be explicitly related to that of 'production'. If this is correct, it is a necessary truth that any viable economic system includes exchange of the output of production; and so in fact true of any actual viable economic system. To determine the kind of system, a Rule of Distribution is then invoked and the taxonomy of possible rules of distribution becomes a part of economic theory also. Our strategy depends on being able to pick out what is conceptually essential and then to insist that what is essential is therefore to be found in practice. This is a rationalist strategy and is merely absurd, unless empiricism is first rejected.

In the sort of system above, outputs of some industries serve as inputs of others. Chains of direct and indirect mutual dependence can be traced. This contrasts with the Walrasian tradition, which stresses the inter-

---

[11] For an illustration of the importance and niceties of applying such a rule, see, for instance, E. J. Nell, Economic relationships in the decline of feudalism, *History and Theory*, vol. 6, no. 3(1967).

[12] For a discussion of various rules of distribution, see E. J. and O. S. Nell, Justice under socialism, *Dissent*, vol. 19, no. 3 (Summer 1972).

dependence of markets, while neglecting the more basic technological inter-dependence of production. Now, it matters much to, for instance, a growth model whether the interdependence stressed is of markets or of production. If it is the former, the arguments of the production function will be factors specific not to technology but to payment of income; supplies and demands will both be tied to the decision-making units, the firm and the household. Yet the technological knowledge and the social conventions underlying production and consumption respectively are part of the common environment of all firms and households and the influence of the common background will be important and perhaps paramount in the long run. Concentration on the individual character of decisions is at the cost of ignoring relevant technological facts.

Classical and Marxian economics focusses on the process of production, and so comes to assess the role of the tradition 'factors of production' differently. They are seen as kinds of income-bearing items rather than as actual productive agents. Although 'capital' and 'labour' receive profits (including interest and dividends) and wages respectively, they do not *as such* enter into production, since they are general categories and need to take particular forms in the production of particular goods. Just the reverse is true in the assignment of income. In equilibrium, the same capital receives the same profit income (allowing for risk), regardless of the particular form it took in production, and the same grade of labour receives the same wage, regardless of the particular job done. So we can distinguish 'factors or production' from 'inputs'. 'Inputs' are goods considered technologically as items in a productive process; 'factors' are collections of inputs held as income-bearing property. This means that neither 'capital' nor 'labour' can be measured independently of prices.

The neo-Classical analogy between the market for factors and the market for final products now breaks down. In the latter value-equivalents (objects differing in use-value but equal in exchange-value) are exchanged; in the former income is paid to those with property rights in the productive process. Even when capital and labour shift in response to differentials in earnings between industries, there is no *exchange* between the recipient of net income and the source of income. The capitalist's sole service to industry is that of allowing it to be his. Although labour receives wages in exchange for work, the level of wages above a basic cost of living, is determined by bargaining power and not, as with ordinary commodities, by a relation between cost of production and value of product. (Evidence is the lack of inherent connection between changes in productivity and changes in the cost of living.) In short, although wage rates and rate of return are made uniform as prices are made uniform and although the return to a factor is normally decided by bargaining, the 'factor market' differs essentially from the markets for goods, in that the payment of net income is not an exchange.

There are also differences among factor markets which matter for distribution theory. For instance, in the market for capital savers compete with investors; the higher the rate of interest, the more savers earn and the less investors profit. Here one set of capitalists gains at the expense of another. Changes in this market redistribute profits among capitalists without directly affecting relative shares. By contrast, competition in the labour market directly affects relative shares, since a gain to labour is a loss to capital and *vice versa*. It might seem that relative shares would then be determined in this market alone and, on certain assumptions, so they will. But the more general case takes note of the point that labour confronts capital again in the market for goods, that the real wage depends on the price level too.

Here we would ask the reader to look again at the Classical-Marxian diagram (Figure 3, p. 17). That diagram was deliberately simple, to bring out the contrast with the neo-Classical picture. Now we must elaborate it. It is no accident that the Classical-Marxian diagram is less abstract, neat and symmetrical than the neo-Classical. There is smoke on the factories in the drawing and factories are concrete, not least in the sense that they cannot be easily adapted. There is a pyramid representing the social system, to remind us that jobs and classes are hierarchical. The profit arrows run between upper levels and the wages arrows between lower levels. Investment decisions are taken at the top of the pyramid, although their effects are felt by those who inhabit the factories, life with the smoke and pollution and risk unemployment. The diagram shows how far we are from industrial democracy.

To elaborate the picture, we will add a separate division for marketing and finance, which some might call 'Wall St.' and illustrate with a Temple of Mammon. We will divide the pyramid into three sections, by inserting in the middle a middle class of employees in the Temple of Mammon, whose work, in the idiom of the old distinction between 'productive' and 'unproductive', is unproductive. This old distinction will be given a new twist by distinguishing the costs of producing goods and services from costs of marketing (or realising) them, including not only advertising, promotion and selling costs but also all costs, like those of finance and lobbying, which have to do with supporting the capitalist system as such. These non-productive costs come out of the 'surplus' generated by productive labour with the instruments, plant and equipment available. This is defined as the excess of total output over and above the goods and services required to support productive labour, to replace the used up means of production and to make up for depreciation of equipment. This surplus will be divided

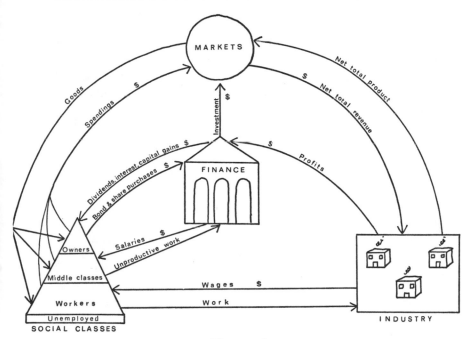

Figure 36

by the financial and corporate managements between ownership income (dividends, interest and realised capital gains), investment and marketing costs, with owners returning a portion in the form of bond and share purchases and spending the remainder of their income on capitalist consumption. Among other things this makes it clear that marketing costs, the costs of running the capitalist system, compete with investment for funds.

The distinction between productive and unproductive labour has often been criticised and not always unjustly. Certainly some cases are hard to classify. Nevertheless work in production is clearly distinct in principle from work in marketing. That a line is sometimes hard to draw does not show there is no line at all. The purpose of the diagram (Figure 36) is simply to exhibit this distinction, indicating its relation to the profit system.

The Social Accounts are now: Wages + Salaries + (Dividends, Interest and Realised Capital Gains) − Bond and Share Purchases = Wages + Surplus = (Worker, Middle Class and Owner) Consumption Demand + Investment Demand = value of Consumption Goods + Value of Investment Goods = Net Total Revenue = Net Total Product.

We could develop our picture still further by showing the State as a platform supporting the pyramid, the Temple of Mammon and the factories, while the market floats above the system independent of 'government interference'. But pictorial metaphors, like crash diets, are best taken in moderation and enough has been said to highlight our points of difference from neo-Classicism. Our next task is a more precise eliciting of implications.

The notion of exchange is perhaps the root notion of economics. The fact that the payment of net income in the factor market is not an exchange in the Classical-Marxian model suggests that there are rival definitions of the notion. In Classical-Marxian thinking a transaction is an exchange (rather than, say, a transfer payment) only if clearly defined, technologically useful goods or services change hands. For the exchange to be in equilibrium, the rate must reflect the relative production costs of the goods, given the competitive requirement of uniform profit on capital. So the Classical-Marxian notion is tied to the technological characteristics of the good and there is no exchange, unless both items have a product equation. In any neo-Classical model, by contrast, an act can count as an act of exchange, if it has an opportunity cost in terms of utility forgone. This distinction will prove to be important when we come to discuss the social ethics of income distribution.

Moreover in neo-Classical theory value is determined 'subjectively', as the result of a series of choices made from motives involving an attempt to maximise a quantity, usually of utility or profit. In Classical-Marxian production models there need be no reference to choices or motives and prices are determined without necessarily maximising anything. The determinant of barter exchange values is that the system exactly reproduces itself in the next production period, given the distribution between capital and labour of the surplus of output over necessary replacements. There is no place here for 'final demand' although it plays an important part in determining the physical composition of the surplus.

Since prices are not determined by maximisation in a Classical-Marxian model, there are also rival notions of equilibrium. A neo-Classical system is in equilibrium, when and only when each individual is, by choice, producing or consuming the quantities he prefers to all alternatives, where 'preference' is construed as, in some sense, maximising. In a Classical-Marxian (or any other) linear production model, this kind of 'choice' is irrelevant and equilibrium is defined in terms of technology and distribution. Exchange equilibrium is a relation between a pattern of production and the pattern of inputs needed to maintain the system, while distributing the surplus in the given proportions.

The rival notions of exchange have different logical forms. In one case 'Equilibrium in exchange' has to do with trading a set of outputs so that, duly allocated, they can function as inputs. Here exchange is an operation to eliminate the difference between the pattern of outputs among industries and the pattern of inputs required for production to take place again. In the other case 'Equilibrium in exchange' means that the set of quantities associated with the prices (or the two sets together) will maximise some index. These two notions have nothing in common. The moral for economists is that some of the least tractable modern problems in welfare economics, growth theory and international trade may prove to be problems less within their particular area than within the value theory commonly presumed to underlie modern economics. When a Classical-Marxian value theory is substituted, many of the problems become more tractable or disappear altogether.

Besides these gains in descriptive theory, there is a significant implication for social ethics. Peace activists and conservatives alike complain that 'their taxes' are used for activities of which they disapprove, like bombing or welfare. Yet they made the money which the government taxes and uses. In similar vein the high-salary earner complains that progressive taxes discriminate against his greater productivity. The underlying idea is that the income earner exchanges a certain productive contribution for equivalent earnings, which should be his to do what he likes with, since society has received full value.

These and similar views share the same fundamental defect. The receipt of income is not one side of an exchange. Income is not a payment in proportionate exchange for a productive contribution, even when it is clearly paid for work performed. Under capitalism even income *as a whole* is not paid out to those who work since those who own property also receive income. Under socialism income would be paid only to those who work (although it also goes to the government) but, even so, the individual payments would not be in proportion to contributions. For in an interdependent system there is no way of isolating any one particular productive contribution. The product is the joint result of the cooperating parties and no specific amount or part can be assigned to any one individual effort. Suppose, following the marginalists, we added an extra worker without adding extra equipment, materials, energy and so forth. He would be merely decorative. Equally, if we subtract a worker but make no other change, his machine will be idle and bring all later parts of the process to a halt. The marginal product upwards equals zero and downwards is the whole product.

Sophisticated marginalists have long admitted that neither marginal products nor any other measure of productive contribution could be assigned to factors in a system operating with a given technique.[13] But they have continued to believe that marginal productivity would be vindicated by considering changes from one technique to another; the extra man works with different equipment and materials. If recent controversy, encouraged, we hope, by our earlier arguments, shows this to be a delusion, the implications for our ordinary ways of thought are enormous. Individual incomes do not result from individual hard work but from exercises of power, political decisions, tradition and other social forces, not least the hierarchical organisation of productive work. But there is no justifiable sense in which any individual 'earns' exactly his income, even though his income may be received for work. Indeed those involved in unproductive work contribute nothing to the size of the total product, even though they may assist in its realisation. The clear implication is that there is no natural nor any efficient allocation of incomes. A competitive scramble for incomes is simply a power struggle and there is no hope of basing an 'incomes policy' on the notion of 'productive contribution' or 'efficiency'.

Programming and prediction models

Finally, in summary of what has been a long and elaborate argument, we shall revert to the kinds of model distinguished earlier. Production, programming and prediction models were introduced in Chapter 7, where we said that a production model gives conditions for the system to continue, a programming model shows how to improve performance and a prediction model forecasts whether the conditions will in fact be met or the improvement be forthcoming. We shall now look at each again, in the light of our case for preferring a Classical-Marxian to a neo-Classical approach to theory.

Production models will show how a society can continue to be viable and how it could adapt to change in its activities, pattern of distribution or state of technology. They are not asked to rank the alternatives and possible adaptations in the light of goals nor to suggest better ways of doing what is being done. That is the task of programming models. Production models only organise possibilities, showing how variables like wages, rates of profit, prices, rents or land values vary as the division of the surplus varies.[14] They are, in Lowe's term, 'homeostatic'[15] and remain indeterminate, when

---

[13] Dennis Robertson, Wage grumbles, *Economic Fragments* (London, 1931); reprinted in W. Fellner and B. F. Haley (eds.), *Readings in the Theory of Income Distribution* (Richard D. Irwin, Inc., 1951).

[14] cf. Sraffa, *The Production of Commodities*.

[15] A. Lowe, *On Economic Knowledge* (Harper and Row, 1970).

applied to a society with differentially rewarded classes, until the division of the surplus is specified. But they do provide criteria of application for theories, to be presented shortly.

When supplemented with a statement of the Rule of Distribution for a type of economy, they can become determinate, although this makes them predictive for only so long as that economy remains true to type. So it might seem only a step to providing a complete theory of distribution. In modern capitalism, for instance, the availability of work, the size of the potential work force, the strength of the unions and the degree of monopoly among employers and corporations all bear upon the money wage rate. Moreover the supply of money, the level of interest rates, the state of aggregate demand and the degree of monopoly all bear upon the level of commodity prices. The real wage rate, and so the share of labour, emerges as the ratio of money wages to price level. Once this is fixed, profits are determined, as it were, residually. Yet, although this much is fairly widely agreed, there results less a single theory of distribution than a class of distribution theories. This should cause no surprise, however, since the exact Rule of Distribution is much disputed and since the institutions administering distribution are normally subject to conflict and change. (The development of the federal Reserve system and the history of the American labour movement illustrate the point.) So, in practice, approximations to determinateness are as much as we can look for at present.

Another limitation on production models becomes clear, when we reflect that systems often in fact fail to reproduce themselves. The history of the trade cycle, for example, is a study in over- and under-shooting the mark, and an accurate model of the trade cycle or of Keynesian underemployment will not be a production model. (Nor will it be a programming model.) We have called a model which attempts to set down conditions in which variables will take specified values a 'prediction' model, whose object is to predict the actual course of events. Its basis will be a valid production model, supplemented by a statement of the goals of the principal agents and of their capabilities. Its success will depend on the degree of constancy in its data. Consumption spending, for instance, is fairly predictable, given disposable national income, since household patterns of living are sociologically fairly stable. Inflation rates are much less predictable, partly because of complexity in the causes, partly because of variations in bargaining strengths and skills and in governmental policies. (Success in prediction also depends on the level of aggregation. For example consumption spending can usually be predicted in the aggregate, despite erratic fluctuations in spending on particular lines but this is not a reliable generalisation. Inflation rates are often indeterminate in general, although price increases in some lines can be forecast with accuracy.)

Prediction models are distinct from both production and programming models. In order to predict, it may be necessary to reckon with inconsistent ambitions among economic agents and social classes, whereas neither a production nor a programming model can tolerate inconsistency. Admittedly the prediction model will in this case presumably predict that a previous constant is about to become a variable, on the ground that something will have to give and conflict is a harbinger of change. But prediction is made difficult rather than impossible by the presence of inconsistencies. A production model shows what has to happen if the system is to remain viable. A programming model shows how best to achieve a stipulated result. A prediction model judges whether the system will actually remain viable and whether the programming strategy will actually be followed. Consequently, whereas production and programming models judge the facts, the prediction model is judged by the facts.

In saying that production and programming models judge the facts, we are casting the economist in the role of magistrate rather than pure observer. In principle the economist and not the consumer is sovereign. It is for him to say whether the system is viable, whether, for instance, given certain exchange ratios reproduction is possible consistently with a proposed Rule of Distribution; whether a proposed diet can satisfy proposed dietary requirements at minimum cost. His yardstick is provided by necessities in in the model. Thus, the method of production, I, which will maximise profits, given the real wage, w* is the one indicated by the arrow in the diagram (Figure 37) below. This is true of necessity and businessmen who choose II must obtain lower profits.

This needs a closer look. The scheme is based on the relationships we first met at the end of Chapter 7, and which we further explored later in this chapter. In the upper right hand quadrant we plot two wage rate-profit rate tradeoffs, representing different techniques, in one of which industry is capital-intensive, while in the other, it is labour-intensive. Just below we have a simple Saving-Investment equation, $g = s_p r$, where s_p is the propensity to run out of profits. We assume that all savings are invested and that all wages are consumed. In the upper left quadrant, though, we have something new: the *duals* to the wage–profit tradeoffs. There are tradeoffs between the growth rate of capital and consumption per head, found by solving the *quantity* equations (just as the wage-profit tradeoff is formed by solving price equations. The system in full

Price Equations	Quantity Equations
$1 = ra + wb\pi$	$1 = ga + c\alpha\lambda$
$\pi = r\alpha + w\beta\pi$	$\lambda = gb + c\beta\lambda$

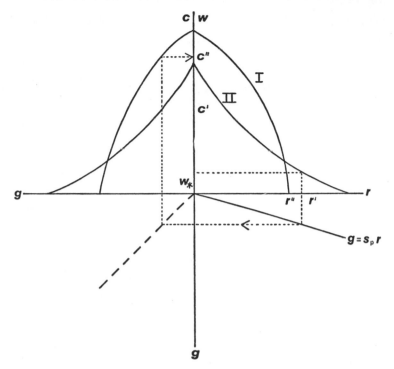

Figure 37

Wage–Profit Tradeoff:

$$\frac{(1/\beta - w)(1/a - r)}{rw} = \frac{\alpha b}{a\beta}$$

Consumption–Growth Tradeoff:

$$\frac{(1/\beta - c)(1/a - g)}{cg} = \frac{\alpha b}{a\beta}$$

Saving equation:

$$g = s_p r$$

where π is the price of the consumer good in terms of the capital good, λ is the output of consumer goods in terms of capital goods, and s_p is the propensity to save out of profits.

The diagram is a good example of a programming model constructed from a production model and also illustrates the futility of defining 'efficient allocation' by profit maximising. Other objectives, like the maximising of per capita consumption, may well require a different choice of technique, as can be seen from the fact that if technique I were chosen, although it would yield a lower rate of profit, $r' > r''$, it would yield a higher per capita consumption, $c'' > c$. Hence, contrary to much neo-Classical thinking, private profit-maximising does not automatically make for efficiency, still less for general social welfare. Indeed pursuit of profits will not, for instance, normally maximise consumption per head since (according to the Golden Rule) the growth rate usually lies below the profit rate. If it is objected that maximising of consumption is an undesirable goal, then we observe that there are other possible goals not all served by pursuit of profit, as current concern with pollution and injury to the social environment makes evident. Efficiency is relative to the goal postulated and we might perhaps be allowed to end with a flourish borrowed from Joan Robinson:

But Marxism can claim the credit for saving the planners from believing in academic economics. Imagine the present state of Russian industry if they had regarded their task as the 'allocation of given resources among alternative uses' instead of 'the ripening of the productive power of social labour' by investment, exploration, and education. (*Collected Economic Essays*, vol. III, p. 153.)

We have now planted enough signposts to show where we hope the road leads. The contrast between neo-Classical and Classical-Marxian theory is radical and pervasive; we have argued both, negatively, that the former is mistaken and, positively, that the latter is right. It remains only to sound a departing horn in the cause of political economy

Summary

Neo-Classical Economic Man is a sovereign individual with utilitarian forebears and is to be first studied in isolation from his fellows and from the institutions surrounding him. The behaviour of social molecules, according to this view, is the effect of combining social atoms. We cannot put it more clearly than John Stuart Mill

The laws of the phenomena of society are, and can be, nothing but the laws of the actions and passions of human beings united together in the social state. Men, however, in a state of society are still men; their actions and passions are obedient to the laws of individual human nature... Human beings in society have no properties but those which are derived from, and may be resolved into, the laws of the nature of the individual man. In social phenomena the Composition of Causes is the universal law.

A System of Logic (Bk. VI, Ch. 7 sect. i)

Nor can we caricature the view of man in society which this conceptual individualism has sometimes been used to support more clearly than Marx does:

This sphere ..., within whose boundaries the sale and purchase of labour-power goes on, is in fact a very Eden of the innate rights of man. There alone rule Freedom, because both buyer and seller of a commodity, say of labour-power, are constrained only by their own free will. They contract as free agents, and the agreement they come to, is but the form in which they give legal expression to their common will. Equality, because each enters into relation with the other, as with a simple owner of commodities, and they exchange equivalent for equivalent. Property, because each disposes only of what is his own. And Bentham, because each looks only to himself. The only force that brings them together and puts them in relation with each other, is the selfishness, the gain, and the private interests of each. Each looks to himself only, and no one troubles himself about the rest, and just because they do so, do they all, in accordance with the pre-established harmony of things, or under the auspices of an all-shrewd providence, work together to their mutual advantage, for the common weal and in the interest of all.

Capital (Vol. I, p. 176)

Our Classical and Marxian rumblings have been directed against Mill's plea for atomism. We believe neither that economic man can be defined apart from his social setting nor that the social setting is, even in theory, created by the combined work of individual wills. The 'individual man', that presocial utilitarian, seems to us a fiction of the enlightened liberal imagination. Nevertheless we are willing to compromise. *Mores faciunt hominem* strikes us as no better than a half-truth. But half a truth is better than nothing and our compromise has been to speak of economic men as essentially individual bearers of economic variables. That will hardly do as a final pronouncement but we have space here only to cast a pebble into the ocean of political and social theory.

Admirers of the clerihew will recall that John Stuart Mill by an effort of will overcame his natural bonhomie and wrote the *Principles of Political Economy*. We judge that he was right to do so and deplore the refusal of his economic successors to do the same. Our quarrel is with the neo-Classical offspring of political economy. Once it is granted that social organisation creates wants, it becomes absurd to aim ideally at organising society so that it serves the preformed presocial wants of its atoms. Individuals do not exist, as what they are, apart from the jobs they do and the services and commodities they produce. Their wants grow out of their daily lives which in turn rest on the work by means of which the system is reproduced and there is no such thing as abstract choice. Political economy is the science of applying sound economic theories to men in a social setting. It will have to combine a sound economic theory with a sound social and political theory. Neo-Classicism, we have suggested, is an unsound economic theory, presupposing an unsound social and political theory, underwritten by an unsound theory of knowledge. In its place we have proposed a kind of rationalism, the first steps in a structural economics and the merest hint of an account of man in society. But we hear the Eumenides on our heels and this is where we halt.

BIBLIOGRAPHY

Allen, R. G. D. *Mathematical Economics*, 2nd ed. Macmillan, 1966.
  Macro-Economic Theory: A Mathematical Treatment. Macmillan, 1967.
Andrews, P. and Wilson, T. (ed.). *Oxford Studies in the Price Mechanism*.
  Oxford University Press, 1957.
Arrow, K. J. The economic implications of learning by doing. *Review of
  Economic Studies*, vol. 29, no. 3 (June 1962).
Aune, B. *Rationalism, Empiricism and Pragmatism*. Random House, New York,
  1970.
Ayer, A. J. *Language, Truth and Logic*. 2nd ed., Dover Publications, 1936.
  The Concept of a Person. Macmillan, 1963.
  Probability and Evidence. Macmillan, 1972.
  (ed.) *Logical Positivism*. Glencoe, 1959.
Bennett, J. *Rationality*. Routledge and Kegan Paul, 1964.
Braithwaite, R. B. *Scientific Explanation*. Cambridge University Press, 1953.
Brody, A. *Proportions, Prices and Planning*. North-Holland, 1970.
Bruno, M., Burmeister, E. and Sheshinski, E. Nature and implications of the
  reswitching of techniques, *Quarterly Journal of Economics*, vol. LXXX,
  no. 4 (November 1966).
Carnap, R. *Der Logische Aufbau der Welt. The Logical Structure of the World
  and Pseudoproblems in Philosophy*, tr. by R. A. George. University of
  California Press, 1967.
Clark, J. B. *The Distribution of Wealth*. Macmillan, 1899.
Collingwood, R. G. *An Essay on Metaphysics*. Clarendon Press, 1940.
Copi, I. Essence and accident, in *Universals and Particulars*, ed. by M. J. Loux.
  Doubleday, 1970.
Cyert, R. M. and March, J. G. *A Behavioral Theory of the Firm*. Prentice-Hall,
  1963.
Debreu, G. *Theory of Value: An Axiomatic Analysis of Economic Equilibrium*.
  Yale University Press, 1972.
Descartes, R. *Philosophical Writings*, tr. and ed. G.E.M. Anscombe and P. T.
  Geach, Bobbs-Merrill, 1972.
Dorfman, R., Samuelson, P. A. and Solow, R. M. *Linear Programming and
  Economic Theory*. McGraw-Hill, 1958.
Dummett, M. Truth. *Proceedings of the Aristotelian Society*, 1968–9. Reprinted
  in *Truth*, ed. by G. Pitcher. Prentice-Hall, 1964.

Durbin, E. *Welfare, Income, and Employment: An Economic Analysis of Family Choice.* Praeger, 1969.
　Education and earnings in the urban ghettoes: comment. *The American Economist* (Spring 1970).
Ellman, M. *Soviet Planning Today.* Cambridge University Press, 1971.
Euclid. *Elements,* ed. by T. L. Heath. J. M. Dent and Sons, 1933.
Evans-Pritchard, E. E. *Witchcraft, Oracles and Magic Among the Azande.* Clarendon Press, 1937.
Frege, G. *The Foundations of Arithmetic,* tr. by J. L. Austin. Harper, 1960.
Friedman, M. The methodology of Positive economics. *Essays in Positive Economics.* University of Chicago Press, 1953.
　A Theory of the Consumption Function. Princeton University Press, 1957.
Goodman, N. *Fact, Fiction and Forecast.* Bobbs-Merrill, 1965.
Goodwin, R. M. *Elementary Economics from the Higher Standpoint.* Cambridge University Press, 1970.
Graaff, J. de V. *Theoretical Welfare Economics.* Cambridge University Press, . 1963.
Gurley, J. G. and Shaw, E. S. *Money in a Theory of Finance.* The Brookings Institution, 1960.
Haavelmo, Trygbe. The inadequacy of testing dynamic theory by comparing theoretical solutions and observed cycles, *Econometrica,* vol. 8, no. 3 (Jan. 1940).
Hall, R. and Hitch, C. J. Price theory and business behaviour, in *Oxford Studies in the Price Mechanism,* ed. P. Andrews and T. Wilson. Oxford University Press, 1951.
Harcourt, G. C. Some Cambridge controversies in the theory of capital. *Journal of Economic Literature,* Vol. 7, No. 2 (June 1969).
　Some Cambridge Controversies in the Theory of Capital. Cambridge University Press, 1972.
Harrison, B. W. *Education, Training and the Urban Ghetto.* Johns Hopkins University Press, 1972.
Harrod, R. F. Theory of imperfect competition revisited, in *Economic Essays.* St Martin's Press, 1972.
Hempel, C. G. *Aspects of Scientific Explanation.* The Free Press, 1965.
Heilbroner, R. L. Is economic theory possible? *Social Research,* vol. 33, no. 2 (Summer 1966).
Henderson, J. M., and Quandt, R. E. *Microeconomic Theory: A Mathematical Approach.* McGraw-Hill, 1971.
Hicks, J. R. *Critical Essays in Monetary Theory.* Clarendon Press, 1967.
Hill, T. P. *The Process of Economic Growth.* O.E.C.D., 1971.
Hobbes, T. *Leviathan.* 1651. Basil Blackwell, 1946.
Hobson, J. A. *The Industrial System.* 1910. New and revised edition, A. M. Kelley, 1969.
Hollis, M. Theory in miniature. *Mind,* 1973.
　Review of *The Principles of Linguistic Philosophy,* by F. Waismann. *Foundations of Language,* Vol. 5 (1969).
Huxley, A. L. *Eyeless in Gaza.* Harper and Brothers, 1936.

Kaldor, N. Capital accumulation and economic growth, in *The Theory of Capital*, ed. F. Lutz and D. C. Hague. Macmillan, 1962.
Causes of the Slow Rate of Economic Growth in the U.K. Cambridge University Press, 1966.
Marginal productivity and the macro-economic theories of distribution. *Review of Economic Studies*, vol. 33, no. 96 (October 1966).

Kenny, A. *Action, Emotion and Will.* Routledge and Kegan Paul, 1963.

Keynes, J. M. *The General Theory of Employment, Interest and Money.* Macmillan, 1936.

Klein, L. R. and Kosobud, R. F. Some econometrics of growth: Great ratios of economics. *Quarterly Journal of Economics*, vol. LXXV, no. 2 (May 1961).

Koopmans, T. C. *Three Essays on the State of Economic Science.* McGraw-Hill, 1957.

Kornai, J. *Anti-Equilibrium.* North-Holland, 1972.

Krupp, S. R. Equilibrium theory in economics and in function analysis as types of explanation, in *Functionalism in the Social Sciences*, ed. D. Martindale. American Academy of Political and Social Science, 1965.

Lancaster, K. *Consumer Demand.* Columbia University Press, 1971.

Leijonhufvud, A. *Keynesian Economics and the Economics of Keynes.* Oxford University Press, 1970.

Levhari, D. and Samuelson, P. A. The nonswitching theorem is false, *Quarterly Journal of Economics*, vol. LXXX, no. 4 (November 1966).

Lewis, C. I. *Mind and the World-Order.* Charles Scribner's Sons, 1929.

Lipsey, R. G. *Introduction to Positive Economics.* 3rd ed., Harper and Row, 1972.

Lipsey, R. G. and Steiner, P. O. *Economics.* Harper and Row, 1966.

Little, I. M. D. *A Critique of Welfare Economics*, 2nd ed. Clarendon Press, 1957.

Lowe, A. *On Economic Knowledge.* Harper and Row, 1970.

Machlup, F. Paper in *Readings in Economic Analysis*, ed. Richard V. Clemence. Addison-Wesley, 1950.

Marcuse, H. *One-Dimensional Man.* Beacon Press, 1964.

Marglin, S. What do bosses do? Unpublished paper, Harvard University, 1971.

Marshall, A. *Principles of Economics*, 9th (variorum) ed. with annotations by C. W. Guillebaud. Macmillan, 1961.

Marx, K. *Capital.* 1887. International Publishers, 1967.

Masters, D. *The Intelligent Buyer and the Tell-Tale Seller.* Alfred Knopf, 1966.

Meyer, J. R. and Kuh, E. *The Investment Decision.* Harvard University Press, 1957.

Mill, J. S. *Principles of Political Economy*, 4th ed. 1847, in *Collected Works* ed. by V. W. Bladen and J. M. Robson. University of Toronto Press, 1965.
A System of Logic, 8th ed., Harper and Row, 1874.

Mincer, J. (ed.) *Economic Forecasts and Expectations.* National Bureau of Economic Research, 1969.

Mises, L. von. *Human Action.* William Hodge, 1949.
Epistemological Problems of Economics. Princeton, 1960.

Morishima, M. Refutation of the nonswitching theorem, *Quarterly Journal of Economics*, vol. LXXX, no. 4 (November 1966).

Nagel, E. Assumptions in economic theory. *American Economic Review*, vol. 53, no. 2 (May 1963).
The Structure of Science. Harcourt Brace, 1961.
Nell, E. J. No proposition can describe itself. *Analysis*, vol. 26, no. 4 (March 1966).
Economic relationships in the decline of feudalism. *History and Theory*, vol. 6, no. 3 (1967).
No statement is immune to revision. Unpublished paper, 1969.
A note on *Cambridge Controversies*. *Journal of Economic Literature*, vol. 8, no. 1 (March 1970).
and O. S. Nell. Justice under socialism. *Dissent*, vol. 19, no. 3(Summer 1972).
Neumann, J. von. A model of general economic equilibrium. *Review of Economic Studies*, vol. 13, no. 33 (1945).
Newman, P. *Theory of Exchange*. Prentice-Hall, 1965.
Newton, I. *Philosophiae Naturalis Principia Mathematica*. 1686.
Packard, V. D. *The Waste Makers*. D. McKay Company, 1960.
Pap, A. *Semantics and Necessary Truth*. Yale University Press, 1958.
Pasinetti, L. A mathematical formulation of the Ricardian system. *Review of Economic Studies*, vol. 27 (2), no. 73 (February 1960).
Changes in the rate of profit and switches of technique, *Quarterly Journal of Economics*, vol. LXXX, no. 4 (November 1966).
Switches of technique and the 'rate of return' in capital theory. *Economic Journal*, vol. 79, no. 315 (September 1969).
Patinkin, D. *Money, Interest and Prices*. 2nd ed., Harper and Row, 1965.
Popper, K. R. *The Logic of Scientific Discovery*. Hutchinson, 1962.
Conjectures and Refutations. Routledge, 1963.
Objective Knowledge. Clarendon Press, 1972.
Putnam, H. The analytic and the synthetic, in *Minnesota Studies in the Philosophy of Science*, vol. III, ed. by H. Feigl and G. Maxwell. University of Minnesota Press, 1962.
Quine, W. v. O. *Word and Object*. M.I.T. Press, 1960.
Two dogmas of empiricism, in *From a Logical Point of View*. Harvard University Press, 1961.
Truth by convention, in *The Ways of Paradox*. Random House, 1966.
Robbins, L. *An Essay on the Nature and Significance of Economic Science*. Macmillan, 1932.
Robertson, D. Wage grumbles, in *Economic Fragments*. P. S. King and Son, Ltd, 1931. (Reprinted in *Readings in the Theory of Income Distribution*, ed. by W. Fellner and B. F. Haley. Richard D. Irwin, Inc., 1951.)
Robinson, J. *The Accumulation of Capital*. Macmillan, 1956.
Excercises in Economic Analysis. Macmillan, 1960.
Essays in the Theory of Economic Growth. Macmillan, 1962.
Collected Economic Essays, vol. III. Basil Blackwell, 1965.
Economic Heresies: Some Old-Fashioned Questions in Economic Theory. Basic Books, 1971.
Russell, B. Mathematical logic as based on the theory of types. *American*

Journal of Mathematics, vol. 30 (1908). (Reprinted in *Logic and Knowledge*, ed. by R. C. March. George Allen and Unwin, 1956.)

On the notion of a cause, in *Mysticism and Logic*. Doubleday Anchor Books, 1957.

Samuelson, P. A. Parable and realism in capital theory: the surrogate production function. *Review of Economic Studies*, vol. 29, no. 3 (June 1962).

Economics, 6th ed. McGraw-Hill, 1964.

Collected Scientific Papers, ed. J. E. Stiglitz. M.I.T. Press, 1966.

A summing up, *Quarterly Journal of Economics*, vol. LXXX, no. 4 (November 1966).

Understanding the Marxian notion of exploitation: A summary of the so-called transformation problem between Marxian values and competitive prices. *Journal of Economic Literature*, vol. 9, no. 2 (June, 1971).

Schoeffler, S. *The Failures of Economics: A Diagnostic Study*. Harvard University Press, 1955.

Seton, F. The 'transformation problem'. *Review of Economic Studies*, vol. 24, no. 65 (June 1957).

Seton, F. and Morishima, M. Aggregation in Leontief matrices and the labour theory of value. *Econometrica*, vol. 29, no. 2 (April 1961).

Shubik, M. A curmudgeon's guide to micro economics. *Journal of Economic Literature*, vol. VIII, no. 2 (June 1970).

Simon, H. A. *Models of Man*. John Wiley and Sons, 1957.

Solow, R. M. *Capital Theory and the Rate of Return*. North-Holland, 1963.

Growth Theory: An Exposition. Oxford University Press, 1970.

Sraffa, P. *Production of Commodities by Means of Commodities*. Cambridge University Press, 1960.

Surgeon General's report, Obesity and fad diets. *The Congressional Record* (12 April 1973).

Sutcliffe, R. B. *Industry and Underdevelopment*. Addison-Wesley, 1971.

Sweezy, P. *Theory of Capitalist Development*. Monthly Review Press, 1942.

Titmuss, R. M. *Income Distribution and Social Change*. George Allen and Unwin, 1962.

Tobin, J. Liquidity preference as behaviour towards risk. *Review of Economic Studies*, vol. 25, no. 67 (February 1958).

U. S. Congress. Senate. Committee on Labor and Public Welfare. Subcommittee on Employment, Manpower and Poverty. *Hunger and Malnutrition in the United States*. Hearings, 90th Congr., 2nd Sess., U. S. Government Printing Office, 1968.

Veblen, T. *The Engineer and the Price System*. B. W. Huebsch, Inc., 1921.

Waismann, F. *The Principles of Linguistic Philosophy*. Macmillan, 1965.

Walters, A. A. *An Introduction to Econometrics*. Norton, 1970.

White, M. G. *Toward Reunion in Philosophy*. Harvard University Press, 1956.

Willey, B. *The Seventeenth-Century Background*. Penguin Books, 1972.

Yurick, S. *The Bag*. Trident Press, 1968.

INDEX